A

DANCE

AGAINST

TIME

As the Snow Prince in *The Nutcracker*

A
DANCE
AGAINST
TIME

DIANE SOLWAY

POCKET BOOKS

New York London Toronto Sydney Tokyo Singapore

POCKET BOOKS, a division of Simon & Schuster Inc.
1230 Avenue of the Americas, New York, NY 10020

Library of Congress Cataloging-in-Publication Data
Solway, Diane.
    A dance against time / Diane Solway.
      p. cm.
    Includes bibliographical references and index.
    ISBN: 0-671-78894-9
    1. Stierle, Edward, 1968–1991. 2. Ballet dancers—United States—
Biography. 3. AIDS (Disease)—Patients—United States—Biography.
4. Joffrey Ballet. I. Title.
GV1785.S77S65 1994
792.8'028'092—dc20
[B]
                                          94-14745
                                            CIP

First Pocket Books hardcover printing November 1994

10 9 8 7 6 5 4 3 2 1

Book design by Stanley S. Drate / Folio Graphics Co. Inc.

POCKET and colophon are registered trademarks of
Simon & Schuster Inc.

Printed in the U.S.A.

For my mother and father
and
for Sylvia

CONTENTS

A

DANCE

AGAINST

TIME

1

EMPYREAN DANCES

On a particularly blustery day in March 1991, twenty-three-year-old Eddie Stierle was determined to get to a black-tie gala at Lincoln Center to see the world premiere of *Empyrean Dances*, the ballet he had just finished making for the Joffrey Ballet.

No patient in his advanced state had ever signed himself out of St. Vincent's Hospital for a night on the town, and his doctors wondered privately whether he'd survive it—still, Eddie was going to get there, dressed for the occasion.

Only six months earlier, Eddie had been dancing outdoors amidst the ruins of the 1,800-year-old Herod Atticus Theatre in Athens and on the stage of the Théâtre des Champs-Elysées in Paris, a star of the Joffrey Ballet. He had fought to turn himself into a ballet dancer; since childhood he had been told that his short, bulky frame was ill suited to the demands of classical ballet. Yet in the four years since Robert Joffrey had hand-picked him for his company, Eddie had streaked into leading roles, quickly establishing himself as the Joffrey's most dazzling bravura dancer, one who tempered speed with clarity and fire with finesse.

When Eddie had been readmitted to St. Vincent's this last time, in late February, he was given a private room with a view of the Manhattan skyline. From his bed, he continued to choreograph his new ballet.

Pausing now before the mirror in his hospital room, Eddie looked himself over—as he'd done hundreds of times before in the Joffrey's rehearsal studios and dressing rooms. Smiling, he fingered the long green silk scarf given to him by Kim Sagami, a Joffrey dancer, on the company's return from Hong Kong. His touch lingered for a moment on the white Chinese characters woven above the scarf's edge: Good Health, they exhorted.

"I want to look really sharp," he said to his sister Rosemarie.

Throughout this past week, Eddie's family had been gathering in Manhattan from scattered locales. The night before, Eddie's parents, three brothers, and four sisters had spent hours in Eddie's midtown apartment, devising a strategy to get him to the gala at Lincoln Center. They knew he was keeping himself alive for this night. With the same attention to split-second timing accorded a presidential motorcade, they mapped out every detail of the fifty-block trip from Eddie's hospital bed at St. Vincent's to his seat in the New York State Theater at Lincoln Center.

Each item of the journey was assigned to a family member and checked off the list. Everyone would have a role to play in the evening's events.

The car sped up Eighth Avenue, and Eddie, sitting in the front seat, sighed as the frenzied sounds and colors of Times Square rushed by. Another moment of reprieve.

As the car pulled up to the backstage door, Eddie's brother Michael, a Catholic lay minister, his wife, Pam, and their four young children welcomed Eddie with colored balloons and a large sign that read, "Congratulations, Uncle Eddie."

Minutes later, Eddie was settled into the viewing room at the rear of the orchestra just as the gala audience began filing into the theater. No one expected him to be there.

"How are you doin', Eddie?" his mother, Rose, called out as she approached the VIP booth, the same perch from where master choreographer George Balanchine had often surveyed his own ballets. "Do you need anything?"

"No, Ma, I'm fine. I'm feeling great," replied Eddie. "You guys are doing a great job."

"Hey, Ed, look this way," commanded his father, Bill, the family chronicler, who had filled innumerable albums documenting Eddie's life on the stage. Adjusting the focus, he snapped the moment and returned to his seat as the houselights began to dim.

The curtain came up on a stage littered with architectural fragments, the facade of a half-finished or abandoned building visible on a backdrop. From the wings, dancers entered the desolate setting and became sculptural friezes themselves, posing on and then soaring from the ruins in a continuous cascade of lifts and leaps. "You are in this destroyed place," Eddie had instructed the dancers during rehearsals, "and you are rebuilding it with your spirit." He had wanted to share with them the discovery of his own spiritual strength, which he was convinced was helping to keep him alive. Hope and rebirth were the twin themes he sought to convey with this ballet; its closing image would feature the entire cast standing in an ascending pattern, gazing upward and offstage, toward a celestial light. In the program underneath the ballet's title, Eddie had added a quote from Thomas Carlyle: "A little gleam of time between two eternities," it read.

As *Empyrean Dances* unfolded onstage, Eddie's thoughts wandered back several months to the day he first came up with the idea for the ballet. He had been walking among ruins in Athens during a visit to the Acropolis in September. He knew he had a grave illness, but he was still dancing at full throttle and had no reason to question that he would be dancing during the New York season the following March. *Empyrean,* his second ballet for the Joffrey, was begun in November and born of his experience in facing death.

By that time he could no longer dance. But he kept himself "in shape" for the day he felt he would return to class by running through all his roles in his mind, "so that when I have the strength in my lungs to go back in, I'll be ready," he'd explained to a reporter. When the strength didn't come, he comforted himself with the thought that he had other bodies to make dances for and threw himself into getting the ballet finished.

Five minutes before the ballet's conclusion, Eddie's reverie was interrupted by his brothers Tom and Bill, who had come to wheel Eddie backstage in time for his curtain call. Earlier that day, the dancers had been alerted that should Eddie show up, Tom Mossbrucker and Daniel Baudendistel, the two male leads, were to hold him up under his arms during the bow, in the same way modern-dance doyenne Martha Graham was suspended by her dancers when she took curtain calls in the final years of her life.*

Tom and Bill maneuvered Eddie backstage, but as soon as they reached the wings Eddie suddenly pulled the oxygen tube from his nose and stood up. His brothers rushed forward to help him, but he shooed them away. "I'm okay, I'm okay," he repeated.

When the curtain came up on the cast, Eddie was standing center stage. Ignoring the hands stretched out to him, he stepped forward, alone, and bowed.

The entire house rose to its feet, witnesses to his triumph. Shouts of "Bravo!" mingled with cries of "Eddie!" The gaunt figure at center stage extended his arms in a gesture of thanks and beamed the showman's smile he had mastered by the age of four.

Then he blew kisses. It was vintage Eddie Stierle.

Back in his private room at St. Vincent's, Eddie was on a postperformance high. He couldn't stop recounting the night's events. "It was a great night, wasn't it? I had my moment. But the music was too fast. I have to tell the conductor to slow it down. Will you bring me the papers? I can't wait to see what the critics say."

---

*Twenty-three-year-old Eddie Stierle and ninety-six-year-old Martha Graham died three weeks apart.

Two days later, on the morning of March 7, Eddie read his reviews. In *The New York Times,* chief dance critic Anna Kisselgoff announced the arrival of a promising new choreographer. "His is a stunning talent," she wrote, adding that *Empyrean Dances* was "a rarity, a visionary ballet, and the vision of the Empyrean or highest heaven that Milton extolled is translated by Mr. Stierle into a burning onrush of hope."

Two days after that, *The New York Times* carried Eddie's obituary.

2

GIRLS' TAP

At 8:40 P.M. on March 2, 1968, Rose Cardamone Stierle gave birth to her eighth child, a boy she named Edward. Eighteen years separated her eldest from the infant she now held in her arms; she knew he would be her last. She was thirty-nine, the same age her own mother had been when she gave birth to Rose, and the years of childbearing had taken their toll. But as Rose saw it, making babies was her creative pact with God. When her doctor strongly advised against more pregnancies, she secretly hoped that Father Fernandez, her priest, would refuse to condone her use of birth control. Instead, he gave her what he called "a dispensation owing to health reasons," or, rather, he agreed to look the other way. But not before instructing Rose to be mindful of her duties: "You still have to think about pleasing your husband," he said as she was leaving the confessional. "But I *have*, Father," Rose explained, concerned that the priest thought her remiss in her affections. "That's why I have such a big family!"

A broad woman, Rose wore her dark brown hair rolled back off her face in the pompadour style of the 1940s. She had little vanity and paid no mind to the toll her pregnancies had left on her body: the once slender legs now marbled with varicose veins, and the waistline, once shapely, that dissolved into thick hips.

By now, Rose was highly attuned to the nuances of her body's rhythms. On the day she realized she would deliver Edward, Rose had been feeling contractions since morning, but refused to leave for the hospital until she had fed her children dinner and washed the three "little ones"—all under the age of six—for bed. She knew Bill was in a hurry to drop her off at North Miami Hospital and she wanted to make sure she left him enough time to get to Chaminade, the Catholic high school near their home. Bill was Chaminade's head maintenance man and, that night, he was to run the time clock for the seniors' basketball game.

As she lay in the darkened room waiting to give birth, the attending nurse suggested she calm the pain by summoning her happiest memory. That was easy. Rose closed her eyes and at once she was waltzing with Bill at Finnegan's, the dance club on Fifth and Cumberland Street in North Philadelphia, where twelve-and-a-half-year-old Rose Cardamone met fifteen-year-old Bill Stierle on New Year's Eve in 1943, after months of admiring him across the floor. "I can't believe he's coming towards me," she thought as Bill Stierle moved past several more likely candidates to ask her for a turn on the floor.

Finnegan's was run by Mom and Pop Finnegan, a middle-aged Irish couple, who opened their living and dining room on weekend nights to the neighborhood kids, most of them the sons and daughters of Irish, Italian, and German immigrants. No alcohol was permitted, but for fifty cents, you could dance to Frank Sinatra, Tommy Dorsey, and Gene Krupa records all night. When it came time for "girls' tap," Mom Finnegan would announce, "Okay girls, this is your chance! Tap the shoulder of the guy you want to dance with," and there would suddenly be a rush on slim, blue-eyed Bill Stierle, for he was Finnegan's resident star. A jitterbug champ known for his impish charm and buoyant ease, the five-feet-four-inch Bill Stierle was *the* partner to snare, and as he shimmied past his friends on the floor, one of them was sure to remark, "You look like Donald O'Connor!"

Bill relished the comparisons to O'Connor, his idol, whose rough-and-tumble street style he preferred to the more filigreed patter of Fred Astaire. "O'Connor is a comer," Bill Stierle (pronounced "Sturl") liked to say. "He isn't top dog. I'm always for the guy who's coming up."

Rose Cardamone, however, admired the suave elegance of Astaire and Ginger Rogers and when watching them swoon on the screen, would say to herself, "I can do that." Her brothers worked in an ice plant chopping blocks of ice to support the family and there was no money left over to pay for the dance lessons Rose longed for. Every Saturday, she had to settle for sneaking into the vestibule of the dance hall down the street from the family's row house. There she would watch the weekly tap class, quietly mirroring the actions of the teacher's feet with her own.

The night Rose met Bill Stierle at Finnegan's, she lied about her age. She told him she was fourteen. Soon after, Bill began introducing Rose to his favorite stars: They saw Louis Prima and Frank Sinatra at the Earl Theater, Woody Herman at the Mausbaum Theatre, and Danny Kaye, Don Ameche, and Donald O'Connor movies at the Kent Theater, where Bill took a job as an usher in the evenings so he could go to the movies every night for free. For many years, until the birth of his first child convinced him to adopt more pragmatic pursuits, whenever Bill was asked what he hoped would become of him, he would always answer, "I want to be a tap and jazz dancer in the movies."

"Your brother will never let us get married," Bill Stierle complained to Rose Cardamone in December 1947. Rose's older brother had become head of the household following the death of their father and didn't think much of Bill Stierle's prospects. "Let's elope," Bill suggested, "and then he'll have to accept it." Rose had dreamed of a church wedding. A pious Catholic schoolgirl, she had been tutored by nuns at St. Edward's Parish and now she worried about what Father Murphy would say when he found out. It was wrong to get married without his blessing, she knew, but there was really no money for a wedding anyhow, and she reluctantly agreed.

Rose Cardamone at age
fifteen, 1945

Bill, Sr., at age nineteen, 1947

On December 15, 1947, Rose and Bill drove to Elkton, Maryland, and eloped. Three days later, Rose went to see Father Murphy. "What do you mean by marrying outside the Church?" he demanded. Rose stammered her way through an explanation and asked for his understanding. Her brother Virgil was equally exasperated.

Yet in her quiet, insistent way, Rose prevailed, as she would learn to do with great skill throughout her married years. On February 7, 1948, Father Murphy blessed the marriage of Rose Cardamone to Bill Stierle inside St. Edward's, while Virgil Cardamone looked on as best man. Rose got her church wedding after all.

It was the first of many small victories.

Edward was only three months old when his brother Michael left home to join a religious order, an event that so upset Rose Stierle that she resolved to hold on to her baby as long as she could. Though thrilled that Michael was going to a novitiate in upstate New York to study for the priesthood, or "going to God," as Rose liked to think of it, she was inconsolable at the thought that her eldest child didn't need her any longer. Bill Stierle was equally discomfited. He had long hoped that his firstborn would join him in his work.

By the time Edward came into the family in 1968, Rose and Bill had been married for over twenty years. Eighteen years earlier, they had taken their first trip to Florida to visit Rose's Aunt Mary and had fallen in love with the lush vegetation and the tropical air, worlds removed from the gritty streets they knew in North Philadelphia. They decided then that as soon as they had saved enough money, they would move their family south. In 1956, they were finally able to leave Philadelphia with their children Michael, born in 1950, and Therese, born in 1952. They settled in Hollywood, moving into the blue, three-bedroom house that Bill never stopped building on Southwest Thirty-eighth Street. He had managed to afford the house by making an unusual deal with the local builder: Rather than pay him the $750 down payment, Bill offered to give the builder $200 toward a half-completed house and agreed to finish plastering the walls himself.

As the family expanded, Bill added on rooms, making sure to involve his kids in every aspect of the construction. He soon had a large crew to help him, for the rest of the Stierle children, "the Florida babies," as Rose dubbed them, came neatly spaced at regular intervals: Rosemarie led the way in 1958; Bill came next in 1960; Kathy in 1962; Tom in 1963; and Patty in 1965. It was not long before each of them was well versed in the fine points of plastering, sheetrocking, and preparing drywall. They teamed up with their father to tile the roof, resod the lawn, hang the kitchen cabinets, and paint the outside of their house coral with brown trim.

To Rose, the house was ideally situated. It stood half a block from Annunciation Parish, which Bill had helped to build; Annunciation School, the coed Catholic elementary school; and Madonna Academy, the girls' Catholic high school. Throughout the day, Rose could hear school bells in the family's kitchen.

Of all her children, only Rosemarie shared her passion for dancing, an interest that developed after Bill got free lessons at Linkletter Tot Dance Studio in exchange for plastering their walls. Rose often confessed to her daughter that she wished she could have "a little boy dancer too."

When Eddie was born, she remembered reading in one of her baby manuals that infants develop a keen sense of rhythm if rocked, so Rose made sure that Edward was lulled to sleep every night in a rocking chair for the first two years of his life.

An affectionate child with reddish brown hair and a face full of freckles, Edward turned immediately to his mother and sisters for support, companionship, and a sense of identity. He looked remarkably like his father, with his sharp features, animated, narrow eyes, and fair coloring, but he shared his mother's demonstrative manner and temperament. "He was a gentle, tender baby," says his sister Terri, who often helped her mother with the bedtime shift by rocking or singing Eddie to sleep.

Edward soon came to be called Eddie by everyone in the family except his mother, who generally insisted on the more formal Edward, out of respect for the Marianist Brother for whom he was named and the Philadelphia church where she was married. Her Edward was a small child for his age, even at four, and preferred the company of neighborhood girls and Barbie and Ken to his brothers' roughhousing. He amused himself for hours staging vignettes for his beloved stuffed animals and his sisters' dolls.

Rose thought little of her son's preoccupation with dolls until her brother Tony, who was visiting from Philadelphia, broached the subject one afternoon while watching his nephew prance around the living room in a pas de deux with Barbie.

"That's not good, Rose," said Tony.

"What's not good?" she asked, at a loss to explain the source of his irritation.

"Well, Johnny Carson was saying just the other night that it's not healthy when boys play with dolls. I think you'd better watch that," he admonished.

"Tony, look at his size," Rose pleaded with him. "Can you see him throwing the football and running around on the lawn with Tommy and the boys? He's just fine."

Several months later, Rosemarie suggested that dance lessons might be the perfect outlet for the energetic, four-and-a-half-year-old Eddie. "Let me put him in my class," proposed Rosemarie, who was about to begin teaching a tap class to four- and five-year-old girls at a new branch of the popular Joe Michaels Dance Studios in North Miami ("Tots to Teens Our Specialty"), just ten miles away from the Stierle home. Rosemarie was then fourteen years old, and considered the best tap and jazz dancer in her class at Joe Michaels' main South Miami studio. Eddie thought dancing looked like fun. He'd seen his sister perform her jazz routines at the annual Michaels recital and he was excited at the prospect of taking part in something his older sister did away from home. "He's a little fireball," Rosemarie told her mother. "Let's see how he does." Rose embraced the idea at once.

Bill Stierle, however, looked disdainfully upon the idea of placing his son in a dance class for little girls. Sports was the only sideline he had ever considered for his sons. As a teenager, Bill had been the smallest and toughest guard on his high school football team and he intended to raise his sons to be accomplished athletes. In fact, when his son Michael was an eighth grader, Bill even took a job as a milkman for a year just so that he could be finished work by 2 P.M. in time to coach his son's basketball team. His encouragement seemed to be paying off: Michael was a fine guard, catcher, and second baseman; Bill, Jr., was on his way to winning a college football scholarship as a wide receiver; and Tom, an all-star guard, would eventually get to the University of South Carolina on a basketball scholarship. "Why does Eddie need dance lessons?" he asked his wife. "We've already got one dancer. We don't need two." When she reminded him of his own prowess on the dance floor, he pointed out that he had taught himself how to dance, and that at age forty-eight, he was still winning contests — he and Rosemarie had won first place in the father-daughter dance at Madonna Academy two years in a row. After much discussion, Bill relented, but only after Rosemarie promised that if Eddie seemed at all disinclined, she'd promptly take him out of her class.

Eddie immediately took to center stage. Not only could he pick up steps quickly, but he loved to move — and he thrived on attention. On Tuesdays and Thursdays, when his mother was busy driving the other children to activities, Eddie spent the afternoon at the Michaels studio watching Rosemarie teach the older students. But sitting still never came naturally to him. As soon as he joined the class, he was outperforming Rosemarie's thirteen-year-old students.

On December 15, 1973, three months after beginning his lessons with Rosemarie, four-and-a-half-year-old Eddie made his debut. The occasion was his parents' twenty-fifth anniversary party, which was held in the cafeteria at Chaminade, the boys' Catholic high school where Bill was working as a maintenance man. Rose wore a long white dress with a corsage of white roses pinned above her heart, while Bill exchanged his work pants for a tuxedo and ruffled shirt. Eddie, wearing a hand-me-down tan suit that bunched around his ankles, a brown bow tie, and a brand-new pair of tap shoes, thrilled his parents and the ninety guests by showing off his latest tap routine. Their noisy approval only egged him on further: Rather than run for his mother's shelter, Eddie spent the rest of the evening by the bandstand, improvising his own steps to the music.

Within weeks, word of Eddie's talent reached Joe Michaels, who convinced Rose to enroll Eddie in one of his classes and offered to let him in for free. When after a year Michaels closed his North Miami studio, Rose agreed to drive Eddie the forty-five miles to his South Miami studio twice and sometimes three times a week.

While the other parents frequently kept their children home because they were sick or had birthday parties to attend, Rose made sure that Eddie never missed a single lesson. Not that he lacked interest. "Eddie had charisma," Joe Michaels remembers. "He just lit up when he got onstage. I'd seen them come and go by the thousands, but Eddie stood out because he had the drive. So many fall by the wayside because it's not really what they want, it's what their parents want." Eddie wanted to be at the Michaels studio because Joe Michaels made dancing seem exciting. "When in doubt, shake!" Michaels would urge his charges, teasing them gently whenever they fell out of step.

A former Catskills nightclub choreographer and dancer, Michaels had once hosted a children's television talent show in New York City called "Joe Michaels' Kids" in the 1950s before settling in Miami and opening his school in 1960. By 1976, the Michaels

Eddie at his parents' twenty-fifth wedding anniversary, 1972

school counted among its students a "Miss Florida Gold Coast"; a "Miss Dance" of Florida (who happened to be Rosemarie Stierle); and a fourth runner-up to "Miss Orange Blossom" (Petite Division). Michaels was a dapper, flamboyant character, who strode rather than walked, and smoked with great flourish, often using his cigarette as a prop. Perpetually tanned and in good shape, he worked as a catalog and runway model for the department stores of Miami and as an actor in commercials for Newport cigarettes and Close-Up toothpaste. He favored leotard tops and tight slacks and occasionally turned up to teach class wearing foundation on his face, his eyebrows discernibly outlined with pencil. His wife and three daughters took classes at his studio, though their presence led the other girls to grumble that when it came to recitals, Joe was more interested in showcasing his own kids than some of the other stars of the studio.

As a teacher, Joe Michaels hoped to instill a sense of showmanship in his students and to that end, he made sure that he got them onstage as soon as possible. The condominiums and hotels of Miami Beach provided him with ample performing venues as well as eager audiences comprised largely of senior citizens waiting to be entertained. The Diplomat, the Doral, and the Fountainebleu Hotel were particular favorites and it was on those stages—far removed from the rarefied atmosphere of the ballet opera-house stage—that Eddie Stierle began to polish his skills as an entertainer. On Saturday afternoons, Eddie tap-danced his way through the revues held for hotel guests and their children, dressed in richly colored satin costumes hand-sewn by his mother. One of the hits of the show was "Bosom Buddies," a number that the six-one Michaels choreographed for himself and tiny Eddie Stierle, who at age six, says Michaels, "looked like he was barely four." Eddie loved sharing the stage with his teacher, whose showmanship he envied.

Eddie's own flair for performance wasn't restricted to dancing. Every Sunday before Mass at Annunciation Church, the Stierle kids helped their father clean up the Chaminade cafeteria from the dance the night before. One Sunday, following a New Year's Eve dance, six-year-old Eddie took all the hats, posters, and banners he could carry, gathered together a group of kids on his street, and organized a New Year's Day parade through the neighborhood.

His freckled face and pixieish charm proved so irresistible—and marketable—that Eddie was soon launched on the children's modeling and commercial circuit. Robin Meredith, a classmate of Rosemarie's at the Michaels studio, had gone to work as a receptionist for a well-known local children's talent scout. When Meredith learned that Keds was looking for kids to model sneakers, she

Eddie's modeling composite

called Rosemarie and suggested that she take Eddie to the casting call. Eddie landed the job, and a week later was walking down a runway at the Americana Hotel in Miami, modeling sneakers during a footwear convention.

A local commercial for Buster Brown shoes soon followed, an assignment Eddie won after beating out more than one hundred other children. Over the next several years, Eddie won commercials for Life Savers, Pet milk, Coca-Cola, and Wise potato chips and began earning thousands of dollars each year. In 1978, after landing a spot in a Doritos commercial and the job of stand-in to actor Ricky Schroder in the film *The Champ*, Eddie earned $6,726, a third of his father's annual income. As it was, the family was just scraping by on Bill's salary as a plasterer and maintenance man and Eddie's earnings would certainly have helped ease the burden. But Bill and Rose decided to deposit them in a bank account for Eddie alone. The proceeds would go a long way toward paying the bills Eddie would accrue on his way to the top of the dance world.

Bill and Rose led essentially separate lives, or so it appeared to their children, none of whom can recall ever seeing their parents go out together alone. "There were a lot of opportunities for them to do things together," says Eddie's sister Kathy, "but it never happened because Mom was worried that we wouldn't get proper care from a babysitter." Rose and Bill had agreed from the start that Rose would focus on the youngest children, while Bill would guide them through their teenage years. But Rose so precisely choreographed the daily routine of meals, chores, homework, and activities that there was little time for contact between husband and wife or father and children.

To Rose, family was all. She immersed herself in her children's lives and drew pleasure and her sense of worth from their successes. She had always admired the devotion of the nuns who taught her at St. Edward's Parish and remembered how the tight fence around the convent walls prevented the sisters from having contact with the outside world. Rose resolved that when she raised her children, she would always keep some imaginary fence around

Christmas 1973. Clockwise from top middle: Rose; Bill, Jr.; Tom; Eddie; Patty; Kathy; and Rosemarie

Hanging out in the front yard. From left: Tom; Bill, Sr.; Eddie; Patty; Bill, Jr.; Michael; and Kathy

her house. In that, she succeeded: "We had no idea that a world existed outside our house," recalls Tom Stierle. Rose didn't read the newspaper, watch television, or get her hair done. She learned that President Kennedy had been shot from her daughter Terri, who heard the news from one of the nuns at her school. Each night after the kids were in bed, she did the day's laundry, prepared the meals for the next day, and scrubbed the linoleum kitchen floor. She rarely went to sleep before 2 A.M.

As soon as her other children were old enough for school, Rose went to work cleaning the rectory at Annunciation Church and running the lunchroom at Madonna, bringing five-year-old Eddie with her every day until he was ready to follow Tom and Patty to the Annunciation elementary school. While his mother served the hot lunches, Eddie performed his latest routines for a captive audience made up of Rosemarie and her girlfriends. "C'mon, Eddie, show us something," they'd cry, rewarding him for his efforts by carrying him around the lunchroom on their shoulders.

Rose had finally got her "little boy dancer" and was enchanted, especially since he was already attracting attention beyond the family circle. "Boy, you're some finale!" she'd tell Eddie. "You're my lucky charm." Rose clung to Eddie, who was naturally happy to have his mother's undivided attention. He could see that his dancing gave her joy; indeed, she seemed to take great delight in the fact that he was as much in love with dancing as she was. What he couldn't see was that he was fast becoming a stand-in for his father.

The Stierle children saw little of their father, who was laboring long hours to care for his large family and frequently taking on whatever small indoor construction jobs he could find to make a few extra bucks. Since time with him was hard-won, they looked forward to the hours they spent with him on fishing trips and building projects, the two activities that brought the family together. A quiet, hardworking man with a strong, burly body and weathered complexion, Bill Stierle would go door to door, asking neighbors if they needed anything fixed. "I was never an extrovert," he recalls, "but I was aggressive enough to ask for work because I needed to survive." He worked as a plasterer, paper hanger, carpenter, and pretzel salesman, though in a year he never earned more than $20,000. Often his income was much less. Following a course at night school, he added photography to his list of services. He built a darkroom for himself behind the kitchen, and began snapping pictures of Little League games, father-daughter dances, local weddings, and other assorted suburban rites of passage.

When he came home at night, exhausted, he had little energy left over for his wife and children. Twice weekly, after dinner with the family, Bill retired to the living room, where he would spend the rest of the night going through two six-packs of Budweiser and watching "Star Trek" or old movies. He would quietly get drunk and fall asleep, his hands resting on his distended belly. As his children came in the door, full of stories about the day's events, they'd take one look at their father and the pile of discarded beer cans at his feet and say to Rose, "I guess I can't talk to Dad." To which she would invariably reply, "No, not right now." On some nights, he would stop off at the bar after work and by the time he arrived home, his kids had already eaten their dinner and were out at the myriad activities their mother encouraged them to pursue: Bill was at football practice, Tom was playing basketball, Eddie was at a jazz dance class, and Rosemarie was rehearsing with The Lemontwist Showstoppers, an all-girl song and dance group that was fast becoming a fixture on the Miami Beach bar mitzvah and hotel circuit, opening for such acts as Jackie Gleason and Bob Hope. Bill would retrieve the dinner Rose had kept warm for him on the stove and await their return.

Eddie resented his father's drinking but knew there was little he could do to stop it. He wished his father showed more interest in his dancing lessons. "Why does Dad have to drink?" he often asked Rosemarie, who found herself searching for an answer. When the other kids confronted their father, he'd tell them not to follow his example. "Whatever you do, just be better than me," he'd say. "That's all I ask." At other times, they would try to bolster him. "C'mon, Dad, you're better than you think you are," they would plead with him. But to little avail. "I knew they were worried about me," Bill remembers, "but I couldn't promise to give up drinking because I didn't think I'd be able to and I didn't want to lie to them or to myself."

Sometimes he would go too far and, feeling contrite, he would try to control his drinking. "I never hit my wife," he recalls, "but once I got so angry that I broke every piece of furniture in the house. I broke the tables, the chairs. I had to go out and buy brand-new furniture. It cost me about $1,500! And I said, 'Hey, there's no way I'm going to do that thing again. It cost me too much money.' I just went berserk. I remember vividly breaking the chairs. I learned how to control myself by reminding myself of that experience."

But his drinking frequently undercut his authority. Eddie became all too familiar with his mother's morning-after refrain: "Dad had a bad night last night," she'd say, never once using the word *alcoholic*. "You could tell it bothered her," says Tom, "but she'd always deny that my father had a problem. She pretended it wasn't an issue."

While not a staunch Catholic like his wife, Bill nevertheless made sure the family went to church every Sunday morning and he welcomed the idea of enrolling their children in strict Catholic schools, where, he felt, they would be put on the right track. "If you put your kids in a nice environment, the chances of them coming out okay are going to be pretty good," he would assure Rose. But unlike his wife, Bill didn't think God's handiwork was always so tidy. "I'm a Catholic," he would say, "but my eyes are open."

By the time Eddie was nine, his brother Michael was studying for his master's degree in theology at St. Mary's Ecumenical Institute in Baltimore. Having spent seven and a half years as a Marianist Brother, he had decided to leave the Catholic teaching order in 1976, opting instead to become a lay minister. Meanwhile, Terri Stierle had married Mike Guttiere, a vending machine repairman, and was living in a mobile home seventeen miles west of Hollywood, where she was raising her two young sons. A quiet, bookish girl, Terri had left the University of Florida at Gainesville after only two weeks out of homesickness and lack of direction, and had taken a job at the Hollywood Library near her parents' house. The other six Stierle children still remained at home, and spent easy hours together when they could find them, sunbathing and swimming at nearby Hollywood Beach. While the older kids didn't mind deferring to Eddie as the baby of the family and even took pride in his local renown, they were beginning to resent his privileges at home.

Eddie's schedule had become crammed with classes, recitals, and auditions, and the busier he became, the more his mother made allowances for him. When his brothers and sisters had to help their father resod the front lawn, Eddie had to save his energy for a class; when they had to wash the dishes, Eddie was excused to do his homework so that he wouldn't have to do it after dance class. While each of his siblings spent time working with their father, accompanying him on his construction assignments or on his pretzel-selling rounds to far-flung ballparks, Eddie was never available for one reason or another, all of them concocted by his mother. At the time, he felt the excuses were justified. It made sense to him that he should reserve his energy for dance class. It wasn't until many years later that he came to realize that by getting out of household work, fishing trips, and construction projects, he missed the few opportunities to form relationships with his brothers, sisters, and especially with his father. As a result, his father would remain at the edges of his life for many years. To Eddie, he and his mother were separate and apart, "their own little team," as Tom recalls.

But Rose's powerful influence was beginning to produce some troubling side effects: Eddie was visited by a recurring nightmare in which he and his mother were dying together in a nuclear explosion. For many months as he kissed her good-night, he would whisper, "I hope you live forever."

3

THE SHINERS

At the same time that Eddie was becoming more involved with his tap and jazz lessons, his brother Tom was proving himself a champion on the basketball court. Tom secretly hoped that if he were successful, his mother would show as much interest in his goals as she did in Eddie's. But Tom's dream to be a basketball star didn't resonate with Rose as forcefully as Eddie's dancing dreams did. To her, Eddie was not simply the most affectionate of her children, but the instrument of her own quelled aspirations. Every night after Rose and Eddie drove off to class, Tom would shoot hoops in the driveway under the lights. "I have this recurring image," remembers Tom, "of Eddie and my mom pulling up in the driveway. I'd look at them in the car and think, 'He's doing his thing with Mom and I'm doing mine on my own.'"

Patty, too, was jealous of all the attention her younger brother was getting, a problem compounded when Rose decided to enroll Patty in the same tap class that Eddie was taking at Joe Michaels'. A broad-shouldered, busty girl who at twelve was in the early throes of an awkward adolescence, Patty quickly discovered she wasn't nearly as cute, coordinated, or skillful as her nine-year-old brother. Not only was her mother paying more attention to him, but so was everyone else. Each year he stole the show at the annual recital the Michaels' studio held at the Dade County Auditorium and at the statewide dance competitions in which the Michaels' students regularly participated. In number after number, he was easy enough to pick out: He was the only boy on a stage filled with tall, blond girls dressed in sequins and feathers—and half their size. Patty would try to improve by practicing with Eddie in the small dance studio—actually a tiny room with a mirrored wall and a ballet barre—that Bill had built for Rosemarie next to his darkroom, but she simply couldn't keep up with him. She stuck with the lessons for three years, but never managed to emerge from Eddie's shadow to cast one of her own.

"My mother seemed to migrate to the kid who was in the spotlight," recalls Patty. "The rest of us called them 'the shiners.' The first one was Mike because he was outgoing and wanted to serve in the Church; then came Rosemarie with her dancing and singing, then Tom who was a basketball star, and last came Eddie. I was in between Tommy and Eddie, so there wasn't much I could do to draw attention to myself."

When Rose realized that her other children were jealous of Eddie, she responded by encouraging Eddie to hide his excitement about the roles and commercials he won. "When Eddie and I were in the car on the way home from an audition, I'd say to him, 'I guess we can't talk about it too much when we get home,'" she remembers. "And he'd say, 'But I'm so happy.' I'd tell him, 'Well, let's get all that bubbly stuff over with in the car and when we pull up, we'll just tell everyone you got it.' It was hard to play down Eddie's success."

Shortly after Eddie's ninth birthday, nineteen-year-old Rosemarie married Kit Worton, a guitarist she had been dating for a year. Rosemarie had been Eddie's protector and adviser; once she went on the road as a singer and dancer with The Right Touch, her husband's show band, Eddie was left to deal with the others still at home.

After Rosemarie's marriage, Bill, Jr., left home for Emporia State University in Kansas, where he would win a football scholarship, leaving Tom to assume the mantle of eldest brother. He and Patty began to retaliate against Eddie. They had already had their fill of Rosemarie's and Eddie's dance recitals and they resented being dragged to more of them in order to admire their already fussed-over baby brother. At the dinner table, they shunned him. They would pass the food to one another over his head until Rose ordered them to stop. Eddie tried to gain their favor by telling jokes or making up silly stories, but he didn't have Tom's command of easy banter and his attempts at humor fell flat. He wanted his brother's approval and he couldn't understand why his brother barely acknowledged him. "Patty and I refused to let Eddie run the show," says Tom.

Their behavior convinced Rose she needed to keep Eddie away from them. "My mother was always worried about Eddie getting hurt," says Patty. "She kept us apart from him and controlled his use of free time." On the occasions when they did try to include Eddie, their mother would prevent him from tagging along. "Eddie would get really excited when we finally invited him to come with us to the beach," says Tom, "and my mother would never let him go. She'd say, 'Well, you know you have to dance this afternoon.' She always wanted to keep an eye on him. When we finally found some common ground, my mother prevented us from sharing."

Eddie wasn't faring much better in the Annunciation schoolyard. Since Rose managed the cafeteria at Madonna, the Stierle children went there every day for their lunch. When the fifth-grade boys at Annunciation heard that Eddie Stierle took dance lessons and went to a girls' school for lunch, they pegged him at once. "You're a girl! You're a fag!" they taunted him. "It bothered him that the kids made fun of him," remembers his sister Kathy, "but he sure wasn't going to stop his dance lessons."

Bill Stierle, however, was troubled by the number of hours Eddie was devoting to those dance lessons. He showed little enthusiasm when Rose and Rosemarie would gush about Eddie's accomplishments—he often complained that Rose was putting

Eddie and the girls from the Joe Michaels studio after winning
first place in 1978

Eddie first, spending more time shuttling him from class to class
than she was at home minding Bill's own needs. Shouldn't he be
considered before Eddie? he asked his wife. Rose quickly saw that
it was going to take a lot of work to "win Bill over to dance," as
she put it, because Bill was "all sports."

Eddie, on the other hand, had never tried any sport. Thinking
perhaps that his son needed some manly encouragement and a
break from little girls, leotards, and tights, Bill signed him up for
flag football. The experiment was hardly a success. When Rosema-

rie came to pick him up after practice one day, she came upon a scene that convinced her that the enterprise was hopeless. All the kids were jogging around the track in their green helmets and padded uniforms except Eddie, who was blithely leaping around the track, practicing his flying splits.

Bill Stierle conceded that flag football was not Eddie's calling. One day he and Tom went to watch Eddie's team play. In the middle of the game, Eddie came off the field, took off his helmet, and lay down on a bench to sun himself. "There's no hope for this kid," Tom sighed.

But Eddie was able to prove to his father that his dancing lessons had turned him into another sort of champion when he won top prize at a national dance contest at the Waldorf-Astoria hotel

Father and son

in New York in July 1979. Eddie had spent weeks preparing for the Dance Educators of America competition, a contest held annually in New York that drew young jazz, tap, and ballet performers from assorted regional studios across the United States and Canada. Eddie had already danced his way to victory in the Florida "regionals" with his performance in a number called "That's Entertainment," wearing a hot pink vest, white bell-bottoms, and a matching pink scarf on his white boater. For the nationals, he danced "Ease on Down the Road," a ten-minute solo Joe Michaels had made to showcase Eddie's brilliant high kicks and breezy

With Joe Michaels
at the Waldorf-Astoria
in 1979

jumps. Set to the song from the Broadway musical, *The Wiz,* "Ease on Down the Road" required Eddie to execute several turns in the air and land on one knee. To protect Eddie's knees, Michaels insisted that he wear knee pads under the costume his mother had ordered from a Miami Beach costume house: a low-cut, black lycra, bell-bottomed jumpsuit with shimmery gold triangles inserted in the sleeves and legs. But in the packed Grand Ballroom of the Waldorf-Astoria, eleven-year-old Eddie danced without knee pads, drawing gasps and applause from the other dance hopefuls and their teachers with his simultaneous turns and head rolls and his skyscraping leaps. As he went skidding toward the audience on his knees, he flashed his smile—by now, the smile of a seasoned professional.

"He could have damaged himself permanently," recalls Joe Michaels, who stood with Bill and Rose Stierle as Eddie was awarded the first-prize trophy in the junior division, edging out the twenty-three other regional finalists from across the country. His victory made the pages of *The Miami Herald,* the first of dozens of press clippings chronicling the promise of Eddie Stierle. To Bill Stierle, the enormous public acclaim—and trophy to prove it— meant not only that his son had talent, but that Eddie was clearly on the road to having the kind of career he himself had dreamed of years before.

The day after Eddie's New York debut, Bill and Rose took him to see a children's talent agent they had met at the competition. The agent pressed the Stierles to keep Eddie in New York, where he felt certain Eddie could get work immediately in commercials. "You've got a winner there," he said, patting Eddie on the head. The fact that a New York agent thought he was special thrilled Eddie; he'd often heard Joe Michaels and Rosemarie talk about New York in awed tones and he knew that his performance there mattered in ways that it didn't in Miami. But when Rose and Bill told the agent that they simply couldn't uproot their family, he urged them to take Eddie to see Mitzi Rader, a former tap dancer he knew who ran a studio in Emerald Hills, a well-to-do neighborhood near Hollywood, Florida.

A compact, earthy woman who liked to play Jewish mama to

her favored pupils, Mitzi Rader was always on the lookout for gifted children she could turn into stars of the musical theater. Since founding the Emerald Hills Studio of Performing Arts in 1969, Rader had been teaching dance to nearly three hundred students each year, but when Eddie Stierle came to audition that year and she saw what he could do, she knew at once that "this kid was the one in a million." At age eleven, he possessed that most elusive of stagecrafts: charisma.

Hungry for more opportunities to dance, Eddie was excited by the prospect of performing on a regular basis and getting paid for it. The knowledge that Rader could help him have the career he wanted made him hungrier still.

Rader put him to work immediately in The Generation Gap, the studio's young performing troupe, which put on shows for local nursing homes and retirement homes. But after a brief apprenticeship, Eddie advanced to The Good Times People, a professional song-and-dance revue produced by Rader and comprised of the studio's best senior students, whose ages ran from sixteen to twenty-six. The group, which later assumed the name Razz Ma Jazz, played the condo, convention, and dinner theater circuit and performed three times a week, for which Eddie earned $50 per show. He had yet to hit five feet and was the shortest and youngest dancer in the leggy lineup—and often the star attraction. "There wasn't anyone who could touch him," says Rader. "He had a magic about him. You can't train people to be wonderful performers. Eddie was born with it. After every show, people would always remember the kid with the freckles."

Chrissie Guastella, the studio's sixteen-year-old female star, recalls that while she and the other members of the troupe were all older than Eddie, they quickly recognized his prodigious talent. They had heard that "this kid" had just won a big dance competition in New York, but the day he came to take class with them, "he blew us away," she says. As Eddie demonstrated his jumps and turns, the rest of the class came to a standstill, finally erupting in cheers. "There wasn't anything he couldn't do," says Guastella. "A few of the guys might have been jealous, but Eddie was never on a high horse. He was used to attention, but I don't think it ever

Wowing local audiences in Miami

With Razz Ma Jazz. Eddie is in the second row, at left; Chrissie Guastella is in the first row, left.

occurred to him how special he was. He became fast friends with everyone, even though we were all at least five years older. He just thought of himself as being like everyone else."

He was hardly like everyone else and the more his talent had opportunities to show itself, the wider the chasm grew between Eddie and his siblings, one that was largely to remain unbridged until the final years of Eddie's life. His schedule had become so jammed with rehearsals and performances, classes at Joe Michaels, and the marathon regimen of voice, drama, gymnastics, jazz, and ballet at Mitzi's studio that he often got home past midnight. To maximize his time while his mother drove him from one studio to the next, Eddie learned to eat, change into costume, and do his homework with a flashlight, all while in a car moving at 60 miles per hour. Now he rarely paused at home long enough to go to the beach or go fishing with his brothers and sisters. Monopoly games would go on for a week, because Eddie could never spare more than an hour each day to continue the game. Week-long Monopoly games were one of the few concessions Tom and Patty were willing to make to Eddie's timetable.

The tension at home had been escalating steadily, but it wasn't until Rosemarie prescribed formal ballet training for Eddie that the family battle lines became so clearly drawn. While at home on a break from touring in early September 1979, Rosemarie went to see Eddie perform with Razz Ma Jazz. She hadn't seen him dance in more than a year, and was anxious to check on his progress. Since she had never had a mentor herself, she was determined that Eddie should benefit from her hard-won experience. "Eddie needs ballet training," she announced to her mother after the performance. "His dancing is great, but his arms are sloppy and he isn't pointing his feet. He's losing his technique. We've got to get him in a strict ballet school."

Eddie was already taking one hour of ballet each week at the Emerald Hills studio, but his sensibility—and that of his teachers, Joe Michaels and Mitzi Rader—was much more rooted in show-biz dazzle than in classical decorum. His apprenticeship in the hotels and condominiums of Miami Beach was only reinforcing that sensibility by teaching him to emphasize flamboyance over subtlety or precision. At age eleven, Eddie was clearly heading for a career on the Broadway or nightclub stage; ballet still belonged to a distant, unfamiliar realm. On the other hand, he valued his sister's advice. He knew he was the best dancer in Razz Ma Jazz and he figured that if she felt ballet lessons could help him excel further, well, why not take them?

Rose Stierle, too, trusted Rosemarie's more practiced eye and had always relied on her daughter for advice about Eddie's training. She wanted only the best for her talented son, even though she had no idea what "the best" meant. Since Edward didn't yet have the perspective or authority to plot his own course, she would be ambitious on his behalf. If Rosemarie said he needed ballet, then she would see to it that she got him into the proper school. But first she had to sell Bill on the idea. Having spent a lifetime mastering the art of avoiding confrontation, she was skilled at evasive schemes, compromises, and behind-the-scenes manipulations. Now when she wanted something done, she would rarely ask for it straight out; instead, she would choose one of her children to run interference. This time she picked Rosemarie.

She suspected that Bill would balk at Rosemarie's suggestion, but she was unprepared for the bitter fight that erupted when she and Rosemarie broached the subject with him one afternoon in the kitchen while he was chatting with Patty.

Rosemarie opened the discussion by explaining to her father why she felt sure that ballet training would improve Eddie's tap and jazz dancing. Rose casually reminded Bill about the ballet teacher they had met the year before in New York at the Dance Educators convention. Her name was Liana and her junior students had won first place in the group ballet competition. Liana, she recalled, had been so impressed by "the little boy in 'Ease on Down the Road' " that she had made a point of meeting his parents so that she could try to persuade them to enroll their son in her school. There was only one hitch: Liana's studio was in Hialeah, a forty-five-minute drive from Hollywood. Rose would have to spend even more time in the car driving Eddie back and forth.

As he listened to his wife and daughter, Bill grew enraged. He had only just come to accept Eddie as a dancer, but he was drawing the line at ballet. "Why are you pushing him into ballet? He's gone all the time as it is," he said, addressing his complaints to Rosemarie. "Rose is always driving him everywhere. And she's terrible on the highway. It's just too much. Too much. I'm the father in this house and what I say *goes*. Eddie doesn't need ballet lessons."

The following Wednesday, Rose drove Eddie to his first ballet lesson at Liana Ballet.

To the ballerinas at Liana's, Eddie was something of a curiosity. They had never had a boy in their class and he didn't speak Spanish, let alone live in their neighborhood. Hialeah had the largest Cuban population in South Florida and classes at Liana's had always been conducted in Spanish—until Eddie Stierle came to study in the fall of 1979 and English was added to the lessons.

Eddie's first ballet friend was a skinny, dark-haired, doe-eyed, ten-year-old girl named Lissette Salgado, who was to become his roommate and confidante several years later when both were members of the Joffrey Ballet. Lissette had seen Eddie dance his "Ease on Down" solo at the regional Dance Educators contest in Ft. Lauderdale and had been impressed with his performance. "I thought, 'He's so little, but he can really dance,'" she recalls. "He had an incredible smile, the kind you remember."

Like the rest of Liana's Cuban pupils, Lissette was reluctant to speak to the eleven-year-old boy in their midst. Eddie broke the ice one day while they sat watching Liana give corrections to another student. "I'd really like to try taking class in toe shoes," he told her. "I think it will help stretch my feet." Girls, not boys, danced on pointe, thought Lissette, who couldn't wait to graduate to pointe shoes herself. "Of course, Eddie ended up taking class in pointe shoes," she says. "It was never what he could do at the moment, he was always concerned about how far he could go."

Twenty-year-old Liana Garcia-Usatorres spoke in rapid-fire sentences, taught class in jeans and white sneakers, and kept her sandy brown hair cropped short. Petite and bouncy, she hardly fit the stereotype of the tall, prim, small-town ballet teacher with a neat chignon on the top of her head and a penchant for correct French terminology. In fact, she seemed more like an aerobics instructor. "La Cola!" she would admonish her students and, at once, rows of little girls would tuck in their behinds and straighten their spines. Liana had studied ballet for ten years at a Cuban ballet school in Coral Gables and her method was based on her schooling in the Russian-Cuban tradition of ballet. In 1977, she opened her own two-room studio in Hialeah's Portofino Shopping Plaza. By 1979, she had already begun to attract some local

With Liana in later years

attention after her eleven-year-old pupils were judged the best junior ballet group at the same dance competition in New York where Eddie Stierle took first prize for best junior jazz dancer. Liana had no boy dancers at her school and though she knew Eddie Stierle was headed for a jazz career, she saw in the charismatic little boy an ideal partner for her fledgling ballerinas.

As a teacher, Liana was an exacting taskmaster who demanded that students adhere to a strict dress code. She wanted her girls in hairnets, black leotards, pink tights, and pink shoes, and Eddie Stierle in white T-shirt, black tights, and white slippers. She also refused to tolerate any distractions from the doting Cuban mothers and grandmothers who waited out the three-hour classes in the lounge adjoining the studio. Before choosing the album of recorded ballet music that would accompany her lesson, Liana would draw the red curtain dividing the two rooms to block their view. Rose Stierle felt left out of the Spanish conversations in the lounge and passed the time by shopping for the satin she needed for Eddie's Razz Ma Jazz costumes or by driving ten miles to Miami to hear Rosemarie's band play at the Doral Country Club. More often, however, she would wait for Eddie outside the studio in her bronze Celebrity station wagon. At 11 P.M., he would open the car door to find his mother fast asleep in the front seat. "Rose really had no choice but to wait for Eddie," says Liana, who became Liana Navarro following her marriage in 1982. "The other mothers could go home because they lived close by, but Rose lived so far away. You could see how tired she was and I was always worried that she'd fall asleep driving home late at night. I'd tell Eddie, 'Make sure you keep your mom up,' and he'd always say, 'Oh, don't worry, I will, I will.' "

Several months after starting his lessons at Liana's, Eddie stopped going to the Michaels studio. There was no time left in a schedule already packed with school homework, casting calls, tap, jazz, and voice lessons at Mitzi's Emerald Hills studio, ballet classes at Liana's, and weekend stints with Razz Ma Jazz. Joe Michaels, who wasn't pleased about losing a promising pupil, considered the move toward ballet misguided. "I thought that Eddie, if he were lucky, would end up in the chorus of a ballet company," says Michaels. "He didn't have the body for ballet."

Nor did his prospects look promising: By the time Eddie's twelfth birthday came around, he still looked like a cute little boy. A mere ninety pounds and four feet ten inches—four inches shorter than his schoolmates—Eddie didn't have the makings of a ballet prince.

To Liana Navarro, he lacked not only the necessary long limbs and high instep, but the technique. During Eddie's first few months at her studio, she doubted that he would ever become a professional ballet dancer. Not that he had expressed any interest. Ballet challenged and stimulated him, but he wasn't about to give up his dream to dance on Broadway. There were no professional ballet companies based in South Florida,* which before the Miami renaissance of the mid-1980s had a decidedly small-town cultural life, and Eddie had never been to see any of the major ballet troupes that occasionally came to town. As far as Liana knew, Eddie's ballet lessons were meant only to strengthen his jazz technique. "Eddie's technique was horrible when he came to me," she says, voicing a refrain commonly heard from teachers who inherit students from other studios. "He had a great jump, but no sense of placement. He'd throw his body all over."

At the end of his first year with Liana, Eddie had not only shed his sloppy habits, but he was beginning to show promise as a classical dancer. "Are you sure you still want to be a jazz dancer?" Liana asked him one day, hoping to woo him to her studio full-time. Unlike her other students, he studied movement, instead of simply imitating and memorizing it, and treated each class as though it were a performance, not a rehearsal. He had an innate sense of his body's capabilities and managed difficult technical

---

*In 1985, when former New York City Ballet star Edward Villella announced he was founding South Florida's first professional classical company, many wondered whether he would flounder in such a cultural wasteland. Today his Miami City Ballet is attracting national attention.

feats with ease, investing every turn and jump with his natural exuberance.

He was also highly competitive. He was intent on showing the flexible ballerinas that he could raise his leg higher than theirs in arabesque and he was constantly adjusting his body as he compared his line in the mirror to that of the other dancers. To Eddie, class was serious business and he relished the rigor, precision, and endless repetition that ballet demanded. "Eddie learned his love for ballet from me," says Liana Navarro. "I made them really dance from their heart." She also demanded strict attention to the details of movement. It wasn't enough to have fun and please the audience, as was the case in Razz Ma Jazz; her pupils had to prove that they could adhere to the strict principles of a centuries-old tradition.

Her method engaged Eddie's mind more thoroughly than his classes at Mitzi's studio did. While tap and jazz had always come naturally to him and allowed him to express his individuality, ballet posed a much bigger challenge. Yet never did he consider it insurmountable, even if he didn't have the ideal ballet body. He would imagine his ideal physique and then try to "make his body look like that picture in his head," says Lissette Salgado.

A year into his lessons at Navarro's studio, Eddie had become obsessed with ballet and soon made up his mind to transform himself into a ballet dancer. From then on, he singularly pursued his goal, one that in 1980 seemed way beyond his reach. It was the beginning of a career built on invented possibilities.

Performing in *Outer Space* with Liana Ballet

4

BALLET CONCERTO

Even as he was emerging as the star of Liana's school, Eddie still managed to outshine the best tap and jazz dancers in Razz Ma Jazz. He was being pulled in opposite directions and Mitzi and Liana each sought to claim him for their own. The two women had much in common with each other and with Rose Stierle: They were emotional, maternal, and possessive, and utterly taken with Eddie, whose success had become their paramount concern. Since Mitzi's own two children had no interest in dance and Liana had no other male pupils, each longed to play a leading role in shaping Eddie Stierle. "I spent more time with him than my own children," Mitzi would say years later. "Neither of them are in show business." Neither teacher had ever taught a student of Eddie's caliber and the better he became, the more central he became to their student showcases. Since Eddie was the only prince-in-the-making at Liana's studio, he was naturally in great demand around recital time. A videotape of a Liana Ballet recital, circa 1981, shows Eddie running around the stage in a work

With Mitzi Rader

entitled "Emotions," valiantly hoisting ballerina after ballerina, showing each of them off like a precious jewel.

Both Mitzi and Liana saw the New York stage in Eddie's future, but while Mitzi envisioned Broadway, Liana dreamed of the Metropolitan Opera House, home of American Ballet Theatre. Just as Rose had relied on Rosemarie to guide her, she now regularly consulted with Mitzi and Liana about his potential. She was not a typical stage mother: She never criticized Eddie's progress, gave him pointers on how to advance, or pushed his teachers to give him leading roles. She didn't need to. Whatever they advised, Rose found a way to provide it.

To build Eddie's strength as a partner, Liana recommended an adagio class at the Academia Cubana de Ballet, known as Ballet Concerto. Every Saturday, Eddie learned to lift, support, and carry Lissette Salgado and several of Liana's older students. This time, Eddie was one of three male dancers in the class, but he was a boy of thirteen, while the other two were young men of nineteen.

One Saturday Rose Stierle was waiting for Eddie in the Ballet Concerto lounge when she caught another mother staring at him, disapprovingly. "Oh, the Americano," the woman said. "If that were my son and he was a good dancer, I'd never put him in ballet because they're all gay." Rose was furious. "That's not so," she protested.

She thought to herself, "If God has given Edward to me, and if God has given him talent, then I'm going to follow through."

On the drive home, Rose related the incident to Eddie. "Something really upset me today. One of the moms told me that if you put a boy dancer in ballet, he could become gay."

"Mom, that's silly," said Eddie. "I'm not gay."

That night, Rose discussed the day's events with Bill. Instead of reassurances, he offered his own homespun theory of homosexuality. To Bill Stierle, there was no debate: It was not genetically determined but socially conditioned.

"I don't think there's a father around who doesn't associate ballet with being gay," he told his wife. "It's environmental. If you put him in ballet, he'll be gay, just like if you put him in with a bunch of gangsters, he'll be a gangster. The odds are not in your favor. I just hope Eddie can handle it." Bill had worried years earlier that his eldest son, Michael, might "turn gay" if he joined the Marianist Brothers, took his vows of chastity, and spent all his time with men. He was concerned that Michael would be influenced by his "environment," but he kept the thought to himself and never mentioned it to his wife.

Rose was going to protect Eddie. She had noticed that Eddie liked to joke around with the guys in his partnering class at Ballet Concerto and she determined that she would keep them away from

Eddie, whether they were gay or not. "I was always worried that the guys would get to Eddie, that somebody would lead him astray, so I kept on my toes," she recalls. "I expected him to be straight, like his brothers. I wanted him to find a lovely ballerina." So did Mitzi Rader, who offered to "have a talk" with Eddie on the subject. "Don't worry," Mitzi told Rose a week later, "I told him that if any guy comes on to him, he should simply say, 'I'm straight and you should leave me alone.' "

Years later, Eddie would tell one of his lovers that on various occasions, he had fooled around in the bathroom at Ballet Concerto with two of the boys in his class, but hadn't then recognized anything meaningful in his urges because he was madly in love with Chrissie Guastella. At thirteen, he had only just become aware of the conflicting desires that would nag at him for the rest of his life.

An outgoing, shapely girl with long eyelashes and dark brown curls framing her face, Chrissie was seventeen and the best female dancer in Razz Ma Jazz. She was also the girlfriend of Brian Kennelly, a twenty-year-old singer and dancer in the troupe. Eddie shared her passion for dancing and in his presence she felt particularly relaxed and playful. She was well aware of his increasing affection for her and while she thought of him as a little brother, she was flattered by his attentions. "Eddie and I used to get into trouble at Mitzi's because we'd get so giddy and try to make each other laugh," she recalls. "You just got addicted to him because he was so much fun. We'd do shows on Friday and Saturday nights and then a bunch of us would go out to the movies or to the beach. My boyfriend became jealous of Eddie because Eddie and I got on so well and spent so much time together."

Her boyfriend's jealousy became even more acute when he noticed that Chrissie preferred to hold hands with Eddie when the three of them went out together. What an unlikely trio they were: Brian was five-ten; Chrissie was five-six; and Eddie, four-eleven. "I could see that Brian was uncomfortable," she recalls, "and he would sometimes make remarks about my holding hands with Eddie." Their situation was even played out onstage in one of their Razz Ma Jazz numbers: While Brian serenaded them from the side of the stage, Eddie and Chrissie tap-danced a pas de deux to "Tea for Two."

Eddie became enamored of Chrissie. "Eddie got swept into this obsession with me," she says. "We were at the studio so much together and maybe I led him on. He would tell me that he was in love with me and I would always tell him, 'I love you too, but not the same way that I love Brian.' I would cry at night because I knew how hurt he was, but there was nothing I could do."

One night, she drove Eddie home from class and agreed to stop in for a visit. As they were sitting on the couch watching television, Eddie tried to kiss her and she relented. He was always trying to kiss her and she felt sorry for him. She regretted her decision almost at once, especially when she saw how ardent Eddie was. Delirious at the thought that he had finally won her over, Eddie figured if she'd kissed him once, she'd want to kiss him again. His elation was short-lived. Chrissie felt guilty about their kiss and advised him there would be no more. "After a while, he just gave up," she says.

Despite his misgivings about the likely effect of ballet on his youngest son, Bill Stierle photographed every one of Eddie's recitals and occasionally accompanied him to Liana's studio to take portraits of the students, which had been commissioned by their parents. But he had no frame of reference for understanding classical ballet. Fouetté, arabesque, tour jeté. The names of the steps were as foreign to him as the Spanish spoken by her students. As a result, he kept his distance and learned what he could through the lens of his camera.

Eddie knew that his father hoped he would become the next Donald O'Connor, but he didn't share his father's dream of becoming a song-and-dance man. At any rate, he spent so much time in the car with his mother and so little time at home that he had few opportunities to stimulate his father's interest in ballet or, indeed, to find any common ground with him.

"Bill really wanted Eddie to be a jazz and tap dancer," says Rose Stierle. "He wanted him to go to Broadway and thought

Eddie was wasting his time in ballet." Practicality also governed Bill Stierle's outlook. He simply couldn't understand how a man could make a decent living as a ballet dancer.

For Eddie, dance was all-consuming. Each day after school let out at 3 P.M., Eddie changed into his tights and went straight to Mitzi's studio for three hours of classes before getting back into his mother's car and driving to Hialeah for another three hours of ballet. On Saturdays, he took classes at Ballet Concerto and then rehearsed excerpts from classical ballets at Miami Dance Theatre, a ballet troupe made up of serious students from several ballet schools in Dade County. Saturday evenings and Sunday afternoons were taken up with Razz Ma Jazz rehearsals and performances.

At the age of fourteen, he had yet to see a professional ballet company or a full-length ballet, except on television. Not surprisingly, he saw his first full-length ballet from the stage, not the audience, when he was cast as a peasant in a Ballet Concerto production of *Giselle* in April 1982. *Giselle* tells the story of a peasant girl who dies of a broken heart and joins the spirit world of the Wilis, young women who died before their wedding nights. Imported for the occasion was the celebrated ballerina Gelsey Kirkland,* one of the ballet world's biggest stars and the frequent partner of Mikhail Baryshnikov, Eddie's idol. The excitement of sharing the stage with Kirkland convinced Eddie that dance would be his life. Shortly after his debut in *Giselle*, the first ballet he danced that wasn't choreographed by Liana Navarro, Eddie wrote to Dahlia Weinstein, a close friend in his tap class. "I love dancing and it's my life. If I couldn't have it, I would die."

---

*Kirkland had been one of American Ballet Theatre's biggest stars, but the company and its director, Mikhail Baryshnikov, were then refusing to renew her contract because she was mired in problems arising from her cocaine addiction. In her memoir, *Dancing on My Grave* (the title is a reference to *Giselle*), Kirkland recounts how in 1982 she was dancing while high from cocaine and so desperately in need of cash to support her habit that she was taking on whatever guest assignments were offered.

5

EPIDEMIC

By June 1982, a year had passed since the Centers for Disease Control in Atlanta had published in its weekly newsletter the first report on an unusual outbreak of a disease affecting homosexual men in Los Angeles. The report was published through the efforts of a young immunologist at UCLA named Dr. Michael Gottlieb and was based on the disturbing cases of *Pneumocystis carinii* pneumonia that he and other referring physicians had seen in five gay men in just one city during the preceding months. Outbreaks of *Pneumocystis* were considered uncommon, since the *Pneumocystis* microbe was known to be held in check by normally functioning immune systems. For some then-unknown reason, the immune systems of the gay men Dr. Gottlieb and others had seen were all out of whack and the men were unable to fight off even mild infections. They all exhibited similar symptoms: swollen lymph nodes, weight loss, fevers, and candidiasis, a yeast infection that was erupting in the mouth. The men were all strangely deficient in T-helper lymphocyte cells, the cells that activate the body's disease-fighting cells and create the antibodies that destroy microbial invaders. The report had noted that "the fact that these patients were all homosexuals suggests an association between some aspect of homosexual life-style or disease acquired through sexual contact and *Pneumocystis* pneumonia in this population." According to Randy Shilts,* author of *And the Band Played On,* staffers at the CDC had been terribly concerned that the content of the report as well as its title—"*Pneumocystis* pneumonia in homosexual men/Los Angeles"—would offend the gay community and fuel prejudice in the medical and political arena at large. As a result, they bumped the entire report to the second page of the newsletter and dropped the reference to *homosexual* in the title. The report earned only a few paragraphs in both the gay and mainstream press. As Randy Shilts has reported, the gay press didn't see much point in giving major coverage to the pneumonia outbreak, since it appeared to be a medical curiosity, whose importance was likely exaggerated by homophobes in the fields of science and journalism.

A month after Dr. Gottlieb's findings were published, the first official report on an outbreak of Kaposi's sarcoma among homosexual men in New York City and California ran in the CDC's newsletter. KS, as it was known, was a rare form of skin cancer that was first discovered in 1871 among Mediterranean and Jewish men in their fifties or sixties. It later surfaced in Central Africa, where it was thought to be geographically confined and relatively benign. The report outlined the common symptoms of the KS patients, all of them young, non-Mediterranean men, twenty of whom lived in New York and six in California. Four of the patients had suffered a bout with *Pneumocystis,* or PCP; others had suffered from severe herpes; candidiasis; cryptococcal meningitis; and toxoplasmosis, a rare parasite. The report noted that "no previous association between KS and sexual preference has been reported."

It didn't take long for the epidemic to be identified by assorted monikers; it was "Gay Pneumonia" if the patient had PCP, "Gay

---

*Randy Shilts died of complications from AIDS in February 1994.

Cancer" if he had KS, and "Gay Plague" if he had the misfortune to be afflicted with both PCP and KS. Soon it had another name: GRID, or Gay-Related Immune Deficiency. By May of 1982, a year after the first CDC report, 355 confirmed GRID cases had been counted in twenty states. It wouldn't be until July of that year that the medical community would finally agree on a name for the epidemic: Acquired Immune Deficiency Syndrome. As Randy Shilts has noted, "That gave the epidemic a snappy acronymn, AIDS, and was sexually neutral. The word *acquired* separated the immune deficiency syndrome from congenital defects or chemically induced immune problems, indicating the syndrome was acquired from somewhere even though nobody knew from where."

Every week, new cases of KS and PCP were popping up in new regions of the country, and not only among gay and bisexual men, although this group accounted for 79 percent of all cases in June of 1982. By then, news of the mysterious disease had made only rare appearances in the nation's leading newsmagazines and newspapers, primarily because the majority of victims were homosexuals and few editors wanted to print stories about gay men, particularly when it involved their sexual practices.

Stigma and neglect were the twin hallmarks of AIDS coverage from the start. As Randy Shilts noted, AIDS became newsworthy only "when it was not killing homosexuals," though in the public mind, it was thoroughly identified as a gay disease no matter whom it was killing. Soon, heterosexual women, Haitians, intravenous drug users, hemophiliacs, infants, and prisoners were added to the list. As new cases were reported, the Centers for Disease Control began dispatching investigators to various pockets of the country in an effort to gather clues to help track the mysterious disease.

Neither the Centers for Disease Control nor Gay-Related Immune Deficiency held much meaning for Eddie Stierle when, in June of 1982, he was asked to attend a special meeting for students at Ballet Concerto following his partnering class. Parents were not invited. Eddie joined the circle of students sitting on the floor of the studio and listened intently as Eduardo Recalt, his teacher, introduced a guest visitor, "a doctor sent by the Centers for Disease Control in Atlanta," he told them. "As some of you know," he went on, "Rogelio Gonzalez, a dancer with Ballet Concerto, died last week from a disease the doctors don't know much about. They aren't sure what killed him. He would like to talk to you to find out as much as he can about him." The doctor spoke to each student privately. Eddie was asked whether he knew anything about Rogelio's sexual partners, his friends, his habits. Did he notice if he looked sick, and if he did, what exactly were the changes he noticed? Rogelio Gonzalez had danced in Ballet Concerto's *Giselle* and though Eddie had met him a few times during rehearsals, he knew little about the older dancer's life and was soon excused from the meeting. But the news of Rogelio's death left him shaken. He couldn't understand how someone could die in his twenties, or how the experts could know so little about the disease that killed him. They had called it a disease, hadn't they? But they still didn't know all the ways it could be transmitted or the length of its incubation period. And they couldn't even diagnose it. (Later that year, it was discovered that the virus could be transmitted through blood.) "Do they think I was exposed to it by dancing in the same room with him?" Eddie wondered. He would discuss his concerns later with Rosemarie, whom he was on his way to visit in Miami. Rosemarie and her husband, Kit, were performing with their band at the Doral Country Club and Eddie was planning to stay with them for the weekend.

Naturally his mother was waiting for him in her car when he came out of Ballet Concerto. "What was the big secret?" she asked as he jumped into the front seat.

Not wanting her to worry, Eddie downplayed his response. "They just wanted to know if we knew anything about Rogelio Gonzalez. He died from some disease, but they don't know much about it. They wanted to know if he hung out with any of us."

"But you didn't know him very well, right?" asked Rose, studying his face for clues.

"Mom, don't worry. It doesn't concern me. It's only something that concerns the older guys."

Rose put Rogelio Gonzalez and his mysterious illness out of her thoughts. It would be eight years before she and Eddie would return to the subject, only by then it had acquired an urgency she could never have imagined, and also, a name.

Practicing with Rosemarie at the Doral Country Club in Miami, 1983

6

BALLET
BODIES

Determined to prove that ballet was his calling, Eddie
flew to New York with his mother in July 1982 to take classes at
the prestigious School of American Ballet. He had won a full
scholarship to the school's intensive six-week summer workshop,
at the end of which the most promising students would be invited
to stay on full-time. Eddie hoped to be among them.

The School of American Ballet was the premier classical dance
academy in the country and the official training ground of the New
York City Ballet, the company led by master choreographer George
Balanchine. SAB, as it was known, had been founded in 1934 by
Balanchine, the last choreographer of Diaghilev's Ballets Russes,
and by Lincoln Kirstein, the visionary patron and tastemaker
who had brought Balanchine to America from Europe and later
established the New York City Ballet with him. "But first, a
school," was Balanchine's now-famous edict on the importance of
training dancers in his style before putting them on the stage. Only
the fittest survived at SAB: Its stringent requirements and ongoing
screening process prompted Kirstein to describe it as "the West

Point of the dance." The school was located on the third floor of the Juilliard School Building at Lincoln Center on Manhattan's west side and numbered among its alumni many of the most celebrated names in American ballet, including Edward Villella, Suzanne Farrell, Gelsey Kirkland, and Fernando Bujones. Eddie had read about them all in *Dance Magazine*, his only contact with the ballet world beyond the borders of South Florida, and he couldn't wait to get to SAB to take his place among them in the competitive hierarchy of New York ballet.

Prior to leaving for New York, Eddie had written to his friend Dahlia Weinstein:

> Going to New York on full scholarship, that sure is luck, but I have worked every day at ballet and this is the break I've been waiting for. It's really not easy taking ballet every day, especially when each class is three hours. But it paid off. It you promise not to tell a soul: If I can stay in New York the whole year round, I'm going to stay, but I don't know if my mother will let me. Whether she likes it or not, if I get another break in New York, I don't know who will stay with me, but I'm staying.

It wasn't long after Eddie and Rose settled into the $700-a-month apartment they had rented on West Forty-sixth Street that Eddie realized that Rose was not about to leave him to his own devices quite so willingly. During his third week at SAB, he wrote to his friend Flavia Carnevale, whom he had met in his tap class. After telling Flavia how much he loved SAB and that he had already been pushed ahead into advanced classes, Eddie noted:

> The only thing that's horrible is my mother won't let me out of her sight. She won't even let me cross the street alone and it's killing me! But I'm learning to put up with it. I mean she just doesn't want anything to happen to me. Getting back to the school, I was standing in the hallway and who do you think walks by but Baryshnikov. I could have died. He was talking on the phone for five minutes and everyone was staring at him.

Baryshnikov was the star and director of American Ballet Theatre and the most highly touted dancer in the world. The air audibly crackled with expectation in every opera house he danced in. Baryshnikov had been to Eddie what Donald O'Connor had been to his father and Eddie dreamed of making it into Baryshnikov's company. The New York City Ballet seemed an unlikely option for Eddie because he knew that Balanchine wanted dancers who were tall and streamlined, with beautifully arched feet, long, elegant legs, and a graceful extension. "Balanchine dancers," they were called. Baryshnikov's height and compact physique gave Eddie hope, for the Russian virtuoso was only five-six. While Eddie was still only five-three, he was counting on gaining inches and longer legs in the months to come, even though both his parents were under five-four.

Every ballet career begins with the body, the dancer's instrument and obsession. The goal is perfection, which is rarely, if ever, achieved. Eddie knew the physical prerequisites of the ballet prince by heart: long neck, long limbs, short torso, good proportions, and of course, height—close to six feet was desirable for partnering willowy ballerinas, who grew five inches standing in their pointe shoes.

For the first time, Eddie began to worry that his body would betray him. At SAB, in the "men's class" taught by the esteemed Danish teacher Stanley Williams, he suddenly found himself face-to-face with dancers who had not only better training than he did, but bodies better suited to ballet. There were Peter Boal and Gen Horiuchi, who would later become principal dancers with the New York City Ballet; Jeffrey Edwards and Michael Byars, who would become NYCB soloists; Patrick Corbin, who would join the Joffrey Ballet; and Parrish Maynard, who everyone agreed had the best and most flexible body. Maynard would become Eddie's rival at the Joffrey several years later. "Eddie and I weren't friends at SAB," says Patrick Corbin, "but I could see that he was in awe of Parrish's body. Later, when we were both in the Joffrey, he told me that he had been really intimidated by the caliber of our class."

Indeed, when Eddie compared his body to Parrish Maynard's and those of the other boys in the "men's class," he found his wanting. His legs were too stocky and not elongated enough from the hip to the knee, his feet didn't have the high, rounded arches that many of the other boys' did, and his nose was too pronounced for his small face. He promised himself that when he could afford it, he would have his nose fixed. But no amount of money, hours logged in the studio, or sheer determination could alter his body's proportions.

Still, Eddie refused to despair and continued to work toward making the reflection in the mirror match the picture of himself he kept vivid in his mind. "I know you want one of us to make it big," he wrote to Liana from SAB, "and I really want to do it for you."

But his break was not to come at SAB. At the end of the workshop, he was told that he was simply too short and stocky to meet the requirements of the School of American Ballet and the repertory of the New York City Ballet. It was his first experience with rejection and, worst of all, it was the first official opinion that his height was a real problem—something he could not control. Eddie returned to Hollywood, determined to find another route back to New York.

In early August 1982, Dan Rather introduced one of the first network news pieces on AIDS, a disease that had been identified a year earlier and officially named only the previous month. (By that time, *The New York Times* had written a total of five stories about the epidemic, none of which made the front page.) In his setup for the piece, Rather identified the biases and paradoxes that would characterize AIDS coverage for years to come: "Federal health officials consider it an epidemic," he noted. "Yet you rarely hear a thing about it. At first, it seemed to strike only one segment of the population. Now, Barry Peterson tells us, this is no longer the case."

That September, Eddie began his freshman year at St. Thomas Aquinas High School, a Catholic school in Ft. Lauderdale whose one thousand students began each day by attending Mass.

Eddie had decided not to follow his brothers to Chaminade

High School because it didn't offer a drama program, but in bypassing Chaminade, he missed another opportunity to forge a link with his father, who was still working at the school as a maintenance man. He certainly wasn't having an easy time at St. Thomas, where gym was compulsory for all freshmen. When Mitzi and Liana heard that Eddie would have to take up football, they dashed off letters to the school's principal and urged Rose Stierle to find a way to keep him off the field for fear that he would injure himself. When the guys in his class at St. Thomas found out that Eddie Stierle was a ballet dancer and that he had been granted special permission not only to skip phys ed, but also to take a drama class restricted to juniors and seniors, they declared open season on him. Like Eddie's brothers and sisters, they, too, resented his privileges. They shoved him against lockers, threatened to pummel him, and shouted after him in the hallways, "Hey faggot, you're a ballerina." Their taunts unhinged and embarrassed him and, worse, reminded him that he didn't fit in with his peers. He tried to steel himself against their taunts and made sure to spend as little time as possible in the hallways, but he considered it futile to report such incidents, thinking he would only aggravate an already painful situation. "What is it about me? Why don't they like me?" he asked Rosemarie on a weekend visit to the Doral Country Club. Their dislike only fueled his attachment to the dance studio, a haven where he felt both admired and understood.

"I'm lucky if there is a day that goes by when I'm not called a faggot," he confided in Chrissie Guastella another day on a break from rehearsing a tap number to *42nd Street*. "It just broke my heart when he told me that," she recalls. "He said he just kept his mouth shut. The guys would get mad at him because he had a much easier time making friends with the girls. Anyone who didn't know him would ask if he was gay because his voice was a little high and we would always say, 'Oh, no.' He wasn't effeminate, but I always felt he was unusually graceful."

Three months into the school year, a classmate who belonged to Eddie's car pool broke her promise to Eddie and blurted the details of Eddie's rough treatment at school to Rose Stierle. He had kept silent about it because he knew his mother would complain to the principal when she found out—which she did. (The offenders were threatened with expulsion and the taunting subsided.)

"Edward, this issue's come up again and you know how I feel about it," Rose told him during the drive to Hialeah. "You're not gay and you're not gonna be gay. It's not right that they call you that."

When Bill Stierle heard that Eddie was being ridiculed by the jocks at St. Thomas, he responded with a pep talk. "Well, Ed, that's a part of dance that you're going to have to accept. If you choose to dance, they're going to say things to you and you're going to have to learn to deal with it."

"Dad, I'm going to be a ballet dancer and what they say doesn't matter," Eddie insisted.

Between pliés, partnering, and performances, Eddie juggled the demands of academia with the same aplomb with which he executed complicated dance combinations. Just as he always stood in the front row of any dance class he took, so he chose the seat that was front and center of every classroom. He was a top student whose strongest subject was Religious Studies; his grade never dipped below 97. "Eddie reminded me of Puck* in *A Midsummer Night's Dream*," remembers Denise Aloma, Eddie's freshman English teacher. "He made witty comments full of puns and irony that only the brighter ones in the class could pick up. Unlike most kids that age, he wasn't in the least intimidated about approaching any adult, but he was naive in thinking that he couldn't draw any negative attention. He never went out of his way to show any interest in his classmates' football games, but he couldn't understand why they wouldn't come to see him dance."

His inexperience ran to romance as well. He desperately wanted to fit in somewhere, to show that he could be one of the gang, and since everyone in Razz Ma Jazz seemed to be pairing off, Eddie figured he might as well find himself a girlfriend. Maybe

---

*The role of Puck in Sir Frederick Ashton's *The Dream*, a ballet based on Shakespeare's play, was to become one of Eddie's signature roles at the Joffrey.

then he would have something to talk to his brothers about. Frustrated in his efforts to win over Chrissie, Eddie soon found a girlfriend more eager for his affections. Sally White,* a sixteen-year-old dark-haired dancer in Razz Ma Jazz, had had a long-standing crush on him and, as Chrissie recalls, "was dying to get Eddie into bed." Eddie, however, considered himself a devout Catholic and even confessed to Chrissie that he thought it was wrong for a man and woman to sleep together unless they were married. After a few dates with the persuasive Sally, he changed his mind and accepted his brother Bill's offer to loan him his dorm room at nearby Biscayne College, where Bill was working in the admissions office. After polishing off a bottle of champagne with Sally one night, Eddie lost his virginity. The next day, his father happened to come by the room to leave Bill, Jr., a message and noticed the empty champagne bottle on the desk with a note from Eddie taped to it. "Thanks for letting us use your apartment," it read. "We had a great night."

Bill, Sr., couldn't have been more pleased. "As soon as I read the letter, I thought, 'Well, Eddie's going with girls.' That threw me off the track of thinking he was gay." Bill had never encouraged his sons to abstain from sex, and when the time came to give each of them his lecture on the subject, he would caution them only against making babies. "I made sure never to mention the girl or marriage," he says. "Just the child that they would have to be responsible for. I never told them, 'Don't do it.' " (Rose, conversely, told her daughters that if they had a child out of wedlock, she'd look after the baby.)

Bill was proud of his own sexual prowess and liked to boast to acquaintances, "Hello, my name is Bill Stierle, but I'm not really sterile, I've got eight kids." Rosemarie remembers her father "as a very sexual presence," someone who was always making pointed remarks about women to his children. He liked to encourage Eddie's interest in the opposite sex by telling him, "There's nothing greater than being with a woman."

Eddie wanted to believe his father, but he was also beginning

---

*Pseudonym.

to recognize his growing attraction to men. He kept his feelings closely guarded, however, and would not recount his adolescent experiments until years later. That summer in New York at the School of American Ballet, several months before he slept with Sally, Eddie and Rose had gone to the Metropolitan Opera House to attend a matinee performance of the Netherlands Dance Theater, the ballet company headed by the Czech choreographer Jiří Kylián. Eddie later told a lover that he noticed that one of the male ushers was flirting with him. Eddie told his mother that he had to use the bathroom and went and fooled around with the usher in one of the side ring seats, a place where they couldn't be seen, then went back to his seat. Eddie would later recall that it scared him at first because he didn't understand what it meant and he knew that his mother was afraid of it happening. "But then he started liking it," a lover remembers him saying.

The following spring, Eddie met Brent Phillips, the only other boy his age in Miami Dance Theatre. Brent and Eddie shared a changing room at the school, just as, years later, they would share a dressing room at the Joffrey Ballet when both were members of the company. Brent recalls that when he and Eddie were at the Joffrey, they would laugh about the early days in Miami, when both of them were so self-conscious that they would face away from each other as they changed into their tights. "When I told him I knew then that I was gay, he said he felt he was gay then too," he says. "But nothing happened between us, even though I was a little attracted to him because we had so much in common. I didn't know any other boys who wanted to be dancers. But we never talked about those things, not then."

The only person with whom he did discuss "those things" was David Bushman, a tall, blond, blue-eyed nineteen-year-old dancer Eddie met that July at a summer workshop he attended at the Milwaukee Ballet School. It was Eddie's first trip away from home without his mother. Like Eddie, Bushman was the product of a sheltered Catholic upbringing. He had started dancing late, at the age of eighteen in Appleton, Wisconsin, and had just completed his first semester at the North Carolina School of the Arts, an arts high school and college in Winston-Salem.

Although Eddie was four years his junior, "he had a real edge on me dancewise," says Bushman, recalling the jealousy Eddie aroused in their classmates when he won the leading role in the final performance, despite his height. One day as he and Eddie were eating lunch together in the park, they tentatively broached the subject of homosexuality in the dance world. "We were both testing the water," remembers Bushman. "Neither of us wanted to relate the subject to ourselves, but obviously we were both thinking about it. I had these feelings, but it was like a fantasy I hadn't named. We talked about how we were brought up to believe homosexuality was wrong and we were each struggling to define our own feelings about it. Eddie wasn't sure how he felt. I told him I thought it was wrong and that I had decided I wouldn't pursue it. So I tried to help him out by telling him that I was struggling to work against the impulse and that he should try to resist as well."

Eddie's sexual confusion was made murkier by his strong feelings for Chrissie Guastella, which seemed to persist even after Sally became his girlfriend. From the Milwaukee Ballet School, he wrote to her:

> I just need you so much and I can't have you. It makes me crazy. Sally and I really are doing great in spite of my feelings towards you. I really do love her. But there will always be that inch more of love for you no matter what happens.

A year before he met Eddie in the spring of 1983, Brent Phillips had watched Eddie partner Lissette Salgado in a special *Nutcracker* highlights program in the middle of a Miami shopping mall. Lissette, the Sugar Plum Fairy, wore a glittering pink tutu and crown; Eddie, her Cavalier, wore white tights. "That guy has a funny body," thirteen-year-old Brent thought to himself. He had been studying ballet for only a year, but he was taller and leaner than the boy in the white tights and his teachers had praised him for his "ballet body." "Eddie's legs were very much out of proportion with the rest of his body," recalls Brent Phillips. "He could kick, but his legs were short and it looked funny. He made *The Nutcracker* very flashy."

Though Eddie was the better dancer, Brent had a superior physique; Eddie quickly came to resent the ease with which Brent would sail through the auditions that the major ballet companies held regularly in Miami to assess the local talent and recruit the most promising students to their schools. While Brent would often win full scholarships to the schools based on his potential, Eddie would find himself cut from the final rounds.

Eddie was deeply disappointed when he was not among the select few chosen—from the one thousand students auditioned nationwide—for ABT II, American Ballet Theatre's junior company. "And that was really *the* place to go," says Phillips, who was accepted into the troupe the following year. "When ABT performed in Miami, the company would give a master class before the regular company class and all of us would take it. Then we used to stick around and watch company class. We all had stars in our eyes about ABT. If you had a nice body, they would try to push you into ABT, and if you had a funny body, they would say, 'You should dance in Europe.' Eddie kept hearing, 'You should dance in Europe.' "

It was becoming clear that Eddie was going to have to find a school that would allow him to combine academia with ballet classes and performances. He had learned all that his dance teachers could teach him and St. Thomas was hardly providing the kind of nourishing environment for which he hungered. He felt out of place at St. Thomas and fantasized about spending his days with those who shared his singular focus. He would later explain to a local reporter that he wanted to be "surrounded by people who knew what it took to become an artist." The distances between studios was also proving to be a problem, because Eddie had to rely on his mother and sister Patty to act as chauffeurs until he was of driving age. His dependency on Rose had become so great that she decided to postpone an operation for a hysterectomy for one month to avoid interrupting Eddie's rehearsal schedule. At the same time, Eddie felt overprotected and began to feel that he wanted his own life.

But where was he to go? The School of American Ballet and American Ballet Theatre's school had already turned him down. Rosemarie's mother-in-law suggested the North Carolina School of the Arts and, though Eddie had already missed the auditions for the coming year, a private audition was quickly arranged in Winston-Salem.

In a studio in the red brick dance building at the North Carolina School of the Arts, Eddie showed dance dean Robert Lindgren and assistant dean Duncan Noble the positions, steps, and combinations he had learned in the schools of South Florida. He pointed his feet, raised his leg this way and that, and demonstrated his ability to move in rhythm to the music. He showed them how high he could jump, how flexible his limbs were, and how swiftly he could turn across the floor. Lindgren and Noble marked off the various categories on their audition sheets. They made notes on Eddie's height, weight, the shape of his head, the quality of his turnout, his musicality (they were to select one of the following: ahead, behind, cannot count), and his presentation (here the selections included a veritable gamut: sullen, blank, unfocused, withdrawn, outgoing). Under the heading "placement," Duncan Noble wrote: "Not quite kosher."

As they sat scrutinizing Eddie Stierle, Lindgren and Noble ruled out the likelihood of a classical ballet career for the outgoing young dancer. "Not a classical ballet body," thought Lindgren, who had danced with the Ballet Russe de Monte Carlo in the 1940s and the New York City Ballet from 1957 to 1959 before becoming the School of the Arts' first dean of dance at its inception in 1965. "He's too short and stocky. He'll never be the prince." Duncan Noble silently concurred. A tall, reedy man in his sixties, the white-haired Noble had made a career out of playing princes during his days with the Ballet Russe in the 1940s. He had also appeared in more than seven Broadway shows, including *Can-Can* with Gwen Verdon. "Not such hot feet. Lots of energy," thought Noble. But what technique! Both men had rarely seen a boy of fifteen with the kind of technique and natural talent that Eddie possessed. "He's still in high school, so we have a few years to see what we can do with him," Lindgren told himself.

As Noble saw it, Eddie's major stumbling block was his accent. He was clearly conversant in the language of ballet, but his pronunciation was inelegant. "Eddie had an outlook on dance that I thought would be hard to break," recalls Noble. "He was a show biz kid, a nightclub performer. He was a very free-form dancer: There was no classic form to his dancing. He had learned that it didn't matter how well you did something as long as you smiled big at the finish and showed a lot of teeth. He could do a lot of pirouettes, but he was moving all over the floor and they were not poetically placed."

Duncan Noble knew it was unwise to try to dissuade ambitious young dancers from the course they had set for themselves. He felt that his job was to train dancers, not to tell them what they would or would not become. "Unless you're God, you don't know," he would say, preferring, like Rose Stierle, to put his trust in a higher authority.

Watching Eddie dance, Robert Lindgren was reminded of a former Ballets Russes dancer he had known. Harold Lang had appeared as one of the sailors in the original production of Jerome Robbins's 1949 ballet *Fancy Free*, before going on to make his career on the Broadway stage in such hits as *Kiss Me Kate* and *Pal Joey*. Lang, he remembered, also had a fabulous technique, but the wrong sort of body for ballet. Fearing that young Stierle was looking at his options from the wrong end of the telescope, he advised him not to narrow his sights. "Here was this short, round-faced boy—a young Mickey Rooney—telling me with all the enthusiasm in the world that he wanted to be a classical ballet dancer," recalls Lindgren, who five years later would become president of the School of American Ballet. Lindgren doubted that Eddie would find a place in a ballet company and advised him not to think "only of being a ballet dancer." Eddie wouldn't hear of it. "I'm going to try anyway," he told the older man.

"He was fighting the odds," says Lindgren, "but *he* never thought so."

7

STAR
SEARCH

Melissa Hayden clapped her hands in delight.

"Oh, Bobby, he is so marvelous. He has so much talent," she whispered to Robert Lindgren as they sat together in Studio 608 assessing the newest batch of dancers.

"But he's not a prince," lamented Lindgren.

It was orientation day at the North Carolina School of the Arts and Melissa Hayden's first day as a teacher at its School of Dance. Hayden had been a principal dancer with the New York City Ballet from 1950 until her retirement in 1973. Known for her speed, attack, and dramatic presence, she was widely considered the City Ballet's prima ballerina and was known internationally through guest appearances with other companies, including American Ballet Theatre, and her role as the Ballerina in the Charlie Chaplin film *Limelight*. Since 1973, she had been teaching at her own school in New York City and directing the dance department at Skidmore College in Saratoga, New York. By the fall of 1983, Hayden had developed a knack for picking out the promising ones and she could see that the Stierle boy had possibilities. There were problems, to be sure: He was short, he didn't have a classically shaped technique, and while most dancers had some kind of "look," Eddie appeared undistinguished. But talent he had in abundance, and she "couldn't wait to get my hands on him."

Hayden set to work at once to retrain Eddie Stierle. "We knew Eddie was pretty raw material," remembers Melissa Hayden, "but you can change a dancer's whole body with proper training. What we had to do was basically force-feed Eddie. He was the most energetic dancer in his class and he had the most facility. He was like a sponge. He was so hungry that he was a challenge to any teacher that taught him. When you have a student like that, you have to teach upwards to the potential without intimidating the rest of the class."

A small, raspy-voiced woman who, at fifty, was still in trim dancing form, "Miss Hayden" quickly earned a local reputation as a feisty and demanding teacher, one who had no time for the marginally talented and readily fazed. Her scathing corrections could reduce students to tears and were frequently the talk of the lunchroom. "Melissa would tell us we were terrible," recalls a ballerina in Eddie's class that year. "She'd say, 'Why are you in this class? You should be a secretary.' Eddie was on a different level with Melissa, though. She loved him to death because he understood everything that she was saying."

In letters home, Eddie called Melissa a genius. He was awed by her reputation and by the close working relationship she had enjoyed with George Balanchine. The fact that she had been a major star made her especially interesting to him. He knew there was a great deal he could learn from her and he was hungry to begin.

To the irritation and envy of the others in his class, Eddie never appeared discouraged with himself. He never seemed to have "down days," says Robert Lindgren. Or rather, as fellow student Brooks White saw it, Eddie's down days "were better than most of our good days." The other boys in his class would be struggling through three pirouettes and Eddie would toss off six pirouettes and announce: "I'm not turning well today." It was hardly the sort of comment that invited camaraderie.

With Melissa Hayden

Indeed, even David Bushman, Eddie's friend from the Milwaukee Ballet School, resented Eddie's presence in class. It was one thing to find a prodigy at a summer workshop and quite another to find him at school with you, "stealing your thunder," says Bushman, by then already a sophomore in the school's college division. "To see someone so sure of himself at that age was hard to take. I was thinking, 'I'm already old, I don't need another whippersnapper here taking roles away from me.'" It was a sentiment later shared by Eddie's senior colleagues at the Joffrey.

Despite his talent, Eddie's teachers saw him primarily as a *demi-caractère* dancer, not the prince, or *danseur noble*. A *demi-caractère* dancer is a performer of great academic virtuosity who lacks the grace, lyricism, and clarity of movement that is the hallmark of the pure classical dancer. *Demi-caractère* roles go to those dancers with a virtuosic technique; but just what sort of dancer is best suited to those roles is an often subjective decision, best illustrated by the case of Baryshnikov. While he came to be regarded as the greatest classical dancer of his day, Baryshnikov was not immediately seen as a pure classical dancer at the Kirov Ballet in Leningrad, where he began his career. The directors of the Kirov, in fact, were reluctant to give him the male lead of Albrecht in *Giselle* because they felt he didn't fit the image of the type of dancer who was ordinarily cast in the part.

As a short, small dancer, Eddie was not considered suitable for many of the greatest male roles in the classical repertoire, such as the Prince in *The Sleeping Beauty* or *Swan Lake*. Nevertheless, Eddie was still in pursuit of the prince's repertoire and, to make his legs look longer in class, would wear black tights with black socks—rather than the traditional white—and black slippers. "Everything was 'Gee Whiz! Isn't that wonderful! Oh Boy!'" says Lindgren. "The whole time he was here, he worked twice as hard as anybody else. He had the rare ability to manifest his ambition. He would say, 'Gee, I want to do ten pirouettes,' and he would make up his mind to do it. There was never a point where his technique wasn't improving. He was never sick. Never hurt. Never out. He had his goals in mind."

Eddie's exuberance was so relentless and undiscriminating that his classmates initially didn't know what to make of him. He wanted everyone to like him, that much was clear. But not everyone did. To some, he seemed loud and obnoxious. He needed to "tone it down," classmate Brooks White remembers thinking. To others, he came across as naive and sheltered.

Eddie, however, was oblivious to the sneers of many of his classmates, in part because he had already found a good deal more in common with them than he ever had with his peers at St. Thomas. He also had a handful of friends, most of them women, and their support and affection seemed to shield him from the envy and disdain of those who found him irritating. An accomplished attention-getter, he exerted a powerful force on anyone who came within his orbit. His charisma and charm were endearing, though in his attempts to be agreeable, Eddie struck some, like Donald Coleman, Melissa Hayden's husband, as "slightly sycophantic."

He came close to alienating Melissa Hayden when he asked her one day after class if she thought he should audition for "Star Search," a television talent show hosted by Ed McMahon. "When a teacher of my stature is told by a sixteen-year-old kid that he is going to go on 'Star Search,' it is shocking and tacky," recalls Hayden. "I said to Eddie, 'Oh, really? What for?' He didn't have too much to say to that."

By the time Melissa Hayden came to the North Carolina School of the Arts in 1983, it was well established as one of the top-ranked arts schools in the country, having produced such graduates as former American Ballet Theatre star Patrick Bissell,* actor Tom Hulce (*Amadeus*), and flautist Ransom Wilson, among others. It was also one of only three state-supported arts schools in the country and the most well-known. Other celebrated arts schools like Juilliard, Walnut Hill, and Interlochen were privately run, while the High School for the Performing Arts, the *Fame* school, was city-supported. The idea for a school of the arts in Winston-Salem seemed most unlikely when then-Governor Terry Sanford proposed it in the early 1960s. A man of adventurous spirit, he had long wanted to put North Carolina on the nation's cultural map and soon set to work campaigning for the creation of a state-supported conservatory. Recognizing that "the artistic spirit . . . demands more room for creativity and self-development," the school's founders envisioned a European-style conservatory, a daring plan that eventually won backing from the state legislature as well as from many of Winston-Salem's leading families and companies, among them Hanes Underwear and the R. J. Reynolds Tobacco Company. Choreographer Agnes de Mille, an early adviser to the school's founders, was invited to Winston-Salem for a tour and later told a local reporter that she was impressed "that the

---

*A tall, handsome principal dancer with American Ballet Theatre, Bissell had been plagued by problems with drugs and alcohol; in 1986, he died of a drug overdose.

In Duncan Noble's dance class at the North Carolina School of the Arts, 1984

entire community [is] absolutely behind it, and fervently and intelligently enthusiastic.

It's new here, this kind of communal enthusiasm for something that is so important and so absolutely unprofitable, except in the spiritual sense. That these rich, rich people were interested now in people's souls, struck me as novel. . . .

The school opened its doors in 1965.

Eddie's life literally revolved around the dance studio. His days were spent running back and forth between his dorm and the dance and academic buildings, a trip that now took him four minutes instead of forty-five. On Mondays, he arose early for an 8 A.M. technique class, which was followed by English at 10:30 and algebra at 11:40 A.M.; men's ballet class began promptly at 1 P.M.; at 2:40 P.M. it was time for science, though by 6 P.M. he was back in the studio for a night of rehearsals. History, math, modern dance, character class, and introduction to makeup filled out his timetable on other days. At St. Thomas Aquinas High School in Ft. Lauderdale, Eddie couldn't walk down the halls without hearing "faggot" called after him; on the campus of the School of the Arts, he could—and did—leap down the corridors in a unitard and ballet slippers without attracting any notice. Whether you pirouetted, trilled scales, or delivered Henry V's St. Crispin's Day speech across the campus, nobody much cared, for nearly all of the school's 750 students were in rehearsal for a career on the stage.

The campus of the North Carolina School of the Arts sat on the edge of a low-income, primarily black neighborhood, surrounded by warehouses and used-car and truck repair shops. The School of Dance was made up of the Agnes de Mille Theatre, dressing rooms, and two long corridors of airy studios, each painted in a primary color. While classes were in session, dancers passing along the corridor could peer through the eye-level windows on the studio doors and check out the competition. Large bulletin boards outside the dressing rooms kept the young dancers up to date on upcoming ballet competitions, company auditions, and the best place to find ice packs.

Surrounded though he was by teachers with stories to tell of luminous stage moments and legendary choreographers, Eddie rarely paused to listen to their anecdotes. The history of dance didn't interest him that much, only dancing did, and he wanted to learn all they had to teach him about moving. He was in a hurry to inherit their legacy.

In November, Melissa Hayden posted the cast list of the school's upcoming production of *The Nutcracker*. Eddie Stierle was to be the prince.

In the midst of rehearsing for *The Nutcracker*, Eddie wrote to his friend Flavia Carnevale:

> I'm sure you heard from my mom that I got the lead in Nutcracker (Cavalier). . . . My teachers are great. Miss Hayden is always yelling and cutting people down in class. She reminds me so much of Liana. I can feel so much improvement in my dancing technically. People don't think you're strange if you do grand jetés down the hall. I love it here, but I really miss my parents.

The months without Eddie had thrown Rose Stierle into a depression. For the first time in thirty-four years, she had no babies at home. Kathy had gone to work as a beautician in Gainesville and Patty had taken up nursing as her major at the University of South Carolina in Columbia, where Tom had transferred two years before. Rose thought she might as well find a job in Winston-Salem so she could "be there for Edward," she explained to her husband, who promptly nixed the idea. "I kept thinking, 'What am I going to do at night?' " says Rose. "I didn't think I'd be able to survive without Edward. I was so lost."

Columbia, South Carolina, wasn't far from Winston-Salem and Patty would sometimes drop by to visit Eddie on weekends. Tom never joined her. He was busy playing guard for the USC Gamecocks and, anyway, he had no interest in driving 180 miles to see Eddie dance in some ballet. Eddie, likewise, wasn't about to get on a bus to watch his brother play basketball. "It was so much easier to be friends with Eddie without my mom around," says Patty Stierle.

But even at a distance, Rose soon gave Tom and Patty new reasons to resent their younger brother. The minute an article or review about Eddie appeared in the Winston-Salem or Hollywood newspapers, Rose would clip it and send off a copy to everyone in the family and to everyone the family knew. (One local feature that made the rounds dubbed Eddie "Hollywood's teenage ballet sensation.") Her mailing list extended to the friends of her children, whether the friends had ever met Eddie or not. "I felt that these were *my* friends, and suddenly articles about my brother started showing up in their mailboxes," recalls Tom Stierle. "I said to my mother, 'It's bad enough that you and him have such a tight relationship, but don't go promoting Eddie to my friends. They don't even know him.' I pulled the plug on those mailings." Rose simply replaced their names with new ones. By the time Eddie got to the Joffrey, she was sending reviews of his performances not only to family members, childhood friends, and Eddie's former teachers, but even to the Joffrey dancers themselves.

Like their son, Bill and Rose also stood out at the School of the Arts. While most of the parents usually showed up for one, maybe two, performances each year, Bill and Rose came to every one of Eddie's performances in the school's fall, winter, and spring concerts, even if that meant seeing the same program two or three times. Eddie was attentive to them during their visits, but he privately worried that his father might drink or betray his blue-collar roots. He was beginning to perceive that there was a gap between the world he had come from and the refined, elitist world to which he aspired. "Make sure you don't drink," he reminded his father when Bill came up to see him as the Cavalier in *The Nutcracker,* the role he had first danced with Lissette Salgado in a Miami Beach shopping mall. "Since I moved up into the ballet world from being a plasterer, Eddie was worried about how I would present myself," remembers Bill Stierle. "Most of the people he was dealing with were much richer and of a so-called higher caliber than myself. He'd say, 'Be careful about what you say to these people because they know a lot about ballet and you don't know much at all.' "

Bill may not have known much more about ballet than the correct positions of the hands and feet, but, as Eddie was to discover, his father had much to teach him about building something out of unlikely materials, as he had learned to do on his fix-it rounds through the neighborhood.

During Christmas break, Eddie returned to Hollywood and went bottom-fishing with his father, alone. Just after sunrise one hot December morning, when they had anchored two miles from shore, Eddie confessed to his father that he wondered whether his height would prevent him from going any further in the ballet world. Despite landing the lead in *The Nutcracker,* he was stuck at five feet six inches and didn't seem to be growing any taller. He had even gone for a bone scan at Wake Forest University's Medical Center, he told his father, to find out his potential for growth. The scan revealed that Eddie had reached his full height. He was devastated. Suddenly it seemed to him that everything about his body was not as it should be: His thighs were too big, his legs were overdeveloped from too much tap dancing, his musculature was wrong for ballet.

Bill listened in thoughtful silence before relating a story he hoped would revive his son's optimism. Once, when he worked at plastering ceilings, he had to learn to plaster on stilts or face losing his job, he explained to Eddie. The other men on the job were at least eight inches taller than he was, and in order to work at the same height, he had to add a nine-inch pipe to the top of his stilts. Not only did he learn to walk higher off the ground than everyone else, an awkward enough feat, but he soon became the most proficient plasterer on the team. He even danced on stilts at a few parties, just to make the others laugh.

The parable inspired Eddie long after he had made his way into the Joffrey Ballet. In a 1989 interview, Eddie was asked about his training at the North Carolina School of the Arts.

"I heard a lot of 'You're short, you're limited, and you've got a lot of obstacles, so if you want to do this, you've got to want to do it more than just a lot,' " he replied. " 'It's not going to be easy for you.' Hearing that just made me work harder.

"Because I was lim—" He stopped and corrected himself.

"Because people *said* I was limited, that made me say, 'I'll show you.' "

Eddie was always saying "I'll show you" in one way or another. Shortly after Christmas, he learned that Duncan Noble had recommended him as a competitor in the International Ballet Competition, the ballet world's Olympics, which that year was to be held in Helsinki, Finland. (The competition rotates annually among Helsinki, Moscow, Varna in Bulgaria, and Jackson, Mississippi.)

Eddie knew that Baryshnikov had won a gold medal at the Moscow IBC in 1968 and figured that the competition's international stage was the ideal place to launch his own career. While the typical route to a dance career is through the ranks of a major company, ballet competitions can bestow international recognition and the opportunity to see and be seen by other dancers and company directors.

Two hundred dancers were to compete nationwide for one of the four slots on the American team. For the next several months, Eddie rehearsed six nights a week with Duncan Noble, who never discouraged him despite his feeling that competition had no place in ballet. Noble helped Eddie with four classical variations, picked to demonstrate his pyrotechnics and versatility. But he soon discovered that while Eddie was deferential in class, he was brash and opinionated in rehearsal.

"He fought me all the way," says Noble. I finally had to say to him, 'If you want me to work with you, you're going to have to do what I say.' He exhausted me." At six-two, Noble had the long, lean lines of the prince and, as Melissa Hayden recalls, Eddie saw himself as Duncan Noble. "Eddie was a stocky five-feet-six-inch young man dancing as though he was in a six-foot man's body," she says. Noble was intent on teaching Eddie the manner and attitude of the prince, but first had to undo Eddie's Miami Beach mind-set, which was no simple matter. Splashy steps mean nothing if they aren't perfectly executed, he counseled Eddie.

In February, three months before the competition, Eddie learned that he had been turned down for the School of American Ballet's summer session ("Sorry, wrong body type.") on the same day that he was invited to join the junior company of the Netherlands Dance Theater, the company he had seen in New York with his mother at the Metropolitan Opera House. While he admired the choreography of Jiří Kylián, the company's director, and was excited at the prospect of joining a recognized company, Eddie realized he still had much to learn at the School of the Arts and decided to finish high school before embarking on his professional career.

His education wasn't limited to dance. At the age of sixteen, he was on his own for the first time and everywhere he looked, he was swayed by temptation. Sex was naturally much on his mind and by February, he had already had a couple of flings with boys he'd met on campus, as well as an encounter with one of his teachers, an older man whose home Eddie sometimes visited on weekends. The teacher was an exceptionally skilled lover, Eddie later told one of his boyfriends at the school.

And yet, Eddie was so intent on keeping his escapades private and hidden even from his friends that few people on campus would have guessed that Eddie Stierle was sleeping with men. The atmosphere of the school was certainly open enough that anyone who wanted to come out did so freely, but Eddie hadn't yet decided which way he saw himself. He was attracted to both men and women and his desires confused him. For the moment anyway, he preferred to work out his conflicts offstage. "Most students at the school were either one way or the other," says David Bushman, who was then grappling with the same issues. "Eddie kept very quiet about his confusion. Some of the gay men knew he was active with boys at the school, but he was so affectionate with everyone and he made such a point of courting women that people were thrown off." As far as most of his friends knew, remembers Bushman, Eddie had a crush on Cydney Spon, a "sweet, virtuous Catholic girl" whom Eddie often accompanied to Sunday services at Our Lady of Mercy, the Catholic church down the street.

In April, the discovery of the AIDS virus made the front pages of the country's major papers, a breakthrough of only passing interest to the students at the North Carolina School of the Arts. No one there yet knew anyone who had been touched by AIDS, even though by then the disease had spread to forty-five states and 4,177 U.S. AIDS cases had been reported to the Centers for Disease Control. Their youth made Eddie and the other students particularly impervious to fears about AIDS. Like most teenagers, they gave little thought to mortality, especially where their raging hormones were concerned. Besides, AIDS was remote, something that couldn't happen to them. They were hardly to blame: At the time, the safe-sex message was directed toward high-risk adults, not teenagers, and education efforts were stalled by national resistance to frank talk about teenage sexuality. It wouldn't be until 1992 that *Newsweek* would devote a cover to the subject of teenagers and AIDS, a decision prompted by the startling statistic that AIDS was by then the sixth leading cause of death among fifteen- to twenty-four-year-olds and that from 1988 to 1992, the cumulative number of fifteen- to twenty-four-year-olds diagnosed with AIDS had increased 77.7 percent.

"My love life is zero and freezing," Eddie wrote to his friend Flavia from North Carolina that spring.

> In other words, nonexistent, nil, depressing, nothing, nix, zip, nowhere to be found, no hope, very cloudy, extinct, unrecoverable, needs help, Indescribable, Fatal, nauseating, worthless, Trivial, Very dead. As you can see I do not have a girlfriend. But I am working on it.

As soon as he got to Philadelphia in June, where the four finalists for the American team were to be selected, Eddie went to work on Shawn Black,* a nineteen-year-old ballerina from the Alabama Ballet who, like Eddie, had her sights set on getting into American Ballet Theatre. Shawn Black and Eddie, together with Damian Woetzel,** a seventeen-year-old soloist with the Los Angeles Ballet, and Peter Taylor, a student of ballet coach David Howard, were chosen to represent the United States at Helsinki. Eddie was elated: He desperately wanted to be seen by the foreign judges, most of whom were directors of major dance companies. He hoped that by making the team, he'd soon get the big breaks he'd been waiting for. "Eddie started making the moves on me," remembers Shawn Black, "but I told him I didn't want to get involved."

---

*Shawn Black is currently a soloist with ABT.
**Damian Woetzel is currently a principal dancer with the New York City Ballet.

Given that the mirror and the pursuit of perfection are constants in the life of a dancer, it's not uncommon for most fledgling dancers to be deeply self-absorbed. While Eddie was certainly ambitious, he struck Shawn Black as being unusually supportive and encouraging. "Eddie pushed me and gave me such confidence," she says. "He stood in the wings whenever I had to dance at Helsinki. It was as if he was as concerned for my success as he was for his own."

To come up with the cash to follow Eddie to Helsinki, Bill and Rose Stierle took out a second mortgage on their home. Rose had always wanted to visit her parents' birthplace in Italy and Eddie took great pride in being the child who provided her with the reason and opportunity to get there. They decided that after the competition they would search out Rose's family roots in southern Italy. Eddie was delighted to have the chance to pay her back in some meaningful way.

Following the first round of the elimination-style competition, the field was cut from eighty-two to forty-two dancers and Eddie was among them. In fact, none of the American dancers made it past the second round, which they attributed to the "political" decision-making on the part of the Soviet-biased jury. But British juror Alexander Grant, a celebrated former character dancer with the Royal Ballet, remembers that the jurors disliked Eddie's short, stocky body. "I was that type of dancer myself," he says, "so it wouldn't have been the sort of thing I'd vote against." Most dancers, once eliminated from competition, tend to sulk their way back home, but Eddie Stierle wanted to know precisely what kept him from winning. So he asked. "Dancers rarely speak to judges. They don't have that kind of gumption," says Grant, who admired the moxie of the sixteen-year-old teenager whom he would eventually come to coach in two of the roles for which he himself had become famous at the Royal Ballet. "I told him that I enjoyed his performance very much and that he did have talent, but he was still young and should use the competition as a learning experience, to see what was required to get to the final round. Great artists are able to overcome their body problems through sheer force of personality."

En route to Rome, Eddie and his parents boarded a train in Stockholm. Somehow, during the cozy two-and-a-half-day family trip, Eddie managed to have an encounter with a Swede he picked up on the train. As he later recounted in his journal:

> I met this really cute guy on the train, Johan from Stockholm. We became really close in a short time, but it was purely a physical attraction.

That fall, Eddie returned to North Carolina with loftier ambitions. He wanted to compete in the Prix de Lausanne, the sole world-class ballet competition open only to preprofessional dancers. Founded in 1973 by a Swiss industrialist named Philippe Braunschweig, the Prix specialized in bringing developing young dancers to international attention. Unlike the other major ballet competitions, which emphasized Olympic-style medals and were open to professionals, the Prix provided its winners with scholarships to top ballet schools in addition to nominal cash prizes. In January of 1985, the Prix was to be held in New York, the first time that it was to take place anywhere but Lausanne, Switzerland, and there was sure to be a good deal of media attention in the dance capital of the world.

Robert Lindgren knew the kind of classical body that got high marks from the Prix jurors and tried to dissuade Eddie from competing. "I didn't want him to be disappointed and I felt sure that he would be." Duncan Noble, however, was more optimistic and, for the next several months, oversaw Eddie's training six nights a week. Prix contestants were asked to select from a limited number of classical solos, but were free to dance a modern work of their choice. Eddie planned to dance the virtuosic male variation from *Don Quixote,* a dazzling nineteenth-century showpiece that is frequently performed to wow gala audiences. For his "free" variation, he decided to dance a jazz solo he choreographed himself to "Far From Over," a song composed by Frank Stallone (Sylvester's brother) for the John Travolta film *Staying Alive.*

Duncan Noble considered it a most unfortunate choice.

"Far From Over" showed Eddie at his Miami Beach condo-crowd razzle-dazzle worst: lots of flying splits, high kicks to the back of the head, and other assorted aerial flights of fancy. "It was tits and ass," Noble says pointedly, shuddering at the memory. "It was the kind of dancing he came from. Everyone here hated it, but we had so little time that we had to go with it. I tried to give it a line and some consistency. That was the best I could do." Eddie, however, remained firmly convinced that "Far From Over" was a showstopper and looked forward to returning to New York, the scene of his first triumph in the ballroom of the Waldorf-Astoria.

In order to cast a wider net than it had in the past, the thirteenth annual Prix de Lausanne had begun in Lausanne before opening at the Brooklyn Academy of Music. Semifinalists had already been chosen from Europe, Africa, and the Near East; in Brooklyn, they were joined by contestants from North and South America and the Far East. Over the next four days, the one hundred remaining dancers were scrutinized by an international jury of fabled ballet personalities and evaluated for their musicality, physique, stage presence, beauty, consistency, technique, and not least, talent. Each night, a list was posted in the lobby of the Manhattan hotel where the contestants were staying, announcing the names of the dancers who had survived the day. On the fourth evening, tears and shouts of anger drowned out sighs of relief, for only fifteen entrants had made it to the combined last round and gala performance on Sunday, January 27. Eddie Stierle was one of them.

As he took to the stage to dance "Far From Over," dressed in a tan lycra unitard and matching headband, Eddie was feeling confident. The elegant Opera House was packed with dance fans and he had just whizzed through the fouettés, multiple grands pirouettes, and scissoring leaps of his *Don Quixote* variation to shouts of "Bravo" and resounding applause. "Far From Over" blared from the speakers and Eddie did a flying split leap to center stage, followed by a fireworks display of high kicks and flashy turns. The audience was screaming with approval.

In *Far from Over* at the Prix de Lausanne, 1985

But not everyone liked what they saw. "The male dancing was too often marked by a disturbing vulgarity epitomized by Mr. Stierle and 'Far From Over,' an MTV-style disco solo he choreographed and performed," dance critic Jennifer Dunning observed that week in *The New York Times*.

Sitting at the long dais reserved for the jury, Patricia Wilde was inwardly grimacing. "This kid is never going to make it into a ballet company," she thought, "but he's going to be great in Las Vegas." A former leading dancer with the New York City Ballet and American Ballet Theatre, Wilde was director of the Pittsburgh Ballet and one of the Prix's eleven jurors. There was no doubt in her mind that Eddie Stierle had an extraordinary technique, but the husky dancer simply wasn't "prince" material. As soon as the performances concluded, she raised her doubts with the rest of the jurors. Yes, they agreed, the jazz solo was vulgar and hardly appropriate fare for the Prix. Juror Violette Verdy, another former New York City Ballet star, had given Eddie top marks for his technique, talent, musicality, and presence, and the lowest marks for his physical attributes and personal choreography. In the box marked "Creativity," she had jotted "Disco!" beside the grade she assigned him.

Still, despite their misgivings about "Far From Over," the jurors agreed that he had performed it well and given the strongest all-around performance in class and on stage. He also had the greatest number of points. But did he merit the gold? The gold medal was the Prix's highest honor and was to be awarded to an exceptional dancer only at the discretion of the jury. It hadn't been given in five years and never to an American male dancer. The jurors faced a peculiar dilemma: As their first male American gold medalist, shouldn't they choose a would-be prince?

"Philippe Braunschweig was very definite that he wanted a gold medal presented that year," recalls Patricia Wilde, "because there was so much attention on the Prix. He really pushed for it. We felt if you're going to give someone the gold, they have to epitomize the classical dancer. Ed Stierle didn't merit the gold solely on the basis of his body. But we gave it to him anyway."

"They thought he was small," recalls Philippe Braunschweig, "but he was so exceptional that it didn't matter."

On the stage of the Opera House, Eddie was stunned to hear Philippe Braunschweig call out his name as the winner of the $2,000 Roberta Pew Bandy/Astral Foundation Award for the most promising American dancer. "Wait," Philippe Braunschweig announced over the cheers and clapping. "Not finished."

In addition to the gold medal, there was another surprise awaiting Eddie on the final night of the Prix de Lausanne. As he strode off the stage, his gold medal fastened around his neck, his father grabbed him in a hug in the wings. "I'm so proud of you, Ed," he told him. Eddie had asked his parents not to come unless he made it to the finals, and during each phone call home that week, they told him they would try to make it to New York if they could. At the last minute, Bill made Rose promise not to tell Eddie they were coming. "Dad, I can't believe you're here," Eddie cried, the shock of winning the gold and seeing his father flooding his senses all at once. "I can't believe it."

8

PAS DE TROIS

Though well on his way to defining himself as a dancer, Eddie was fumbling in the dark with his sexuality. Still drawn both to men and women, he would vacillate between them for the next several years. In the fall of 1984, two months before winning top honors at the Prix de Lausanne, Eddie had met Anita Intrieri while standing in line in the school cafeteria. A squeaky-voiced ballet major with waist-length brown hair, Anita was a newcomer to the School of the Arts and Eddie quickly took it upon himself to show her the ropes. They were soon spending most of their time together, in ballet class, at the library, and at Our Lady of Mercy on Sunday mornings. When *Nutcracker* rehearsals were called that November, Eddie pushed the shy Anita to try out, even though her name wasn't on any list. "I assumed I wasn't good enough," she recalls, "and Eddie told me I should go to Mr. Lindgren [the dean] and ask for an audition. I kept saying, 'No, no,' but Eddie pushed me, so I went. And I got noticed and ended up with several parts in *Nutcracker.*" In addition to his role as the Sugar Plum Fairy's cavalier, Eddie was paired with Anita in the Chinese Tea variation.

In short order, she became his partner offstage as well. "Eddie was just so positive that I was sure I was in love with him," she says. "He just knocked everyone's socks off and I loved that about him."

Eddie was also preoccupied with rehearsing for the Prix and when he wasn't at her side, Anita assumed he was rehearsing. But when the school's first Prix medalist returned from New York in late January 1985, Anita discovered that she had competition from unlikely quarters.

"I probably shouldn't tell you this," a male friend of hers baited her in the cafeteria one day, "but I think you should know that Eddie is gay."

The thought had never crossed her mind. She had never met anyone who was gay. "What do you mean?" she demanded, suddenly overcome by confusion and embarrassment.

"I've heard that he's been with other guys."

Eddie had started seeing a drama student named Mark who lived in the college dorms, which were off-limits to the school's high school students. By sneaking into the dorms, Eddie had managed to keep Mark a secret from his dance friends, that is, until a classmate divulged his identity to Anita Intrieri.

Not knowing what to do, Anita decided to avoid Eddie until he finally confronted her as she was on her way to the cafeteria. "Someone told me you're gay," she said icily. "Is it true?"

"I can't believe anyone would say that to you," he answered angrily. "Who was it?"

Reluctantly Anita divulged the name. Marching into the cafeteria, Eddie grabbed a pitcher of milk, made a beeline for the informant, and promptly poured the milk over his head. Then he took Anita outside and tried to explain.

"Eddie told me that he was very confused," she recalls, "because he didn't know himself sexually. He said he loved me, but that he had feelings for someone else, a man. I was so hurt; I thought I'd never get over it. I didn't want to know who it was. I didn't want to compete with anybody and the fact that I was competing against another man . . . How could I win?"

The gossip about Eddie quickly made the rounds, only to be fueled a month later by even juicier news: Eddie, a high school junior, had dumped Mark for Richard Register, a college junior who had previously ignored his advances. Not only were they an item, but they were suddenly everywhere together and visibly in love. "It was a fairly big deal on campus," recalls David Bushman. "Everyone wanted to know, 'What's going on with Richard and Eddie?' "

Eddie had pursued Richard as ardently as he had gone after the Prix de Lausanne. They first met in the cafeteria in January of that year, though Richard's impression had not been favorable. He thought Eddie "extremely young and tacky, with moussed hair." But Eddie was taken with the exotic-looking Richard, with his dark eyes and straight jet black hair, and began deploying his considerable charms to seduce him. He taught him to tap-dance, he flattered him, and even sent him roses to wish him luck on the opening night of a play he was in. "I thanked him for the roses and then sat him down and said, 'This is not going to happen,' " Register recalls. And yet, soon after Eddie began seeing Mark, Richard's next-door neighbor, Richard had a change of heart. "At first I thought of him as a tacky kid and then he became this cherub," he says. "He was my first serious boyfriend and even though he was four years younger than me, he was a lot more experienced. I was still squeamish about some things and Eddie was so patient. He taught me to make love to a man. His body was like an anatomy lesson and his sensuality was just so pure; it always had this innocent quality."

Since high school students weren't allowed in the college dorms, Richard had to sneak Eddie into his room. One night they tied the sheets together so that Eddie could shimmy down from Richard's window. Another night, one of the residence monitors suddenly walked in on them. It was Richard's worst fear. "I was thinking, 'I could be arrested, he's just seventeen and it's against the law.' " Embarrassed, the young man asked Richard, "Have you signed in?" Yes, he had, the startled Richard answered. "Fine," said the man, and promptly left the room. Richard was mortified. Was he going to be reported? Eddie, however, thought the episode amus-

With Richard Register in Winston-Salem, 1985

ing. "Don't worry, he's gone, it's fine," he kept telling Richard, trying to calm him.

After a few months had gone by, Anita Intrieri had overcome the shock of being dropped for a man and became friendly with Richard. "At first I thought it was disgusting and gross," she explains. "I didn't want to be around Eddie. And then I started to accept it. In a way, it helped me accept gay men because I started understanding."

In the journal that he began soon after leaving the School of the Arts for the summer, Eddie described the ménage in which he had found himself months before. Yet despite his rapturous celebration of his love for Richard, he remained conflicted about his overpowering attraction to men and his desire to be a husband and father, an issue he would never resolve.

> My personal life is not one of the ordinary because I am in love with a man. . . . Although I have had relationships with women, there has never been anyone in all my life who I have loved more.

It is so hard to explain, but it is just now that I am beginning to see that this is not "wrong." All my life, I have thought it to be "wrong" and a "problem," but now I realize that love is so deep that it doesn't matter who you love; it is giving and sharing of yourself with someone. . . . Most of my family thinks I am straight because of the women I have dated in the past, but it is becoming harder and harder to hide and lie with them, especially with my parents. God, I pray that they will love me just as much as they do now, when they find out. But, deep down I always think I will have a family someday with a woman that I love more than anything. . . . I just wish people could understand my feelings. I love Richard so much, and if I didn't have a career, I could probably spend the rest of my life with him. That scares me in a way and makes me happy in a way. It scares me because I am only seventeen, but it makes me happy because just the thought of him fills my heart with bliss.

The news that Rock Hudson had AIDS hit the front page of virtually every newspaper in America that summer. The rumor had persisted for months despite heated denials from the actor himself, but the diagnosis was confirmed by Dr. Michael Gottlieb,* Hudson's doctor, who on July 30 announced to the world that Hudson was being treated for complications of AIDS at UCLA Medical Center. It had been four years since Gottlieb had first reported five unexplained cases of the disease to the Centers for Disease Control and he had since treated two hundred AIDS patients, most of whom were dead. But none were as famous as Rock Hudson and Gottlieb was dismayed to discover that it took the diagnosis of a move star (and friend of President Reagan) to wake up the world to the urgency of the epidemic. Not until basketball star Magic Johnson divulged his own HIV status to the nation in the fall of 1991 would the news of an AIDS diagnosis again have such a far-reaching impact.

No sooner did the Hudson story break than people began asking the question: How did he get it? The answer was first

---

*Hudson had become a patient of Michael Gottlieb the previous summer, soon after learning that he was suffering from Kaposi's sarcoma.

provided by *The San Francisco Chronicle,* which published quotes from Hudson's friends about the actor's anguished years in the closet, a secret he had successfully kept hidden during his long career as Hollywood's matinee idol. Papers around the country followed up with reports of Hudson's homosexuality. As thousands of AIDS patients had already discovered, the means by which one acquired AIDS either inspired pity or provoked disdain, and it wouldn't be long before the phrase "innocent victim" entered the AIDS controversy.* (In fact, when Magic Johnson went public with his HIV status, he made sure to emphasize that he wasn't gay.**) Disavowals of homosexuality drew a line between gay men and others and only reinforced some people's notion that AIDS was God's punishment for immoral behavior.

For all the media attention devoted to the AIDS epidemic as a direct result of Hudson's disclosure, the disease still carried a tremendous stigma. By the summer of 1985, 12,067 Americans had been diagnosed with AIDS and the federal government still had no coordinated AIDS prevention program. It wasn't uncommon for obituaries of AIDS patients—well-known or otherwise—to attribute the cause of death to something other than telltale AIDS-related illnesses. Susan Sontag has observed that "[AIDS] brings to many a social death that precedes the physical one." Prominent personalities such as Liberace, fashion designer Perry Ellis, lawyer Roy Cohn, and *Chorus Line* choreographer and director Michael Bennett died of AIDS soon after Hudson, but embarrassed by their illness and the shame attached to it, they instructed their publicists to lie about the true cause of their ailments. Nobody wanted a tarnished public image, even a posthumous one.

The other major news on the AIDS front in the summer of 1985 was the introduction of AIDS testing. (Nobody could be

---

*In 1991, Kimberly Bergalis, a young Florida woman who became infected via her dentist, appeared at a congressional hearing shortly before her death to denounce the medical establishment and proclaim her "innocence." "I didn't do anything wrong," she said, implying that many others with AIDS did.

**In the early years of the epidemic, 69 percent of those affected were gay men.

given the test without written consent and the results were to be kept confidential.) The AIDS antibody test could determine whether a person was infected with HTLV-III,* the agent that infects and destroys the T cells that are a key component of the immune system. But researchers still faced many unanswered questions: Did the virus act alone? Did its presence mean that the person would automatically develop AIDS? How long was the latency period between infection and the onset of medical symptoms? The fact that testing was being conducted on a public scale meant researchers could begin to track and project the scope of the epidemic. Until then, their statistics had reflected only the number of people manifesting AIDS-like symptoms or who already had full-blown AIDS. The problem confronting scientists was twofold: Many people were reluctant to be tested for fear of learning the verdict, one that was final and irreversible, and they feared that discrimination would follow if their results were made public. To allay public fears, doctors and scientists played up the important role the test was to play in AIDS prevention. Blood banks were now required to test donated blood and people who tested positive for the lethal virus could take precautions to ensure that they didn't pass it on to anyone else. As far as was known, the virus could be transmitted only through direct contact with infected blood, semen, or vaginal secretions. "Safe sex" campaigns promoted the use of condoms as the most effective prevention against HIV infection, but it was proving difficult to break down taboos about discussing sex.

The summer of 1985 may have seen the dawning of AIDS consciousness in America, but in Europe, where Eddie Stierle was about to embark on a series of guest appearances, AIDS was viewed as primarily an American problem. European health authorities had reported nearly one thousand AIDS cases by then, but safe-sex measures were not widely advocated, nor, as a result, were they followed.

---

*In 1987, an international committee settled on one name for the AIDS virus: HIV, or Human Immunodeficiency Virus.

Stretching at the Princess Grace Academy in Monaco

9

DISTANT STAGES

"After I won the gold medal so many doors began to open in my career," Eddie wrote in the journal he began en route from Ft. Lauderdale to London with his mother on July 9, 1985. His summer itinerary included stops in London, Paris, Monte Carlo, and Cape Town, where the promise of a $1,500 fee had enticed him to agree to perform as a guest artist with Cape Town University's Youth Ballet for five weeks. In London, he was to decide whether he wanted to enroll at the Royal Ballet School, to which he had won a scholarship as a result of the Prix; in Paris, he was to make arrangements for his performance that September in a Prix highlights gala; and in Monte Carlo, he was to study at the Princess Grace Academy of Classical Dance with Marika Besobrasova, a much-admired teacher who had been a juror at the Prix. Rose was to get Eddie settled in Monte Carlo and Bill was planning to accompany him to Cape Town.

Excited as he was by the prospect of his European tour, Eddie was heartsick without Richard, whom he wasn't going to see until Christmas. Just before leaving for his trip, he'd managed to sneak in a week with Richard, who was working at the Virginia Shakespeare Festival in Williamsburg, by telling his father that his new girlfriend was performing in a play there and he "would go crazy" if he didn't see her. "That week was like a honeymoon," recalls Richard. "We were in bed every minute. We were so happy."

Eddie carried the memory of that week with him throughout Europe. Despite his heavy schedule, he wrote Richard long letters nearly every day and wrote about Richard in his journal nearly every night. His journal bubbles with declarations of his love and lust:

> On the morning of the thirteenth, my mother's birthday, my first words were "happy birthday." She didn't think I would remember, but I did. She went out to try and call my father, and I masturbated on the bed. I hadn't ejaculated since I had last been with Richard about eight days ago. I was just fantasizing about his weighted body on top of mine and the way he holds me, his gentle touch in his lips. God, I love his lips. With those thoughts, it took about ten seconds without exaggeration. By the way, I mailed his letter the minute we got to Paris.

Four days later, on his first visit to the beach at Monte Carlo, women's bodies battled for possession of his fantasies:

> I gasped at my first glance at the beach, and when I got closer I gasped even more because the women were topless. I may love men, but women's bodies still turn me on. I picked a place near this beautiful blonde with gorgeous breasts and put all my stuff down.

Keenly aware of the incendiary nature of his journal should it fall into his mother's hands, Eddie inscribed a warning label at the start of the journal he kept that summer and one can safely assume that it was intended for Rose: "Request: Please, this journal is very private. My thoughts and personal life are expressed thoroughly." The two years in North Carolina away from Rose had given him a strong sense of independence and a newfound appreciation of his mother's devotion. The resentment would come later.

For her birthday, Eddie gave Rose a copy of *The Giving Tree,* a children's book about a tree that continues to give her leaves to a young boy until none remains on her branches. The dedication to Rose, moving in its profound simplicity, reads like a Sunday sermon:

> Mom, this book symbolizes so much in our relationship . . . it is only now that I realize, after reading this book many times, that *Giving* is what makes the tree happiest. Making the boy happy, supplying him with his needs, is what made the tree happy, as it made you with me. . . . All this time all your children have wanted you to do for yourself, thinking that that would make you happy. . . . I hope that through my success and acceptance of your loving and giving nature, I can make you happy. . . .

It took only three days for Eddie to see that his desire for independence was completely at odds with his mother's desire to play the "Giving Tree." She wasn't ready for him to cut loose and, perhaps, neither was he. Their relationship would always remain emotional. Two days after Rose's birthday, Eddie and Rose got into an argument after Rose kept him waiting for more than an hour outside a store prior to her departure from Monaco. As described by Eddie in his journal, their argument suggests a lovers' quarrel more readily than it does a typical dispute between teenager and parent.

> The plan didn't work. She missed her train and I was pissed because I stood outside the store for about an hour. We missed each other somewhere. The next few hours I treated her so poorly. She checked into a hotel and I went in with her. I took a shower and then fell asleep on the bed. When I woke up, we discussed what happened, and I was impossible. I went back to my room and lay in my bed from 1 A.M. till 2 A.M. and couldn't sleep. I decided to go back to the hotel and convince Mom to come and stay the night with me regardless if she would get me in trouble with the school. I realized how badly I was treating her and I wanted the next day to be nice and something she could remember for the rest of her life. So we walked to my place at 2 A.M. and she stayed with me. We talked and cried and I told her I loved her and wanted to

Getting a tan on the Riviera

have a nice time in the morning. We woke up about 8:30 and went and had a nice breakfast. I told her I was glad that she missed the train yesterday and was glad we had a nice time that she will remember for a long time. . . . I saw her crying as the train pulled away and I felt a tear come to my eyes. She has given so much of herself to me. I owe her so much.

Just before leaving Monte Carlo himself, Eddie learned that Swiss choreographer Heinz Spoerli, the director of the Basel Ballet, was looking for a short male dancer to fill a slot in his company. Spoerli had been a juror at the Prix and wanted Eddie to come to Basel to audition. Though he was a few courses shy of his high school diploma, Eddie was eager to start his professional career and had decided against spending a year at the Royal Ballet School. He considered auditioning for the Monte Carlo company, but the nagging doubts about his body persisted. He knew the company preferred tall dancers.

> The whole company is for giants, which really frustrated me. I couldn't believe that I couldn't get in just because of my size. I can't stand the fact that before I even audition people say, "I'm sorry, but you are just too short." Anyway, it's not going to stop me . . .

In Basel, Eddie auditioned for Heinz Spoerli. Since his body type prevented him from fitting into the uniform line of the corps de ballet, he was signed to a five-month soloist's contract at $1,350 per month. Doors now seemed to be opening wherever Eddie approached, and with each opportunity, he began to imagine an even greater career for himself.

He was so taken up with himself that the real world of politics and history rarely intruded on his self-absorption, even when he happened to be in South Africa during the unraveling of apartheid.

The day after arriving in Cape Town, he was dreaming of distant stages:

> Right now I just finished looking at books from the New York City Ballet and American Ballet Theatre. In these books I saw so many photos of the stars of Classical Ballet and it has put me in such a mood of question. Will I become one of the stars of the future? I want so desperately to become the Baryshnikov of America. The dancer from America who even the people who are not interested in dance know to be great. My desire to improve has just influenced this feeling. I don't feel that it is wrong or selfish to want to be #1 and it also doesn't take away any feeling of wanting to be an "artist," for it is the ones who make it to the top who are the real artists. I am just burning inside with this feeling of success. . . . To dance is my life and the more I strive to get to the top the happier my life is going to be.

Both Eddie and Melissa Hayden had been invited to Cape Town by Mignon Furman, the engaging blond director of Cape

Town University's racially mixed Youth Ballet and school. Eddie
and his father stayed in Furman's home ("Wow, what a palace,"
Eddie noted in his journal) and the fact that she had a cook, maid,
and driver made more of an impression on them than did the
country's political turmoil. "Bill, Eddie, and I would talk about the
flowers and the botanical gardens and Eddie's training, but Eddie
never mentioned politics to me," remembers Melissa Hayden.
"How could you be right there and not make any comment?"

The trip to Cape Town provided Eddie and Bill with their first
real chance to spend time alone. Perhaps they needed to be 7,700
miles from home—and Rose—before they could see their way to a
closer relationship. Each day, Bill accompanied Eddie to the theater, where he would stay and watch rehearsals and snap photos
until Eddie was ready to go home to the Furmans' for dinner.

> Tonight was one of the most moving nights of my life. We had
> dinner with Mignon, her husband, Boy, and their son and his wife with
> their son, and Melissa and her sister. I went downstairs and told them
> about writing in my journal. We had a fantastic meal, but the best part
> came when we went into the living room and talked. At one point while
> Pop was speaking about the family and all about our stories of growing,
> he stopped and said to everyone on the verge of tears, "You know, I
> have met a lot of terrible people in my life, and when I had my family, I
> just decided that it was time to put some good guys on this earth." He
> looked at me for a while and I saw him beginning to cry very quietly. I
> think what a hard life he had just for us kids. Before writing in this
> journal I went to him in his room and said, "Thanks for all the
> compliments," and he said, "Thanks for making it possible." I sat down
> on the bed and we hugged and he started to cry. I don't think I have
> ever seen my dad so emotional before.

Eddie's reputation had preceded him in Basel. By the time he
showed up for the first day of class, the Basel dancers had already
pegged the gold medalist from the Prix de Lausanne as cocky.
Every dancer feels threatened the minute a talented young dancer
joins the ranks with advance press. The Basel dancers scrutinized
Eddie's technique. He was the youngest member of the company.

"We all thought he was showing off," remembers Linda Roth,* an American dancer who had joined the troupe the month before. "He had so much energy that we all thought he seemed overly ambitious." A few hours later, Linda met Eddie while they were standing in line for lunch in the Basler Theater's canteen, the same way he had met Anita Intrieri the year before. The spunky kid struck her as boyish and innocent and she immediately felt a desire to help him. "I ended up spending the day with him helping him find a furnished apartment," recalls Linda Roth. "I quickly realized that he really wasn't cocky, he was just very young. I felt as if I had known him forever. When we met up with a few of my friends later that day to go to the movies, they said, 'How long have you two known each other? It seems like you're old friends.' We both looked at our watches. 'Oh, about five hours.'"

Like Eddie's classmates at the School of the Arts, the Basel dancers were taken aback by his ingenuousness. Their director, Heinz Spoerli, was a rigid taskmaster whose severity made the dancers tense and paranoid. A chubby man with a charming smile, Spoerli would scream at the dancers he didn't favor and humiliate them in rehearsal by dismissing them from a ballet in which they'd been cast. "Eddie was like this burst of sunshine in that theater," recalls Linda Roth. "People were shocked by him in the beginning because he was so different from anyone there. Most of them were European and reserved and Eddie was so bubbly and open. He would talk to anybody. But he started to grow on people and in time everybody loved him, especially the girls."

The men, naturally, were more wary, since the young hotshot dancer spelled competition. Naive about the strict hierarchy of ballet companies, Eddie arrived in Basel assuming that major roles would readily come to him. He had already skipped the corps de ballet—the starting point for virtually every dancer—and was given soloist roles to learn, but there were other accomplished dancers ahead of him in line. As the resident company of the Basler Theater, the Basel Ballet performed six nights a week; Eddie was

---

*Pseudonym.

on stage for only half of the company's performances. In Basel, he was getting an education in patience, humility, and the politics of ballet.

Linda Roth was seven years older than Eddie, and Eddie liked to tell her that she reminded him of his sister Rosemarie. They quickly became confidantes, remaining close even during Eddie's overlapping relationships with Stefan, a man he met in Basel, and Catherine, a beautiful dark-haired French ballerina in the Basel company who was seventeen years Eddie's senior. At the same time, he was still writing impassioned letters to Richard, professing his singular love and encouraging him to visit at Christmas. "Just thinking about spending a whole two weeks together," Eddie wrote in November,

> makes me think that dreams really do come true. Richard, you are my dream come true. . . . Our love seems as though it can really last a lifetime, yet we have to take it one day at a time. I have never loved someone as I do you, and it is hard to believe that I could ever love a woman more than I love you.

"Eddie was very conflicted about his sexuality," remembers Roth, who believes it was Eddie's unusual blend of little-boy enthusiasm and old-world graciousness that made him so appealing to both sexes. "We talked about it a lot. He liked both women and men and he couldn't choose between the two. He was very attracted to men and more confident with men, but he couldn't imagine not getting married and having a family and it scared him to think he might not have that. It was very painful for him, but he kept it a secret. Eddie gave very mixed signals, so it was really hard to tell whether he was gay or straight. He looked so young that I think most people thought he didn't have much experience, but he did."

While AIDS was not widely discussed among the dancers, Roth recalls broaching the subject with Eddie on a few occasions. "Eddie was just beginning to become aware of how important it was to be careful," she says. "He told me that he knew he wasn't careful enough. He wasn't always practicing safe sex. He felt it couldn't happen to him."

Eddie had been in Basel for only six weeks when Rose Stierle came to visit. One morning, when Eddie was at rehearsal, Rose stayed behind at his apartment "tidying up," as she puts it, and came across a letter in Eddie's desk drawer. The letter was from Richard. Rose read the letter again and again.

"I have to find out how we can change him back," she repeated to herself as she read several pages of a love letter written to her son by another man. She was stunned. "I had no idea how into sex they were," she recalls. "I thought Richard was just his friend. I probably should have known, but I wasn't watching the talk shows."

Rose copied the letter by hand. She didn't want to "say words that weren't there." But she kept her discovery from Eddie because she didn't want to spoil their visit. She would call Rosemarie when she got home and see how they could help him "get back on the right path."

The transatlantic calls began. "My mother called me in tears," remembers Rosemarie. "What are we going to do about Eddie? she wanted to know. I was naive then and thought I could convince Eddie to be straight." As soon as Rose returned home, Rosemarie rang Eddie in Basel. "Mom knows about Richard. She found a letter in your desk," she told him. "It's okay if you love a guy, but do you feel you've given women a chance?"

Eddie called his mother: "Mom, I know you know." Rose began to cry. "It's very hard for me," she sobbed. "I didn't want to spoil our visit, but I'm not happy about this." "I know, Mom," Eddie answered, evenly, wondering what it would take to convince his mother to accept Richard. He knew she couldn't get past the idea of Richard, so he hoped that by making him real, she might see just how much Richard meant to him—and thus, change her mind. "He's such a great person," he pointed out to her, "and I really love him."

Rosemarie called her father. "Dad, I'm sure if you talked to him it would help. I'm sure if he knows how you and Mom feel, things will start changing. He hasn't had much of a male influence on his life."

Bill Stierle had trouble believing that a son of his could be truly homosexual, and stuck by his environmental theory. "Nothing's definite," he told his wife and daughter. "He's still growing and experimenting. But as long as he's in ballet, there's no way you can keep him from that."

The next week, Rose went to see Sister Sue Fitzpatrick, a thirty-two-year-old Sister of Mercy at the Catholic Charities in Ft. Lauderdale. "I'm here to find out how I can change my son. He's not normal," Rose announced.

The nun advised Rose that the Church needed to do "some work in this area." She urged Rose to stop trying to change Eddie and to accept and support him.

"That doesn't sit right with me, Sister," Rose protested. "How do the bishop and the Pope look on this?"

Preferring to give her own answer, Sister Sue returned to the theme of acceptance.

Rose thought she might as well get a second opinion. On his next visit, she spoke to her eldest son, Michael, who headed the Catholic Campus Ministry's Department of the Archdiocese of Miami and taught Scripture at St. Jude Catholic Church in Boca Raton, where he had moved with his wife. "Mom always went to the Church for advice, but she didn't always take that advice," says Michael Galligan-Stierle, who had added his wife's surname to his own. "My mother wanted me to lead Edward to the decision that he would be happier choosing a life-style with women rather than with men. I said I would listen to him when the time was right, but I wasn't going to steer him."

In a spur-of-the-moment decision, Eddie decided to come home for five days while on a layoff from performing. Richard was coming to visit at Christmas and he was getting tired of trying to explain himself to his family over the phone. "Eddie was sure that his parents would never accept his gay feelings and he was afraid that they would never understand," recalls Linda Roth. Rose tried hard to follow Sister Sue's advice, but disappointment over-whelmed her one morning when Eddie announced that he was spending Christmas with Richard in Basel. It was the first time Rose had ever felt cut out of Eddie's life and, all at once, she lost her bearings. "A mother likes to be in control and all of a sudden, I'm helpless," she remembers. "I asked Bill to talk to Eddie, but he never told me if he did." Out on a plaster and patch job with Eddie, Bill had a tête-à-tête with his son. As they rode in Bill's pickup truck, Eddie told him about Richard. "Ed, you have to give the girls a chance," Bill exhorted, making sure not to raise his voice. "It's too early to choose. You don't have to do it just because it's acceptable in your profession."

Bill felt unhappy about Eddie's "being on the gay side," but consoled himself with the thought that he didn't "make him that way." "If I was brought up a nonbeliever in God, it probably wouldn't have made any difference to me," says Bill Stierle. "I hoped I made an impression on Eddie, but that's all I could do. I told him I didn't approve of it and I told him to keep his sex life personal. I said, 'It's not a thing you go around bragging about.' "

Before leaving Hollywood in November 1985, Eddie went for a checkup with Dr. Newman, the family doctor. He asked his mother to leave the room. "I'd like to get an AIDS test," seventeen-year-old Eddie informed him.

That November, Richard Register also told *his* mother that he was going to Basel. He had never spent Christmas away from his family and his mother wanted to know why it was important for him to go. "That's when I told her about Eddie," he recalls. "She realized I was in love with a man. She started weeping and said, 'Well, I guess we'll welcome him into the family.' "

His trip to Basel was a disaster. "Eddie knew it was a mistake the minute Richard arrived," says Linda Roth, who soon replaced Richard in Eddie's affections.

The visit was awkward from the start. Despite Eddie's long, pining letters, Richard found him distant and preoccupied. He figured they just needed time to readjust to each other. Eddie, however, was confused by his reaction to Richard and wondered whether he was still in love with him after all. He was frightened by the intensity of Richard's feelings once face-to-face with him, and feared the rupture with his family that his continued relationship with Richard might cause. A week into their reunion, Eddie broke up with him. Over lunch in a Burger King in downtown Basel, Eddie confessed that he was still questioning his sexuality. "I don't think we can continue this relationship," he announced suddenly to Richard. "I couldn't tell you over the phone or in a letter, I had to see you."

Shattered, Richard began crying, pleading with Eddie to give them more time together. He wasn't due to leave for another week. Couldn't they "just pretend everything was the way it used to be?" Eddie agreed to try, but two days later, Richard saw he would have to leave. When he couldn't get through to the airline to change his ticket, Eddie called Rose.

It was the phone call Rose had been praying for. "Richard and I broke up, Ma. I'm having trouble getting through to the airline. Could you book him a reservation out of here?" Within twenty-four hours, Rose had put the ticket on her credit card and sent it Express Mail to Basel. "Wait till I tell Sister Sue," thought Rose. "Maybe he'll revert back to liking girls. Maybe Anita from the School of the Arts will start loving him again."

Two weeks later, Rose sent Eddie a letter. As he opened it, a picture of Anita Intrieri fell into his lap. Rose had gone to see Anita dance, she wrote. "She was lovely."

The turnabout from Richard to Linda left Eddie confused. He couldn't understand why the intensity of his love had subsided so dramatically; two months later, he would write to Richard of his confusion. By that point, however, Richard was furious with Eddie for having invited him all the way to Basel just to break up with him. He was hardly interested in Eddie's rationale, particularly when he was now writing to tell him that he had begun a relationship with Linda.

> I am not by any means telling you that I have completely changed, but I have definitely experienced something that has shown me so much about love between a man and a woman. Richard, I am still searching, but I have taken a step into the heterosexual life-style, and I really was fulfilled, not just physically, but mentally and emotionally too. . . . There are so many things that I need to find out before I can love a man like you loved me. . . . You have given me so much, and this I will *never* forget. I don't really know what the future holds for me, but no matter what it brings me I will never forget the love we had.
>
> Thank You So Much,
> Eddie

The end of their relationship came just as Eddie began to experience nagging foot pains. X-rays would later reveal that calcium deposits had formed an extra bone in the back of his ankle, but at the time, Eddie knew only that he felt sharp pain every time he tried to point his right foot.

His unhappiness was compounded by his frustration at seeing the plum assignments go to senior dancers. He was dancing the stool dance in Spoerli's *Chäs,* a soloist variation that required him to perform virtuoso feats with a stool attached to his bottom by a belt, and he had minor parts in *Coppélia* and *The Nutcracker.* But when he didn't get to dance Puck in *A Midsummer Night's Dream,* a role Spoerli had promised him, and found himself spending too much time off the stage, he blamed his small, stocky body and set to work on lengthening his muscles, improving his line, and strengthening his feet. "Eddie had the ability to excite audiences," recalls Heinz Spoerli. "But he put so much energy in his dancing that the precision of his technique sometimes got lost in his dynamic dancing."

The only heartening news Eddie got that winter came in the mail. His lab results showed that he had tested negative for the presence of antibodies to the AIDS virus.

Performing *Lacrymosa d'Amore* in Jackson, 1986

10

AMBITION

After five months in Basel, Eddie longed to return to New York, where he hoped finally to land a job with Baryshnikov's ABT. The day he arrived in New York, he went to see Baryshnikov's orthopedic surgeon, Dr. William Hamilton. To Eddie, it mattered less that Hamilton had strong medical credentials than that he was the doctor to the biggest names in the ballet world. Dr. Hamilton repaired Eddie's foot by removing the extra bone.

Two weeks later, Bill Stierle underwent triple-bypass heart surgery following a heart attack he suffered on the day the space shuttle *Challenger* blew up. Father and son recuperated together in Hollywood, where one weekend Eddie accompanied his brother Michael on a Catholic retreat in Miami. On a walk in the woods together, Eddie told his brother that he was having trouble defining who he was. He was attracted to both men and women, he said, and didn't know how to choose. He felt he had to choose one or the other and thought perhaps he would focus on women for a while. "So I said, 'Great! Let's give it a try, I'll be glad to help, affirm, or whatever you need me to do,' " remembers Michael. "He felt that I was more open-minded than he had thought I'd be, but not that I was for his being gay."

As his foot began to heal, Eddie set to work choreographing his next steps. He wanted desperately to jump-start his career in America and figured the ideal vehicle was the International Ballet Competition, which was to be held in Jackson, Mississippi, in June. He was counting on his performance at Jackson to land him an audition with ABT. But he knew he needed help to get there. Just before his foot operation, he had gone to see David Howard, one of New York's best-known ballet coaches, whose roster of celebrated students had included Gelsey Kirkland and Natalia Makarova.

Howard's first impression of Eddie was mixed: The boy was talented, he thought, but he had lousy proportions. Nonetheless, he agreed to take him on, primarily as a partner for his fourteen-year-old prodigy, Jennifer Gelfand, a student from Boston who regularly flew to New York for Howard's coaching. Howard was grooming Gelfand for a big-time career and hesitated about pairing the delicate, ninety-pound ballerina with Eddie Stierle. "I was very edgy that Eddie would throw her off because he wanted to be noticed so badly," says the British-born David Howard, a member of the Royal Ballet in the early 1960s. "It was very important for him to win you over. He was a bit of a con artist, but with an honest passion."

Eddie's ambitions were all too familiar to Howard. Every talented student vying for a place at the barre in his studio harbored the same ones. Howard tried to convince Eddie that ABT was unlikely. Although Eddie was the same height as Baryshnikov, his proportions were entirely different. Baryshnikov had unusually long legs for his body, which gave him the illusion of height on stage. "I told Eddie there was no point in thinking of ABT because Misha wasn't interested in a dancer like him. I said, 'Mr. Joffrey will be at Jackson and if he's interested in you in any way, don't let it go.' " And he said, 'That's not what I want to do.' He would not be put off. So I said, 'Eddie, it's not what you want to do, it's where you can fit in.' "

Eddie's sense of movement and love for dancing were immediately apparent to Howard, who worked with him five hours a day, five days a week, from April to June, refining his technique and lengthening his bulky muscles by giving him stretching exercises, putting him on a low-fat diet, and working on his placement. By learning to stand forward on his legs instead of on his heels, Eddie was less inclined to grip—and thus, shorten—his muscles. Howard prepared a program of works for Eddie and Jennifer Gelfand that would present different aspects of their stage personalities. He chose the pas de deux from the comic classic *La Fille Mal Gardée*, to showcase their youth and effervescence; the pas de deux from *Hunchback of Notre Dame*, to highlight their dramatic potential (Eddie danced the role of the Hunchback); and the pas de deux from *Don Quixote*, to finish off with a fireworks display of technique.

For his solo, Eddie once again decided to choreograph his own variation, which he developed with Howard's help. He called his solo *Lacrymosa* (meaning "Tearful") and set it to a movement from Mozart's *Requiem*, which had absorbed him ever since he had seen the film *Amadeus*. What moved him most about the *Requiem*, he told his sister Rosemarie, was Mozart's determination to compose it even while dying.

As he worked on his solo, Eddie fretted endlessly about whether his small, compact body would keep him out of a classical company. "Why did God give me this gift and put me in this body?" he complained to his mother one day through tears.

Prior to the competition, Eddie wanted to try out *Lacrymosa* on an audience and promised his brother Michael to perform it at a benefit for the Archdiocese of Miami. (The program for the event proclaimed Eddie "Miami's Own International Ballet Star.") "It's about being judged and forgiven," Eddie remarked of *Lacrymosa* to *The Sun-Tattler*, though in an interview with a writer for the Archdiocese of Miami's newsletter, Eddie played up the ballet's religious overtones by pointing out that it was about "God's forgiveness." Several years later, when he incorporated the solo

Robert Joffrey presenting Eddie with the gold medal in Jackson

into an expanded version of *Lacrymosa* for the Joffrey, the work and its title had come to reflect a different personal dilemma. "It's about coming to terms with death," he would say.

At Jackson, Eddie won not only the gold medal in the junior men's division, but the astute eye of Robert Joffrey, the copresident of the twenty-member international jury. Eddie's strategy had paid off: He got the attention in America he was seeking, and from a distinguished panel of dance personalities, several of whom were directors of major companies. Robert Joffrey's praise was especially flattering, for Joffrey was known for his ability to ferret out possibilities in dancers. He told David Howard that Eddie's performance in *Don Quixote* was the best he'd seen "in ages." Like Eddie, Robert Joffrey was short and stocky and had been told early on that he would never succeed as a classical dancer. An outsider to a club that wouldn't accept him, he simply formed his own club and opened up the membership to dancers who were athletic, youthful, and versatile, whatever their body type. He cared about exuberant dancing, not strict uniformity to an ideal.

Prior to leaving for Jackson, Eddie was asked about his prospects by a reporter from *The Miami Herald*. When the reporter noted that his height was "still a problem," Eddie corrected her at once. "I'm going to shoot for the top. My attitude is 'I'll overcome.' Just watch me."

At the closing ceremonies, Robert Joffrey approached Eddie. "How would you like to come to New York and join my company?"

As Alain in *La Fille Mal Gardée,* 1987

11

THE

JOFFREY

Eddie and Scott Barnard, the Joffrey's persnickety ballet master, got off to an uneasy start before Eddie had even set foot inside the Joffrey's New York studios. "Hello, this is Edward Stierle calling," a voice informed Barnard, who was on tour in San Francisco with the company. "I won the gold medal at Jackson and Robert Joffrey has offered me a contract. I'm supposed to find out when I start."

Barnard was taken aback. This wasn't the way things were done at the Joffrey and Barnard was hardly one to break with protocol. Dancers usually came up through the Joffrey School or the Joffrey II, the company's junior troupe, and rarely were unknown quantities out-and-out offered a contract. As ballet master, Barnard, a former Joffrey dancer, taught company class, oversaw rehearsals, made casting recommendations, and kept a close watch on company standards. Yet even in a profession built on meticulous attention to detail, Barnard was known to be overexacting and methodical to such a degree that several dancers called him "the Martinet" behind his back. Of course, few dancers approached Barnard head-on, and did so only if they had the stature or seniority to back them up.

"I had no idea who this *child* was," recalls Barnard, "and my first thought was, 'Oh, yes, one of *these.*' I figured he was a young kid who wanted to dance and had all that fire and vinegar but no substance."

Barnard told Eddie he'd have to first speak to "Mr. Joffrey" when he returned to New York. "Bob" to his friends and colleagues, Robert Joffrey was always "Mr. Joffrey" to his company.

"Oh, no," Robert Joffrey corrected him when Barnard suggested that Edward Stierle was an upstart. "He was at the competition. He's very gifted. We *must* look at him."

Eddie was invited to take company class by way of an audition, but by the time he arrived at the Joffrey studios at City Center on West Fifty-sixth Street, Eddie had first stopped by American Ballet Theatre to audition for Baryshnikov. "I don't need any more short dancers," Baryshnikov told the disappointed Eddie after seeing him in company class. When Robert Joffrey learned of Eddie's ABT audition, he was apparently so put out that Eddie didn't head straight for *his* company that he decided to punish him by giving him the runaround for two weeks.

"Bob knew that Eddie had tried ABT," remembers Gerald Arpino, the Joffrey's cofounder and then its associate artistic director and principal choreographer. "He told me Eddie was an operator. He knew right from the beginning that Eddie was his catch, even before Eddie realized it. He said to me, 'Let him make the rounds, he'll be back.' " In Eddie, it seems, Joffrey recognized a kindred spirit. "Bob understood Eddie because they were so much alike," observes Gerald Arpino. "They both had definite goals and knew what they wanted to accomplish. They both could have been great politicians."

Scott Barnard, however, still had reservations about Eddie's body. He could see that he was a gifted and natural dancer, but he considered Eddie "exceptionally" short and, worse, raw material. "He had brute, gut strength but there was nothing polished," he recalls. "But Mr. Joffrey and I felt that Edward was very good for this company, because this company is made out of dancers who don't have the absolute body. Edward had one of those bodies that any classical company would look at and say 'No' at the sight of him."

Although the Joffrey had already filled its allotted quota of forty-one dancers for the year, Robert Joffrey was so excited by Eddie's promise that he simply added an extra slot. He made room for Eddie. It wouldn't be long before the Joffrey dancers would be asked to make way for him as well.

The day Mr. Joffrey introduced Eddie Stierle to his company as its newest member, the dancers immediately recognized the glint in their director's eye. "The buzz was that Mr. Joffrey loved Eddie," recalls Patrick Corbin, who was three years older than Eddie and would soon be competing with him for leading roles. "It wasn't so much what he said about Eddie, but the way he said it with such excitement." Everybody in the Joffrey wanted Mr. Joffrey's attention and approval and while they didn't set much store in medals, Eddie Stierle's gold medal meant something to them because Mr. Joffrey had been head of the jury that awarded it to him.

To his family of dancers, Robert Joffrey was a paternal figure, a stocky, bearded man of visionary zeal, who was their leader, never a colleague. "He was a presence," points out the ballerina Tina LeBlanc, "not a friend." Quick-witted and boundlessly robust, he personified American ballet. The son of an Italian mother and an Afghan father, a restaurant owner, Joffrey had grown up in Seattle, where he first began dreaming of founding his own ballet company composed of American-trained dancers. From a small band of six dancers who toured the country in a station wagon, the troupe he founded with Gerald Arpino in 1956 eventually grew into the third major ballet company in the United States—and the most distinctly American. Where American Ballet Theatre was known for dance theater and its stagings of the nineteenth-century classics, and the New York City Ballet was known for Balanchine's neoclassical ballets, the Joffrey stood for youth, exuberance, and eclecticism. The company had introduced ballet to a whole new public with its wide-ranging, accessible repertory, much of it choreographed by Arpino, who as resident choreographer replenished the repertory each season. While his hard-driving, spirited dances had shaped the Joffrey's reputation for pop ballet, they had also led critics to dismiss both the company as trendy and Arpino's choreography, in particular, as sometimes glitzy and facile.

Though himself a choreographer of some note (his rock ballet *Astarte* was the first ballet to make the cover of *Time* magazine, in 1968), Robert Joffrey was more interested in playing the role of impresario, curator, and missionary for the dance. In addition to producing works by Arpino, he was committed to commissioning works from both emerging ballet choreographers and maverick modern-dance choreographers who had no experience in ballet. He wasn't a snob and he knew that to popularize ballet, he had to open the company's repertoire to a variety of movement styles and musical choices. He had given Twyla Tharp her first major break in 1973 with *Deuce Coupe,* a landmark pop ballet that caused a sensation with its unlikely blend of pas de bourrées, the Beach Boys, and the Boogaloo; later he had followed up with assignments for Laura Dean and Mark Morris, long before they became fashionable in ballet circles. But Joffrey was also intent on preserving dance history and made his company a showcase for distinguished revivals of twentieth-century classics that ranged from creations made for Diaghilev's Ballets Russes, through works by Kurt Jooss, Agnes de Mille, and Jerome Robbins, to the largest American collection of the ballets of Sir Frederick Ashton.

Despite his exuberant public persona, Joffrey was an intensely private man who communicated little about his offstage life to his dancers. Still, bits and pieces trickled down to them from time to time. It was widely believed, for example, that Joffrey and Gerald Arpino had once been lovers and continued to live together in their Greenwich Village town house, even though both had moved on to other relationships. When Eddie joined the company in the summer of 1986, Joffrey was rumored to be involved with Richard Englund, the director of the Joffrey II Dancers, who was married to that troupe's ballet mistress.

The former director of American Ballet Theatre's junior troupe, Englund was already well acquainted with Eddie's dancing by the time Eddie arrived at the Joffrey. He had auditioned Eddie for ABT II several years earlier in Florida (and rejected him for consideration), and had been a member of the jury at both the Prix de Lausanne and Jackson competitions the years that Eddie won the gold.

Robert Joffrey kept close watch over his dancers and faithfully studied their performances from his aisle seat in the last row of the orchestra each night, rushing backstage at each intermission to encourage, correct, or rebuke them. He once reprimanded a dancer who wore clear nail polish onstage (the lights picked it up, he said) and another for not wiping away the barely discernible trace of dirt on one of her pointe shoes. "We came to rely on his eye in the audience and in the studio," says Leslie Carothers, then a star of the company. "He was the person we tried to excel for." Over the years, as he had become more intimately involved in directing every aspect of the company's activities, he spent less and less time in the studio, and had increasingly left company class in the hands of Scott Barnard. But every now and then, he surprised his dancers by showing up to lead morning class. "When you heard he was going to teach, you wore your best leotard, you smelled good, and your hair was pulled back just right," says Joffrey veteran Jodie Gates. "Everything had to be perfect. Nothing escaped his notice." Indeed, even after he'd been absent from the studios for several weeks, Joffrey would be able to pinpoint the particular nature of a dancer's progress, as if he'd been there to see it all along.

Every newcomer to the Joffrey was expected to obey certain unspoken rules. In class, the front lines were reserved for the company's senior members. During rehearsal, no one was allowed to leave the studio nor take phone calls. And, at all times, novitiates were to keep a low profile.

In his first two weeks, Eddie broke all the rules. Not having come up through the ranks, he didn't have occasion to learn them and, anyhow, subservience had never come naturally to him. He stood front and center in company class, he did six perfect pirouettes to everyone else's four, and he took phone calls during rehearsals, which, according to Patrick Corbin, was unheard of: "The rehearsal studio was considered a sacred temple." Rather than hold back in class and rehearsal to save himself for the stage as most dancers do, Eddie always danced "full-out," throwing himself into his new assignments with his signature aplomb. Like some sort of superconductor, he had the ability to charge the other dancers around him. "He was an elemental force," recalls Leslie Carothers. "Energy just emanated from him. It was as if there was no room big enough to contain him." To those less favorably inclined, it seemed as if Eddie simply took the room over. As Joffrey veteran Carl Corry remembers, Eddie was "a steamroller" in the studio.

In a company where dancers were expected to blend and humbly obey, Eddie's magnetic personality stood out at once. His biggest faux pas was in exuding an air of supreme self-confidence. "Here was this little shit doing all these tricks," recalls Jodie Gates, who had been a company member for ten years. "We thought, 'Who does he think he is?' " Given the competition for roles, the men were particularly hard on Eddie. In the dressing room, they would point up his imperfections to one another: He didn't have good feet, he was chunky, he was short. But what they couldn't overlook was the fact that he moved with remarkable speed and power. Patrick Corbin had joined the Joffrey the year before Eddie and remembers that the dancers were "awed" by Eddie's technique, especially by his ability to do "buttery multiple turns from any position and in any tempo or direction." That didn't make it any easier to like him, however. "There's always fear when someone new comes into the company," explains Corbin, "especially when they're good, because you worry that you're going to fall by the wayside, that your career is over, and you'll never do another leading part."

Compounding their fears was the knowledge that they had only a short time to make their mark. All dancers wage a losing battle against gravity and time, their bodies the instruments of betrayal in a world obsessed with youth and fairy-tale illusion. Careers in ballet assume a certain urgency because, in due course, the body will simply refuse to perform as the mind wills it to. A dancer can expect about ten years of peak performance; if recognition and fulfillment of one's goals don't come by age thirty, they are unlikely to come at all, for most dancers are professionally finished by forty, at a point when those called to other vocations are just making their mark. Unlike actors, dancers cannot make up for lost time with "mature" roles later in life.

It took less than two weeks of Eddie for several of the Joffrey's rising male dancers to begin fearing for their roles. Among them was Mark Goldweber, who at five-seven was the company's shortest male dancer. Despite his talent, he had remained with the Joffrey II Dancers for two years before finally getting into the Joffrey's main company in 1977, in large part because the company's directors were concerned about his height. "Here Eddie, at five-six, shows up from nowhere and gets into the main company," says Goldweber. "I figured I had better watch this guy because there must be something special about him if he's that short and they want him."

Standing at the opposite pole of the physical spectrum was Ashley Wheater, a tall, blond dancer with chiseled good looks, whose broad experience and stature enabled him to see through the flak about eighteen-year-old Eddie Stierle. At twenty-seven, Wheater was firmly established in leading princely roles, having already performed as a principal dancer with the London Festival Ballet and the Australian Ballet before joining the Joffrey in 1984. To Wheater, Eddie was "a naughty little boy," whose refreshing candor stirred the ranks. "Most dancers cling to the walls in their first weeks in a company," recalls Wheater. "They don't want to ask anyone what to do. Eddie simply asked. A lot of people were envious of him, so they stripped him down for not having good feet or good legs or for being too short. The fact of the matter was that he was a very talented boy."

The very talented boy didn't lack for humility, though it was hardly his strong suit. He had never learned to pace himself in any area of his life and, anxious for acceptance, he tried to win over the Joffrey dancers. He had a sense of himself as a special person and saw no reason to conceal his accomplishments from his peers. But they didn't always want to hear about them, especially when they already considered him ambitious and competitive. That impression was soon held by a number of dancers around town after Eddie showed up at several parties with both his gold medal *and* a videotape of his Jackson performance in hand.

Kyle Ahmed met Eddie the week he arrived in New York and remembers how surprised he was by Eddie's audacity the night he was introduced to him at a birthday party for a dancer with American Ballet Theatre. "Dancers are so snobby and everyone said, 'Who is this guy showing his video? This isn't even *his* party.' Eddie didn't notice. He was very caught up in the whirlwind of himself." Ahmed had just moved to New York from California to study at the Joffrey School and was looking for a roommate. When two friends at ABT offered to sublet their Upper East Side apartment to him, he asked Eddie to room with him and before long, the two became friends. To Kyle, a handsome young dancer with thick, midnight black hair and brown eyes, Eddie was a big star. He and Eddie were the same age and yet Eddie had gone straight into the Joffrey's main company with two gold medals to his credit, while Kyle was still a student at the Joffrey School. Lonely for a friend, Eddie was excited to find an appreciative audience in Kyle. Where others had snickered or feigned indifference, Kyle happily sat for hours studying Eddie's competition performances on videotape. "Here he was living my dream right there in front of me," he recalls.

Eddie was also living out Lissette Salgado's dream. Eddie's childhood ballet partner and friend at Liana's, Lissette had grown into a beautiful, curvaceous dancer with large brown eyes and dark, lustrous hair. She had kept in touch with Eddie over the years via Rose Stierle's mailing list and Eddie's visits home, but hadn't had a chance to spend much time with him. That year, however, their career paths finally converged. The same month that Eddie joined the Joffrey, Lissette was accepted into the Joffrey II Dancers, after Eddie helped arrange for her audition. Having led a sheltered life in a close-knit Cuban family, Lissette had never been away from home before arriving in New York and was naturally nervous about finding her place in the Joffrey. She looked to Eddie to guide her and since the Joffrey and Joffrey II occupied studios in the same building, they began meeting regularly for lunch. Over her lunch of cottage cheese and fruit and his of peanut-butter-and-jelly sandwiches, they would compare notes on their progress. According to Lissette, Eddie would push her to overcome her shyness and make herself known in the second company. But when she, in turn, tried to encourage him to scale down his expectations, he would snap at her, "I see these other people in the company and they're not as good as I am."

As in all ballet companies, choice roles at the Joffrey generally went to the dancers who had served apprenticeships in minor roles. Likewise, dancers who had paid their dues were rewarded by being cast in the "first cast" of a production, which gave them special perks: They got to work personally with the choreographer or person staging the ballet, they got the only dress rehearsal, they got opening night performances of the work (the performance most often attended by the major critics), and they got to dance their role more often than their alternates in the second- and third-cast rotation. At the Joffrey, the casting lineup usually became clear to the dancers within the first few days of rehearsal when they saw who had been assigned to work directly with the choreographer.

During Eddie's third week at the Joffrey, rehearsals got under way for a big, splashy production of Sir Frederick Ashton's full length pastoral comedy *La Fille Mal Gardée*. Refashioned by Ashton in 1960, the original *Fille* had been choreographed in 1789 on the eve of the French Revolution and had since been staged numerous times as a vehicle for many of the greatest dancers of the day. The ballet tells the story of a spunky farm girl named Lise, and her sweetheart, Colas, who during the course of the action try to outwit Lise's mother in her attempts to marry her daughter off to the son of a rich farmer. The son, a seemingly dim-witted fellow named Alain, fails to understand why everyone mocks him and clings to his red umbrella like Linus to his blanket.

There were at least four possible candidates for the role of Alain, all of whom had been in the company longer than Eddie. Mark Goldweber and Carl Corry were chief among them and they, along with Eddie, Patrick Corbin, and Parrish Maynard, were called to the rehearsals led by Ashton's original Alain, Alexander Grant, who was staging the production for the Joffrey.

Both Carl Corry and Mark Goldweber privately considered themselves front-runners for the role. "I had my heart set on the part before we had even started rehearsing," remembers Corry, who was twenty-eight. "I had worked so hard on it before the rehearsal period. I thought I was at least going to do second cast. All of a sudden Eddie appeared and I was out of the picture completely. It was really, really disappointing."

Alexander Grant, the veteran Royal Ballet star who had been a juror at both Helsinki and Jackson when Eddie competed, was delighted on his first day of rehearsal to find young Eddie Stierle at the Joffrey and doubly so when he learned that Eddie was to be the first-cast Alain. "Oh, marvelous, you've got Eddie," the portly, flush-faced Grant remarked to Robert Joffrey, whom he hadn't seen since the Jackson competition the previous month. "He's just absolutely perfect for Alain."

And so, with the imprimatur of Ashton's definitive Alain, Eddie set to work learning the role, while Mark Goldweber, the second-cast Alain, and Patrick Corbin, the third-cast alternate, marked the steps and learned what they could from the sidelines. From that point on, and with rare exception, whenever he danced in a new production or major revival, Eddie was always first cast.

Eddie's ballet family soon began to echo the resentments first harbored by Eddie's brothers and sisters. Like many of the Joffrey men, Carl Corry felt Eddie hadn't paid his dues and didn't deserve preferential treatment. Having been overlooked in the role of Alain altogether (he was cast, instead, in the *travesti* role of the Widow Simone, Alain's mother), Corry was hardly feeling generous toward

Eddie and Rose with Alexander Grant in Washington, D.C.

him. "Everything was Eddie, Eddie, Eddie, all day long. He was a master at getting attention," he says.

For six hours a day for two weeks, Alexander Grant worked directly with Eddie, resetting his role on the younger dancer. All the while, he tried to convey just what Ashton had in mind when the choreographer tailor-made the role for him. "Don't make the mistake that many dancers have, of playing him as if he's the village idiot," cautioned Grant. "He's childlike, not stupid." Grant encouraged Eddie not to copy *his* interpretation, but to understand the essence of the character and then make it his own.

Certainly, there were traces of Eddie's own life in the fictional life of Alain. "Because he is so childlike," Grant further advised him, "the world laughs at him and the way the role is wonderfully sympathetic is that we're all frightened of being laughed at and being rejected. The boy is rejected, but he overcomes it with his own spirit. He's always trying to please his father, the girl, and her mother. He's looking all the time to see that they're pleased with what he's doing."

Eddie worked hard to please Grant—and, by proxy, Ashton—who was impressed with Eddie's ability to absorb all he had to teach him with such ease. "Eddie was a choreographer's dream," allows Carl Corry. "They would whisper the steps to him and he could perform them right there and then."

Just as he had the audacity to approach Grant at Helsinki and ask for his advice, Eddie now wasted no time in asking Grant out to lunch after rehearsal one day. There was nothing inappropriate in his invitation, it was just that the Joffrey dancers, particularly new ones, rarely if ever fraternized with the artistic staff, let alone famous guest artists. But Eddie wanted to hear Grant's stories about the making of *La Fille Mal Gardée*. "I was rather taken aback," admits Grant, who nonetheless accepted his invitation and joined him at the Stardust Diner, a coffee shop near the Joffrey. "I was so much older than Eddie and here he was inviting me to lunch."

To the other dancers in *La Fille Mal Gardée*, it looked like brownnosing. During a company meeting that season, Gerald Arpino gave the dancers one of his rambling pep talks. "I need more *zah* from my babies," he prodded them. "Then he pointed to Eddie," remembers Jodie Gates. "He said, 'For inspiration, we should all look to Eddie.' I was sitting there thinking, 'Hey, I'm working my ass off too!'"

Eddie sensed that many of the dancers disliked him, but he couldn't understand why. It was important to him that people like him, and for the first time in his life, he was having a hard time convincing them that they should. "Everyone seems so distant," he wrote in his journal. "They have been the hardest group of people to make friends with." At St. Thomas, the girls had liked him even if many of his male classmates had made fun of him and at North Carolina, he had never had trouble charming the people he liked. Having always been rewarded by his mother, Liana, and Mitzi for standing out, he couldn't understand why he offended other dancers by getting cast ahead of them or why many of the company members seemed reluctant to embrace him or his talent. But then, in his rush to be noticed, Eddie hadn't yet learned the art of diplomacy.

Returning to his apartment at night after a nine-hour day at the Joffrey, he would vent his frustrations to Kyle Ahmed. "People would be nice to him to his face and then talk badly about him behind his back," says Kyle. "He got a reputation for being loud and full of himself." Kyle also began to share that view when he found himself listening to Eddie talk about himself on the phone night after night.

La Fille Mal Gardée opened the Joffrey's thirtieth anniversary season at New York's City Center on October 16, 1986. Teenage dancers in their first year with a ballet company are lucky to get cast in a major role in a new production, but as was quickly becoming his custom, Eddie got even more: He was singled out in several reviews.

"The wonderful surprise of the evening was the young Edward Stierle's* brilliantly danced and moving performance as Alain," wrote dance critic Anna Kisselgoff in *The New York Times*. Tobi Tobias in *New York* magazine felt that Eddie gave the role "the right sort of grotesqueness and poignancy, as well as stunning physical virtuosity," while Clive Barnes, who had seen the original Royal Ballet production in London, observed in *The New York Post*: "Another of the performance's special virtues was young Edward Stierle, who was making his New York debut with the company. He was both brilliant and touching in Alexander Grant's original role of Alain. . . ."

Bolstered by his enthusiastic notices, Eddie resolved to work even harder, intent on quickly adding many more roles to his repertoire.

---

*Prior to Eddie's debut in his first leading role, the Joffrey Ballet's press office asked Eddie how his surname should be pronounced. While his family pronounced it "Sturl," Eddie decided that his name would sound more European and more dramatic if pronounced "Stirlee."

In New York

12

THE MAN MAGNET

Lauren Rouse had been dancing with the Joffrey for nearly twelve years when eighteen-year-old Eddie Stierle joined the company, becoming its youngest member. At thirty-two, Rouse was approaching the end of her career; she knew that only a few prime dancing years remained and had already begun to think about retiring. Blond and leggy, she was considered one of the company's sexiest ballerinas and it didn't take Eddie long to notice her. Indeed, within six weeks of joining the Joffrey, he was sneaking into her room while on tour in Houston. "Give me a call if you like, and maybe we can visit before turning in," read one of the late-night notes she slipped under his hotel room door. Though they tried to be discreet by meeting only late at night in hotel rooms or in her studio apartment in Chelsea, word got around.

This was one piece of gossip that was too good to keep under wraps. It wasn't simply their age difference that had people talking; conflicting perceptions of Eddie's sexual preference soon became a subject of debate as well. "People were mortified," remembers dancer Parrish Maynard, who assumed that since Eddie was seeing

Lauren, he was straight. "They couldn't believe she'd go out with this guy who's half her age." Others, however, assumed that Eddie was gay—and confused. Among this group was Patrick Corbin, who had just broken up with his girlfriend because he had fallen in love with a man. "I thought, 'He's just trying to look really cool by bedding down with this outgoing beautiful blonde," he recalls. Rima Corben, the Joffrey's longtime publicity director, remembers how surprised she was by the power of Eddie's "macho body language" when she caught sight of him in a restaurant, cozying up in a booth with Lauren Rouse. Still others couldn't get over how crazy they seemed about each other. "They were such a hot

Lauren Rouse

item," says Tina LeBlanc, recalling the powerful physical connection between them. "I heard it was a pretty wild relationship."

Given his penchant for older ballerinas, it wasn't surprising that Eddie gravitated toward Lauren Rouse. He had always had an easier time making friends with women, in part because he had grown up surrounded by them, but also because he was never in direct competition with them for roles. His boyish charm and old-world manners made him particularly appealing to women with a maternal streak. Few could resist the ardor of his affection when it was directed toward them; as a result, he almost always won over anyone he actively sought out. "Eddie couldn't be close to more than one person at a time, because he got so involved," says former Joffrey dancer Victoria Pasquale.

A month into his relationship with Lauren, as he was lying with her in her loft bed looking out at the Empire State Building, Eddie confessed that he'd "experimented" with male lovers. "I wish I had known earlier," she says in hindsight. "I was leading my life with my heart and not my head. AIDS was something we were all just learning about and I thought, 'I should have been more careful.'" They continued to see each other through Christmas, long enough to visit Rosemarie at her new home in West Atlantic City. Both Rosemarie and her husband, Kit, worked in the casinos, Kit as an arranger and guitarist in his band, The Right Touch, and Rosemarie as a singer in the band and as a dancer at Merv Griffin's Resorts. Following family tradition, Rosemarie and Kit had managed to get a great deal on the fire-damaged house and had rebuilt it with the help of Bill Stierle and several Stierle siblings. Eddie and Lauren rarely emerged from their room the whole weekend, leading Rosemarie to conclude that Eddie was "back on track" with women. "I called my mother and told her Eddie was visiting with a girlfriend and that they seemed to be crazy about each other," she recalls. "We were both so happy."

Michael Galligan-Stierle also happened to spend an evening with Eddie and Lauren that fall and remembers how convinced he was that Eddie's sexual preference had swung decisively toward women. "The last time he and I had talked, he was confused sexually," he says. "But when I went out to dinner with them that night, Eddie and Lauren were all over each other. I figured he'd worked out the girl thing."

The relationship was over two months after it began. Rouse was ready to consider marriage and children and she saw that Eddie was far from making a commitment to anything but his dancing. "We always felt happy together, but we knew it would never be anything more than this soul-mate type of friendship," says Rouse. Four months later, she became engaged to the man who was to become her husband.

Eddie's sexual preference still remained something of a mystery, to himself as well as to the dancers and staff at the Joffrey. But as modern dance choreographer Senta Driver promptly discovered after meeting Eddie that December in Winston-Salem, shortly after his breakup with Rouse, his sexuality wasn't an either/or proposition. "Eddie was charismatic to all genders and ages," she says. "He wasn't afraid of that." Like many of Eddie's confidantes, Driver was struck by the way he projected a sensuality that was at once innocent and erotic. "Eddie had a tremendous amount of sexual energy," remembers Driver. "He had this intelligence and capacity to focus and a genuine interest in other people. There was no skin on him—he got right through to you. It was probably some kind of electrical capacity. It was as if all the waves could go in one direction. His physicality, his sensuality, and his artistic energy came all in one package."

A frank, intense woman known for her fierce intellect and cerebral dances, the forty-three-year-old Driver met Eddie in Winston-Salem, where both had been invited to work with the North Carolina Dance Theater. Eddie was to perform as a guest artist with the company in New York later that month and had come to Winston-Salem for two days of rehearsal with the troupe's leading ballerina, Joanna Sands.* Shortly after he arrived, Sands and her husband asked Eddie and Driver to dinner at their home.

_____
*Pseudonym.

They hit it off at once. "I had known him barely an hour and he came over to me and started hugging me," recalls Driver. "He did not know how to proceed slowly. He came at me like a tornado." Despite the considerable difference in their ages and experience, Driver found Eddie to be unusually curious about the world and well informed, "like a European college student." Though Eddie was not dancing in Driver's work, he found time to sit in on her rehearsals and watch her at work. He already had plans to become a choreographer and dedicated himself to studying the methods of more seasoned dance-makers. Driver, in turn, was moved by Eddie's understanding of her objectives, especially since they seemed to be incomprehensible to almost everyone else present. "In my work, I like the dancers to make emotional choices. And I kept saying to them, 'Don't be afraid if you have one feeling and the person next to you has a different one. It will work. It seems odd, but it will look the way I want.' And they found that puzzling. And Eddie said, 'She wants them to make their own choices. How exciting.' He understood exactly what I was trying to get the dancers to do and from a director's point of view. He got all of that watching, not dancing in it, which is pretty remarkable."

Eddie and Senta Driver quickly became close friends, but never lovers, though she remembers there was a lot of sexual energy between them. In fact, his presence was so compelling and seductive that she says she still recalls the feeling of kissing him, which she had occasion to do on the North Carolina troupe's opening night in New York at the Joyce Theater. As she walked by Eddie's dressing room backstage, he motioned to her to come in and then asked her for a "good luck" kiss. Eddie turned around and said, "That was wonderful," and asked for another. "It had a lot of energy in it," she says.

The North Carolina engagement couldn't have been any more loaded: Eddie had been brought in to partner Joanna Sands, the troupe's sultry leading dancer, with whom he soon began an emotionally charged affair. Sands, however, was married to another dancer in the company, who also happened to be her customary partner in the ballet Eddie had been invited to dance. In short order, Eddie displaced Sands' husband both onstage and off, a turn of events known to no one except Senta Driver, who recalls feeling jealous when asked to cover for them one afternoon. "At first I didn't know what was going on," she recalls. "He asked me to come over to his apartment because he needed to talk to me. I had a distinct suspicion that there was something about to happen between him and me. And then he told me that he and [Joanna] had become involved. And I said, 'Don't get me into this.'"

Several days after returning to Winston-Salem, Sands sent Eddie a letter. "I just can't stop thinking about you," she wrote. "I never knew that you could have this kind of effect on me. I feel that I am absolutely losing my mind over you." Eddie soon responded in kind a few weeks later, while on tour in Los Angeles. "Needless to say you are always on my mind. . . . Is it love? Hell, I don't know, but how can this feeling that I have for you get any better with someone else?" Distance, touring, and the matter of Sands' marriage soon conspired to leave those questions unanswered and within a few weeks, the relationship had faded.

Senta Driver was surprised to discover that Eddie, in fact, was more secretive about his relationships with women than he was about his liaisons with men. "Eddie would walk in the street with the men that he was sleeping with. That was no problem, but he would meet the women in secret places. He seemed to treat women as illicit and very often they were older. It wasn't about hiding them from each other. It was about hiding them from the world."

Eddie's attraction to women quickly won him his family's endorsement. Finally his father had stopped calling him to ask, "So, are you working on that girl problem of yours?"

Soon after his breakup with Joanna, though, Eddie began to have nagging doubts about his sexual identity. In the journal he kept for only six weeks beginning in February 1987, he voiced the self-doubt and insecurity he rarely showed to others:

> My personal life here in New York has been a bit of a mess, I guess because of my never-ending search for what and who I am. It many times seems to engulf my total existence. Sometimes I feel so completely confused. I feel as though I'm not going to be able to handle it any longer.

And yet, despite his private confusion, he had no trouble sending out very clear signals to the men who interested him. He wanted desperately to fit in somewhere and went out of his way to find affection and company where he could. On tour in early 1987, the Joffrey's male dancers couldn't help noticing that Eddie always seemed to have some great-looking man waiting for him backstage after a performance. In fact, they were convinced that Eddie wanted them to notice.

If the gay men in the company were jealous of his dancing, they were at least as envious of his ability to attract handsome men. Eddie, they joked, was a "man magnet." What particularly puzzled them was how Eddie, whom they considered cute and spunky, managed to "get these gorgeous guys," remembers Parrish Maynard, Eddie's roommate on tour that year. Though he had a strong muscular body and intense blue-green eyes set off by smooth, freckled skin, he was hardly anyone's idea of *GQ* perfection. "We would be like, 'What?'" explains Maynard. "Eddie was just okay attractive. But he had this beaming personality and he loved to go out and meet people. He wasn't afraid to walk up to people he didn't know and just start talking to them or buy them drinks. And I would be, oh, God, running in the other direction." Maynard was something of a clotheshorse and considered Eddie a sartorial disaster. While Maynard had grown up pampered and projected a sophisticated air, Eddie had grown up on hand-me-downs and had never developed a sense of style. To Maynard, Eddie seemed to be caught in a late 1970s disco-era time warp: bell-bottoms, silk shirts, "very John Travolta," he remembers. "I would always say to him, 'Eddie, we're going to have to change your wardrobe, babes.' But Eddie was always counting his pennies. He didn't like to spend money."

Following evening performances on tour, the younger dancers liked to go to clubs to unwind, where they could improvise their own choreography. Eddie often went out with a group that included Maynard, Jodie Gates, Tom Mossbrucker, Patrick Corbin, Mark Goldweber, and Brent Phillips, Eddie's childhood dance friend from Miami. Exhibitionists at heart, they all loved to show off on the dance floor and no one more than Eddie, who didn't

Parrish Maynard (at left) and Ashley Wheater

restrict himself to the floor. He would get up on top of the speakers, pull his shirt half off, and run his hands over his body as he moved. "He'd do very erotic dancing," recalls Maynard. "He was very outrageous with his dancing in discos. It was campy and funny and we would all egg him on." Often the other men on the floor would crowd around Eddie and cheer him on as he danced high above them on the speakers. "It was as if he were saying, 'I may not be the best-looking guy here, but I can really move,'" remembers Brent Phillips. "He didn't just dance, he did steps. It was like 'Dance Fever.'" One night at a gay club, the Rage in Los Angeles, Phillips noticed a crowd gathering. "I turned to Mark [Goldweber] and said, 'What's the commotion over there?' and then we said in

unison, 'Oh, it's Eddie.' " Dancer Tom Mossbrucker recalls that
Eddie "got high from people watching him." Indeed, the dance
floor belonged to Eddie, just as it had to his father, forty years
earlier in North Philadelphia.

Eddie's club-going was not restricted to the Joffrey tours. In
New York, he sometimes hit the Works on the Upper West Side,
or the Spike, a leather bar on Eleventh Avenue, where he met and
briefly took up with a blond actor named Christian. On weekend
nights, particularly Sundays when he had the next day off, he and
Parrish Maynard liked to go dancing at the Tunnel, the Palladium,
or Private Eyes. Among the Joffrey men, Eddie had a reputation
for sleeping around, but to Ashley Wheater, Eddie's lack of re-
straint was born of a desire to keep falling in love. "The thing
people misunderstood about Eddie was that he wasn't out for a
quick fuck. He just fell in love with people. He would say, 'This
one is so great, I'm in love with them,' and I'd say, 'You don't even
know what the word *love* means.' And he'd just laugh."

By early 1987, 20,000 Americans had died from AIDS-related
illnesses and another 36,000 had contracted the AIDS virus. Still,
according to AIDS chronicler Randy Shilts, the only major Western industrialized nation that had yet to launch a coordinated
AIDS education campaign was the United States. In the fall of
1986, Dr. C. Everett Koop, the country's surgeon general, had
galvanized the media the moment he went public with his then-
controversial report on the AIDS epidemic. In strong and direct
language, Koop confronted the problems of the epidemic head-on
by framing AIDS as a public health issue, not as a political hot
potato. He called for AIDS education at the earliest grade possible
for children, urged the widespread use of condoms, and advocated
public testing, but only when accompanied by guarantees of confi-
dentiality and nondiscrimination. Koop's call to arms took the
Reagan administration and Koop's ardently conservative backers
by surprise. After all, the surgeon general had won his post in 1981

largely on the strength of his record as a leading player in the antiabortion movement. With his white beard and stern features, Koop looked like a Shaker Elder, though in fact, he was a Quaker; he certainly wouldn't have struck anyone as a likely advocate for sex education and condom use.

As Dr. Koop continued to wage his campaign in the face of opposition from conservative quarters, the general public continued to regard the disease as a remote and strictly homosexual concern. Though the dancers at the Joffrey were by then well acquainted with the term "safe sex," no one in the company had died from AIDS and so, for the moment, the disease still remained at a remove. "AIDS hadn't hit home with any of us, so we had no real reason to talk about it," says Brent Phillips.

In 1987, it was still possible to come up with theories, however implausible, about why AIDS happened to other people. To the heterosexual dancers at the Joffrey, AIDS was something that the gay men in the company needed to worry about. To the younger gay dancers, AIDS was viewed as a menace only to the older, "Studio 54 generation" of sexually active gay men, the ones who, according to their definition, frequented clubs, did a lot of drugs, and had anonymous sex in the gay bathhouses. The theory then making the rounds was that these older men had depleted their immune systems by not taking care of themselves.* "We thought as long as we stayed away from people who seemed to have had a string of one-night stands, we were safe," says dancer Adam Sklute. "We figured, 'We're healthy, we're clean living, we couldn't possibly get the disease.'"

In the journal he kept from February through mid-April 1987, Eddie discussed his sexual confusion and never once mentioned AIDS or safe sex. He may have been using condoms, but it seems that his use of them was inconsistent.

---

*The theory first began gaining ground around May of 1982. In an article in *New York* magazine entitled "The Gay Plague," the writer noted: "The fast New York gay life-style may or may not be the root of this mystery disease. And the homosexual community may or may not be concerned enough to alter that life-style as a precaution."

Performing in Costa Mesa, California, in the spring of 1987, Eddie was billeted with patrons of the Joffrey, who lived in a house overlooking the ocean in nearby Laguna Beach. One night Eddie stopped in at the Little Shrimp, a piano bar in town, and noticed two striking men talking together at the bar. Eddie approached them. "You two make a handsome couple," he ventured coyly to the boyish-looking one, who promptly broke out laughing. "Hi, I'm Eric, and this," he said, introducing the man next to him, "is my father." Eddie was astonished, particularly when the younger man told him that he and his father frequently

Eric Castellano

went to gay bars together. Eddie spent most of the evening talking to the father and son, and went home that night with twenty-six-year-old Eric Castellano, a handsome commercial makeup artist with curly dark hair and blue eyes. By then a number of links had been reported between the early AIDS cases in Los Angeles and Laguna Beach; however, Castellano and his friends didn't pay much attention. They were too busy having the time of their lives. "Our hormones were driving us, and Eddie and I both thought we didn't need to worry about AIDS," Eric said. "No one we knew had it."

Within the year, Eddie, Eric, Eric's father, and Eric's best friend would all test positive for HIV.

Even on tour, Eddie continued to attend Mass whenever he could. His faith still offered him solace, for he had yet to openly declare himself gay and suffer the judgmental sting of Catholicism. He wrote in his journal:

> I've been going to church again, and it seems to be helping me a lot. It truly is amazing how God always makes you welcome. It's so hard sometimes because I don't even feel worthy to be in His presence, but he is only there to give you strength, and that is so true. I always feel such an inner strength after I take the time to pray. I'm happy for that possibility.

His moments for reflection were few, for Eddie was on a fast-rising trajectory at the Joffrey. Beginning at 10:30 A.M., he had company class, rehearsals all afternoon, and rarely got home at night before 7:30. In early 1987, Eddie learned that the company was planning a major revival of Gerald Arpino's antiwar ballet *The Clowns*, and that he was to be cast in the bravura central role of the little clown. A multimedia parable about the end of the world, *The Clowns* was made in 1968, a year of protests and assassinations, and reflects that era in its use of inflatable plastic forms and electronic music. Arpino's vision of apocalypse opens with the sounds of an atomic explosion as dummy corpses fall from the sky. A little

Making up in the men's dressing room. Kyle Ahmed is facing the
camera at center.

clown, the lone survivor of the holocaust, coaxes his fellow clowns
back to life by dancing, only to see them turn on him and torment
him before their own final collapse. In the end, a plastic bubble
fills the stage and devours all but the little clown. In the late
sixties, the ballet had proven enormously popular with critics and
audiences who responded to its then-daring theatrical power. In
1987, however, critical opinion was divided between those who
dismissed it as a cloying period piece and those who considered it
a bold work with renewed relevance in a world devastated by
Chernobyl and AIDS.

Following his first rehearsals of *The Clowns*, Eddie described in
his journal the feelings that overcame him while dancing the role

Gerald Arpino rehearsing Eddie and dancers in *The Clowns*

of the little clown, a Christlike figure who prevails over the brutality around him. He didn't appear to recall the dream that haunted him as a young child, in which he and his mother were dying in a nuclear explosion. But his observations are eerily prophetic:

> It's as though I completely absorbed myself in an atmosphere of death and hatred. I felt so many emotions run through my body as the ballet progressed, and even when it was all over, I couldn't seem to shake the feelings. That is the first time that has ever happened, and I'm sure it's not the last.

Eddie's immersion in the ballet led him to consider how quickly his life could be "snatched away" in the event of a nuclear war. "I'm Catholic," he would later tell *The Los Angeles Herald Examiner*,

> and there are so many times in the ballet when Christian symbols, such as the crucifixion, appear. At the end, I cannot help but think of the phrase, "Forgive them Father, for they know not what they do." It's very difficult emotionally. I think about war all the time, about being called to action . . . *The Clowns* touches those fears.

The process of reviving *The Clowns* gave Eddie his first of many opportunities to work closely with Gerald Arpino, the Joffrey's effusive, if somewhat flighty, resident choreographer. A magpie of a man given to long-winded speeches about his craft, Arpino took at once to Eddie's precociousness, to the way he "chewed the movement with a vengeance." He also welcomed Eddie's constant questioning, which he felt enriched his own working process. Since there was no videotape of the ballet in existence, and only incomplete notes to work from, Arpino had to rely on his own and others' recollections in bringing *The Clowns* back to stage life. Among those present at its creation was ballet master Scott Barnard, who had danced the role of the little clown in earlier productions. The ballet, Arpino advised Eddie, "is about nuclear holocaust, but it's also about the pollution of self, about a man polluting himself with all the wrong ideals."

In the ballet's closing moment, the little clown walks on top of an inflated plastic bubble, inside which his tormentors are slowly suffocating to death, their anguished faces pressed up against the plastic. Seeing their suffering, the little clown lifts his arms over his head and opens his mouth in a silent scream. Both Arpino and Barnard felt that the clown's final supplication should imply acceptance. Eddie, however, soon made it clear that he had a different conception in mind. "Eddie didn't agree that the clown would feel compassion for them after what they'd done to him," remembers Barnard, "so he screamed in anguish only for what *he'd* been through, not with acceptance and horror at what *the others* were going through."

Unlike Arpino, Barnard was more irritated than amused by Eddie's independent streak. Having danced in the original production and taken over the lead role from Robert Blankshine and Gary Chryst in later years, he no doubt felt a certain claim to the role. He also had an understanding of it that, in his view, Eddie was only beginning to grasp. A stickler for precision, Barnard disliked the fact that Eddie seemed to prefer to follow the spirit, rather than the letter, of the choreography at hand. After all, dancers, generally did what they were told by the choreographer or rehearsal director and rarely offered their own views on how they should dance. "Scott would want Eddie to do things the way he did them," remembers Parrish Maynard, who played one of the brutish clowns. "And Eddie would say, 'No, I want to do it this way,' and then they would go back and forth constantly. He was the only person I ever saw at the Joffrey who could speak back to Scott and Jerry and get away with it. No one else had the guts."

Jodie Gates recalls that Eddie got away with things because of his talent. "If any of us had spoken out the way Eddie did, we would have been excused from rehearsals," she says.

Having fought so hard for his ballet career, Eddie was not about to let anyone interfere with what he saw as his artistic progress. But in his effort to impose his youthful will on whatever challenge faced him, he frequently mistook direction for disapproval. "Edward felt that if he listened to Jerry or to me too much, that he was being robbed of his artistic senses," recalls Barnard.

"He felt that he'd be doing my clown, not his. He was still at a point in his life where he couldn't trust. He thought that every time I said, 'No, that's wrong,' that I was admonishing him, not *helping* him." In fact, Eddie had convinced himself that the only way he could make a step his own was to change it slightly. To Barnard, Eddie's liberties were inappropriate, particularly for a dancer in his first year at the Joffrey. "I would say, 'Edward, I don't care if they told you that you could do it that way, you should learn to do it the right way,'" says Barnard. To which Eddie would reply, "I want to do it the way I want to do it. I'm the artist."

He's not the first dancer to think he's Isadora, Barnard thought.

Eddie, meanwhile, felt Barnard was reining him in. While he admired the ballet master, he was still intimidated by him, though in due course, Eddie would begin to intimidate Barnard. "It's amazing how much power this man has in the company," Eddie wrote in his journal.

> As a coach, he is one of the most giving and devoted coaches you can come across in this business, but as a teacher, he is very restricting and limited. . . . H has this way of intimidating people like I've never seen before. . . . I mean if I said or disagreed with anything that Scott said, opportunities could be whipped away faster than I could spit.

He was clearly not losing any roles over disagreements. In addition to learning *The Clowns*, Eddie won the lead in the second revival of the season, *La Vivandière Pas de Six*, a ballet that had been revived especially to showcase the talents of Eddie and Tina LeBlanc. "Just when I thought I had gotten the best, this came along," Eddie noted in his diary, reflecting on the insecurity and lack of self-worth prevalent among the dancers he'd known.

> It's funny how when I write of how humble I am to be given these opportunities, I realize how silly it is. Why should I think that I'm nothing? Is that the way developing Artists should feel? How absurd. Yet this is how most dancers feel.

Nothing could provide a greater contrast to the highly stylized, darkly theatrical *Clowns* than the gossamer-light, strictly classical

La Vivandière, a reconstructed fragment of a once-lost Romantic ballet. Reminiscent of a scene from Degas, the ballet was choreographed by Arthur Saint-Léon, the nineteenth-century dancer and choreographer best known for *Coppélia*. Technically, the ballet demanded lightning-quick changes in direction, crisp footwork, and precise, clean lines. The man's variation was particularly taxing because it combined many of the most difficult steps from the male dancer's canon. "You're either on or you're off," says Scott Barnard. "It separates the men from the boys." Eddie was to partner the petite, five-foot-one-inch Tina LeBlanc, an exquisite dancer who was on her way to becoming a star of the company. Even though Eddie was cast as the Cavalier, the role was not a straightforward heroic or romantic princely role, in that he was not meant only to show off the ballerina, but to execute the bravura feats of the virtuoso.

Tina LeBlanc had never seen Eddie look nervous before going onstage, except before going onstage to perform *La Vivandière*. In the wings, she would smile encouragingly at him as she watched him calm himself down with deep breaths. "*La Vivandière* made him so nervous because he had to be classical," recalls LeBlanc. "For him, it was like being naked up there. Eddie didn't have the ideal body, but he could make you believe anything onstage." While the other dancers agreed that Eddie was probably the only male dancer who could master the technical demands of *La Vivandière*, several of the men looked askance at the company's decision to "put a body like that in white tights." After all, only the best bodies were shown to advantage in white tights. On the other hand, it had become evident to them that the company was pushing Eddie Stierle. He wasn't just getting lead roles, but lead roles in important showcase ballets. "Mr. Joffrey was watching to see how far Eddie's talents and gifts would go," recalls Scott Barnard. "He was watching to see how much his presence added to the overall strength of the company."

Competition colored Eddie's relationships with all the male dancers of his own rank, but nowhere more acutely than in his friendship with Parrish Maynard. Eddie and Parrish were soon to

In *La Vivandière*

compete for a number of roles. Eddie would always win first-cast placement and more press attention, though, a situation that not only aggravated tensions between them, but eventually ended their friendship. From the start, each measured himself against the other. As the company's youngest dancers, they were often thrown together and as roommates on tour, they couldn't help but stay current on each other's progress. "In my first year in the company, I didn't do any leads, and in Eddie's first six months, he was doing three of them," remembers Maynard. "I couldn't understand why people would pick him over me because I had a better body."

While Maynard envied Eddie's technical facility, Eddie was in awe of Maynard's superior physical gifts, which he had first admired in class at the School of American Ballet, several summers earlier. Parrish had been the boy in his class thought to have the best ballet body. To Eddie, Parrish possessed all the attributes he had long dreamed of having: He had thin, sinewy muscles, hyperextended legs, high arches, and long limbs. "Parrish was everything that Eddie wasn't," says Patrick Corbin. "He was more suited to leading male roles, whereas Eddie was more suited to *demi-caractère* roles." Eddie was particularly jealous when Parrish was cast in Frederick Ashton's *Monotones*, a classical ballet showcasing the line and sleek bodies of its three principals. Despite their different body types, however, Eddie and Parrish were usually considered for the same roles. In the studio, they tried to make light of their competition by engaging in friendly one-upmanship. One day, however, Maynard inadvertently went too far. "We were joking around and I said to him, 'Well, at least I don't have a pair of spatulas for feet.' The minute I said it, I realized I'd hit a really sensitive nerve."

Though geographically separated, Eddie and Rose were in constant communication. They spoke on the phone five nights a week and Rose regularly followed up with notes, care packages, and photocopies of Joffrey reviews (which she also sent off to everyone on her growing mailing list). A few days before leaving on his first major Joffrey tour, a four-month sweep through

Chicago, Clearwater (Florida), Washington, Los Angeles, San Diego, and San Francisco, Eddie called his mother in Hollywood. Rose was planning to bring a group to see him in Clearwater and talked of flying out to Chicago to catch his debut in *The Clowns*. When Eddie casually mentioned that he'd gone out shopping for a winter coat, Rose interjected: "Oh, I wish I could live up there and be there for times like those, for when you need me."

"I don't need you here," Eddie protested. "I need you right where you are. It's lines like that that make me think you are not letting our relationship go to another plateau. We are still mother and little son in your eyes and that must change. I mean change in the sense of becoming friends who make the most of their time together."

On the opening night of a new work, revival, or season, Robert Joffrey made a special point of sending his dancers cards to wish them luck, handpicking them himself. On March 20, 1987, the night Eddie was to make his debut in *The Clowns* in Chicago, Joffrey sent Eddie a card featuring a vintage photograph of Nijinsky, a dancer whose legend would soon absorb Eddie. "Dear Edward," Joffrey had scrawled. "My very best for a special night for you and Jerry and *Clowns*. —Robert Joffrey."

Eddie soon provided his own assessment of that "special night" a few days later in his journal.

> The premiere of *Clowns* was a great success. There were a couple of small mistakes but I was pleased. . . . No one in direction said anything to me until finally Mr. Joffrey said, "Very good tonight, Edward, you made me really proud." Scott ignored me all night and Mr. Arpino was too busy being such a social butterfly that I was the last thing on his mind.

His debut performances in *The Clowns* met with strong reviews, some of them ecstatic. *The San Francisco Examiner*'s longtime dance critic, Allan Ulrich, raved that with his performance in *The Clowns*, Eddie "made the most brilliant Joffrey debut in this town in years,"

VASLAV NIJINSKY IN DANSE SIAMOISE FROM LES ORIENTALES
STAGED BY THE DIAGHILEV BALLET, 1910
PHOTOGRAPH BY DRUET

March 20 - 1987
Chicago

Dear Edward
     My very best. for
a special night
for "Son and Jerry
and "Clowns"

                    Robert Joffrey

and pointed to his "extraordinary pantomime and mercurial technique."

During the third week of April 1987, the Joffrey flew to Los Angeles to begin its three-week spring season at the Dorothy Chandler Pavilion of the L.A. Music Center, which since 1983 had been the bicoastal Joffrey's second home. One afternoon during a *Clowns* rehearsal, Parrish Maynard pulled Eddie aside and told him he needed to ask a favor. He had just started a relationship and had promised to get an AIDS test. "But I'm scared to go," he said. Having already tested negative sixteen months before during his visit home from Basel, Eddie thought he might as well offer to go along with Maynard as a show of support. "Look, I'll even take the test too," he said. "It's no big deal." The next day, he and Parrish Maynard went off to have their blood drawn and sent out for testing.

Then they went back to work and awaited their results.

13

FREE FALL

Eddie was on his way to the men's dressing room when Dr. Robert Stone* approached him in the backstage hallway of the Dorothy Chandler Pavilion. He was still sweating from rehearsal and in a hurry to change and go on his dinner break, since he had only one hour before he would have to start warming up for the evening performance. Tonight he was dancing *The Clowns*.

"I'm not happy about telling you this," Dr. Stone, one of the company's doctors, began in his measured voice, peering at Eddie through his wire-rimmed glasses. "Your test results came back positive. You've really done it this time."

Eddie stared up at the heavyset doctor in stunned silence. Dr. Stone continued speaking but Eddie could barely hear his words. He couldn't help feeling that there was something accusatory in the doctor's tone. He heard the doctor say that his T-cell count was in the normal range, so evidently his immune system was still in good shape. That was hardly consolation.

---

*Pseudonym.

Patrick Corbin, who was also dancing in *The Clowns* that night, was about to leave for his dinner break when he noticed Eddie talking in hushed tones to the company doctor down the hall. "Dr. Stone was looking down at Eddie and pointing his finger at him," remembers Corbin. "I thought it was odd because I hadn't heard anything about Eddie being injured. I soon forgot about it, but two years later, when Eddie told me he was HIV-positive, I asked him about the scene I had witnessed that day in the hallway and he said, 'Yes, Dr. Stone was telling me right at that point. Can you believe he would tell me in the hallway before a performance?'"

From that point on, AIDS was to accelerate Eddie's already crowded agenda. On March 2, he had celebrated his nineteenth birthday. Now, just two months later, he felt that the end of his life was close at hand, that his life was being snatched away. *Snatched away.* Wasn't that the very phrase he had used in an interview to describe how *The Clowns* forced him to reflect on the fleeting nature of life? Well, here it was. His worst nightmare. He had barely begun his career in a profession known for its brevity and intense physical demands. Now he was facing a much more daunting prospect: He was carrying a virus that would not only shorten his life, but likely sap his strength in his dancing prime.

For the next two hours, he tried, in vain, to calm himself down. He sat alone in the men's dressing room, savoring the quiet hour he could claim for himself before the room filled up with the clamorous voices of dancers getting ready for an evening performance. He studied his face in the mirror of his dressing table and silently plotted his transformation into the little clown. Opening the lids of his myriad pots of greasepaint, he began to obscure the boyish, freckled face with the "Clown-white" pancake makeup he sponged generously over his skin. In a few moments, his face was blank and anonymous. Next he outlined his eyes, sprayed his hair black, and colored his mouth red. All the while, he tried to make sense of the questions flooding his thoughts. The questions merged.

In the wings, he inhaled deeply before going on to dance the little Clown. It was the most charged performance he had ever given. This time when he opened his mouth for the clown's final silent scream, his whole body shook with the anguish of his private horror. He was sobbing when he came offstage. What a grotesque sight he must have made, his tears streaming down a face caked in white, an exaggerated scarlet smile painted wide over his lips. The other dancers took one look at him and rolled their eyes. "Eddie's being overly dramatic," someone whispered. "What's with *him?*" wondered Parrish Maynard. Earlier that day, Maynard had been given a clean bill of health by Dr. Stone. "No need to worry," he had said. "Your test came back negative." Maynard wouldn't know for four years that Eddie had not been given the same news. It never occurred to him that Eddie's results could be different from his own.

By the time Eddie managed to get Ashley Wheater alone in the dressing room, he was hysterical. Wheater had seen him crying in the shower and knew instinctively that Eddie's AIDS test was the cause of his distress. Eddie and Parrish had told him they were going to get tested. They had mentioned it in passing to a few other dancers as well. "He was beside himself," recalls Wheater of their late-into-the-night conversation. "He made me promise not to tell anyone. I had friends who'd died of AIDS, so he knew I wasn't frightened by it." At twenty-seven, Wheater knew at least ten people who had died of AIDS in their twenties and thirties. Despite his youth, he had helped many of them grapple with the sudden realities of illness and mortality, subjects he now accepted as a part of his daily life. As he listened to Eddie, he tried to calm him by pointing out that there was so much still to be discovered about HIV. "What's important right now is to get the maximum out of life," he advised him. "I'm sure that it's frightening to know that there's something in you that's not going to go away, but the only way you'll get on top of this is to find out as much as you can."

Eddie ran through a list of everyone he'd slept with since his first test in November of 1985. Since the virus took anywhere from three to six months to show up in an antibody test, it was likely that he had been exposed to the virus sometime in the past two years. He knew that he had to tell Lauren Rouse right away. He waited until they both had a break from rehearsals the next afternoon and knocked on her dressing room door. "We need to talk," he told her somberly, straining to sound optimistic as he conveyed his news. "I was in a total state of shock. It was like a spear through my heart," remembers Rouse. "I thought, 'He doesn't deserve this.' What struck me the most was that he seemed to be as worried about me as he was about himself."

The chain of reaction didn't stop with Rouse. She had become engaged six weeks earlier, and was in a panic about what to tell her fiancé. They were to be married in July. She was relieved that he was back in New York. The distance would make it easier for her to keep quiet about Eddie until she had gotten herself tested and learned her results. The next day, Eddie held her hand while her blood was drawn at a lab in West Hollywood. "Both of us were scared to death," Rouse remembers.

With a few hours to spare before the evening performance, they drove around L.A. in silence. Heading through Temple-Beaudry, a predominantly Hispanic neighborhood across the free-way from the Music Center, Eddie spotted a tiny Catholic church and called out to Rouse to stop the car. It was late in the afternoon and the church was empty, save for two elderly women lighting candles for the dead near the altar. Lauren and Eddie settled into the back pew. "We held each other and cried," she says. "Then we had to go back to the theater. We were both performing that night."

Two weeks later, while the company was in San Diego, Rouse learned that she was negative. Relieved, Eddie still had other ex-lovers to call and, during the next month, got in touch with several of them, including Christian, the blond actor he'd picked up at the Spike. "I just found out that I have AIDS," Christian informed Eddie over the phone. While Eddie would never know for certain just which of his lovers gave him the AIDS virus, he told friends that he suspected it was Christian. But he gave them different accounts: While he explained to Linda Roth that his condom had ripped during sex, he told Kyle Ahmed that he and Christian never had safe sex.

When Eddie called Linda Roth in Basel to tell her he was HIV-positive, he surprised her by announcing, "This means I'm never going to be with a woman again." According to Roth, Eddie considered AIDS a gay disease and believed that his HIV status somehow stamped him as homosexual.

Kyle Ahmed remembers that Eddie was shocked and angered at the realization that he would never have children, an option he hadn't ruled out prior to his HIV diagnosis. "Eddie always hoped he could be gay, but have a wife," says Kyle, who was an apprentice to Joffrey II that summer and was spending time with Eddie on tour. Eddie, however, soon became convinced that he would find sensitivity and understanding about his HIV status only in the gay community. He knew how much fear the subject aroused and he knew, too, that the straight community still perceived AIDS as a gay problem. By then, the gay community was the only community with both an extensive support network firmly established for people with HIV and AIDS, and with a keenly developed understanding of the myriad challenges facing those infected with the virus. Eddie felt he could still be sexually active in the gay community "without people freaking out," says Kyle Ahmed. "He realized that it would be a lot more difficult if he tried to be with a woman."

Six years into the AIDS epidemic and three weeks after nineteen-year-old Eddie Stierle discovered that he was HIV-positive, President Ronald Reagan delivered his first speech on AIDS. The occasion was an AIDS fund-raising dinner held in the nation's capital on the eve of the Third International Conference on AIDS. Dr. Michael Gottlieb, Elizabeth Taylor, and a who's who of the scientific and medical AIDS establishment were on hand that night to hear their president give a speech that was long on political rhetoric about AIDS testing and the need for compassion, but short on solutions. Dr. Gottlieb was there as the cochair of a new foundation that his most celebrated patient, Rock Hudson, had launched with a $250,000 contribution. It was called the American Foundation for AIDS Research (AmFar), and Elizabeth Taylor was its spokeswoman. By then Gottlieb had become one of the world's leading AIDS clinicians, and more than six years had passed since he reported the first AIDS cases to the Centers for Disease Control. He had recently left UCLA as a result of academic infighting and gone into private practice in Los Angeles. There were as yet no FDA-approved AIDS treatments available to the 36,058 Americans already diagnosed with the disease.

Still struggling to define himself sexually and artistically, Eddie was not about to let AIDS take over his life. He wanted to keep dancing and decided to do whatever he could to remain hopeful. He did his best to appear unchanged, but beneath his optimism and bravado, he was terrified.

He was afraid to tell his parents about his HIV status because he didn't want to repeat the family anguish brought on by the Richard Register episode and, perhaps more significantly, he feared the pain would be too great for his mother to bear. He began to wonder whether his childhood nightmare, the one in which he saw he and his mother dying together, might not have been prophetic. He also worried that his family's concern would rob him of his remaining dancing years. He had waited six weeks before calling Linda Roth in Basel because he didn't want to alarm her with his panic, nor was he ready to deal with *her* panic once she learned he was HIV-positive. "I was really upset that he didn't tell me right away, because I knew how terrified he must have been," she recalls. "But he said he didn't want to tell me until he was strong enough. He said, 'I realize I have to be very careful about who I tell. The minute I tell somebody that I tested positive, they'll start imagining me dying.'" He couldn't tell his parents, he told her, because "they'll kill me with their fear."

Eddie had just returned from a brief, two-day visit home, which he had slotted in between the Joffrey's Los Angeles and San Diego engagements. The trip home only intensified Eddie's fear of isolation: He was devoted to his nieces and nephews and began to worry that his sister Terri, the volunteer director of Respect Life, a church-sponsored right-to-life organization in Hollywood, and his brother Michael wouldn't let him near their children if they knew he had the virus. And he feared that his other siblings would push him even further out of their tight circle.

"Promise me," he asked Linda, "that you'll only think about me positively."

It wasn't only his family that concerned him. He worried that the Joffrey's ballerinas would refuse him as a partner, for fear getting the virus through sweat* or open cuts, and that the company's directors would stop grooming him for an important career if they thought for a minute that his future might be jeopardized. He was right to worry. Scott Barnard would later acknowledge that if the Joffrey's directors had known that Eddie was HIV-positive sooner than they did, they "would still have used him and given him what was rightfully his, but we may not have designed in the future so much."

Though Eddie had always planned to concentrate on his dancing first and leave choreography for later, he concluded that with his life foreshortened, he would have to throw himself into making dances as soon as possible. He kept thinking about *Lacrymosa*, the solo he had done at the Jackson competition, and wondered how he might expand it into a larger work. To Eddie, choreography was essentially personal, a public expression of private experience. He had set *Lacrymosa* to the *Requiem* Mozart had composed while dying, and he thought the music might now strike too close to home. In fact, the stigma of AIDS, with all its attendant Catholic guilt, and the pain of hiding a life-threatening secret from his family, so gnawed at him that he considered making a ballet based on *The Scarlet Letter*. Nathaniel Hawthorne's classic story, set in seventeenth-century Puritan Boston, tells the tale of Hester Prynne, whose adulterous entanglement and pregnancy lead her to public disgrace. Forced to wear a red *A* to mark her as an adulteress, she becomes a defiant outcast, her life forever shaped by her struggle to overcome the letter's meaning. In Eddie, AIDS aroused feelings of shame, and while he decided to keep his diagnosis hidden from all but a few well-chosen friends, he couldn't help but recognize the implied moral judgment surrounding any

---

*In the fall of 1992, a year after basketball legend Magic Johnson announced to the world that he was HIV-positive, several NBA players complained of being afraid to guard him because they feared contracting the AIDS virus through cuts or sweat. In response, Johnson retired from basketball. There have been no documented cases of HIV transmission through sweat.

discussion of the disease.° Within the year, he would begin to plan his exile from the one place that had always given him a sense of community: the Catholic Church.

Despite the existential questions now before him, Eddie refused to dwell on his mortality. He believed that if he fought hard enough, thought positively enough, and danced fully, he could defy illness, just as readily as he had once defied the limits of his own body. He was determined to prove that he could assume the challenges of any role, no matter how foreign its requirements might be to his physique. He was soon given that opportunity when the Joffrey relocated to the University of Iowa for the month of June, to begin the intensive process of reconstructing Nijinsky's *Le Sacre du Printemps* ("The Rite of Spring"), perhaps the most infamous ballet of the century.

The first performance of the ballet by Sergei Diaghilev's Ballets Russes is famous for the riot it set off on May 29, 1913, at the newly opened Théâtre des Champs-Elysées in Paris. The catcalls began soon after the first notes of Stravinsky's driving, dissonant score were struck. The primitive rite represented in Nijinsky's choreography, Stravinsky's groundbreaking score, and Nicholas Roerich's sets and costumes was a far cry from the ballets to which Parisian audiences had grown accustomed. In short order, mayhem erupted. Bejeweled ladies and tuxedoed gentlemen jeered and howled at the ballet's scenes of pagan Russia, while the aesthetes in the crowd engaged in fistfights over the work's avant-garde merits. Backstage, Nijinsky stood on a chair shouting counts to the dancers, while out front, the impresario Diaghilev tried vainly to

---

°As Susan Sontag writes in *AIDS and Its Metaphors:* "Cotton Mather called syphilis a punishment 'which the Just Judgment of God has reserved for our Late Ages.' Recalling this and other nonsense uttered about syphilis from the end of the fifteenth to the early twentieth centuries, one should hardly be surprised that many want to view AIDS metaphorically—as, plaguelike, a moral judgment on society. Professional fulminators can't resist the rhetorical opportunity offered by a sexually transmitted disease that is lethal. . . ."

restore order. The artist Jean Cocteau, a friend of Diaghilev's and an eyewitness, considered the frenzied fallout inevitable:

> Every possible ingredient of a *scandale* is here: a society audience, décolleté, festooned with pearls, aigrettes, ostrich plumes; and along with the tailcoats and the tulle, daytime jackets and women's hair that never saw a hairdresser—the ostentatiously drab trappings of that race of aesthetes is more intolerable than the sincere boos of the society folk . . . were I to continue, I would have to describe a thousand shades of snobbism, supersnobbism, countersnobbism, which would fill a chapter by themselves. . . .

A cause célèbre, the revolutionary ballet later came to be regarded as the harbinger of modern dance. At the time, however, it was dubbed *"Le Massacre du Printemps"* by the French critics and performed only seven more times before it disappeared from view.

Soon after the ballet's premiere, the twenty-three-year-old Nijinsky alienated Diaghilev, his mentor and lover, by marrying a young corps dancer named Romola de Pulszky.* Upon hearing the news, Diaghilev was thrown into a black rage: He promptly fired Nijinsky, his most brilliant star, and dropped *Sacre* from the repertory. It wasn't long before Nijinsky suffered a breakdown from which he never fully recovered; with his sanity in turmoil, his ballet seemed destined for oblivion. He died in London in 1950, spending the last thirty-one years of his life in and out of sanitariums.

What had so provoked that first-night audience was the way both Stravinsky's score and Nijinsky's movement broke all the rules. Where classical ballet promotes a turned-out position, an unbroken flow of movement, and the ideal of transcending gravity,

---

*Eddie felt an affinity with Nijinsky, which may not have rested solely on a physical or artistic identification, though these were of paramount importance. "As Diaghilev's lover," Ballets Russes scholar Lynn Garafola has noted, "[Nijinsky] was a homosexual hero; leaving Diaghilev to marry Romola de Pulszky—the event that occasioned his dismissal from the Ballets Russes late in 1913—he became no less notorious as a homosexual turncoat."

Sacre emphasized the natural and primal: Feet were turned in; shoulders were hunched; and hands, elbows, and faces pointed down toward the ground. The dancers drove their weight into the floor, emphasizing their connection to the earth, not their affinity for the sky. As Nijinsky saw it, his *Sacre* was "the soul of nature expressed by movement to music."

As developed by designer Nicholas Roerich, the action of *Le Sacre du Printemps* revolves around a series of games and rituals, during which a maiden finds herself selected for sacrifice. Surrounded by the tribe's elders, she dances herself to death to awaken the spring.

Sacre would have remained the stuff of theatrical lore if an energetic Berkeley graduate student named Millicent Hodson hadn't decided in 1971 to try to unearth its missing pieces. With no definitive source to study, Hodson, a choreographer, designer, and dance historian, spent sixteen years seeking out clues, sketches, photographs, letters, scores, and personal reminiscences. In the process, she met art historian Kenneth Archer, Roerich's biographer, who was also researching *Sacre*, and the two joined forces. (They later married.) In 1981, Hodson and Archer approached Robert Joffrey with their plans to re-create *Sacre*, and in Joffrey, long a champion of ballets from the Diaghilev era, they found an enthusiastic ally. Joffrey invited them to set the work on his company and eagerly awaited the results.

Given their director's unabashed enthusiasm for the historic re-creation of *Le Sacre du Printemps*, the Joffrey dancers were surprised not to find Robert Joffrey in Iowa when they arrived for the first rehearsals in June of 1987. He was getting over a cold in New York, they were informed, and would join them later in the month.

From the start, the *Sacre* rehearsals proved difficult and painful, just as they had in 1913 for the dancers of the Ballets Russes, who were likewise unaccustomed to the pigeon-toed positions, stamping, and clenched fists demanded by the choreography. Musing on those first rehearsals, Nijinsky's assistant, Marie Rambert, had exclaimed to Millicent Hodson: "It was a torture."

Eddie was cast as one of the tribal Youths, and though merely a member of the ensemble, he was the first dancer to catch Millicent Hodson's eye. "I noticed this young kid, this very muscular dancer," she recalls, "and I thought, 'He's got Nijinsky legs.'" What particularly struck her about Eddie was how much he seemed to revel in the ballet's challenges. The most complicated task facing the Joffrey dancers was the process of breaking down the ballet's complex rhythms—which Eddie mastered at once. The dancers had to learn how to employ two different systems of movement counts simultaneously: While their head and arms moved to one set of counts, their feet moved to yet another. "Eddie just smiled as I demonstrated the steps," says Hodson. "He reminded me of a highly gifted child who had just been given an advanced toy. I said to him, 'Maybe this is all meant for you because you have the body type for doing that really compact jumping, where you really pull your legs up into your body,' and Eddie surprised me by replying, 'Yes, I've always felt as if I was somehow like Nijinsky.'"*

Eddie became preoccupied with Nijinsky. He asked Hodson for a background reading list and soon invited her out to dinner, just as he had Alexander Grant several months earlier. Hodson's husband had just flown back to England and, seeing her looking glum one day, Eddie made the offer to cheer her up. Over supper in Iowa City, he listened raptly while Hodson recounted stories about Nijinsky, occasionally pressing her for details about his methods as a choreographer. Did he keep notes of his ideas? he asked. Hodson explained that while Ballets Russes choreographer Michel Fokine made sequential drawings as he was devising *his* dances, "none of us are really sure what Nijinsky did." She told him that according to Jean Cocteau, Nijinsky wrote to his mother every day after rehearsal, and sent her drawings of the day's work. "We looked everywhere for those drawings," Hodson confessed. "Nijinsky's daughter left them in a sewing basket, which she

---

*A living legend in his twenties, Nijinsky was known for his unprecedented technical brilliance and his unrivaled elevation.

Eddie (at far left) as one of the Youths in *Le Sacre du Printemps*

entrusted to a friend when she left the Soviet Union for Paris in the twenties." Eddie was so intrigued with the idea of drawings that Hodson suggested that he, too, should make drawings in a notebook when he started to choreograph. (That advice would prove valuable to Eddie during the making of his final ballet.) The conversation turned to Nijinsky's inner crisis and, as Hodson began describing the diary Nijinsky kept while on the verge of mental collapse, Eddie suddenly blurted out, "I wonder what it would be like to write from that kind of desperation?" His absorption in Nijinsky, then just beginning, was to intensify over the following years and would lead him in the final year of his own life to begin making plans to choreograph a ballet about the life of Nijinsky. "I want people to see what Nijinsky went through," he would later tell Hodson as he described a ballet built around the image of doors closing.

Just how Eddie's own private turmoil informed his work on *Sacre* is impossible to assess, but it's likely that *Sacre*'s themes resonated with him as he struggled to come to terms with the meaning of his HIV status, the news of which was only a month old. Nijinsky's *Sacre*, as Ballets Russes historian Lynn Garafola has noted, "exposed the barbarism of human life: the cruelty of nature, the savagery of the tribe, the violence of the soul."

Nijinsky's choreography for the ballet's fourth scene, "Ritual of the Rival Tribes," called for the tribal Youths to engage in martial arts–like combat. Since Hodson was finding it difficult to translate the movement from her annotated drawings on to several bodies at once, she asked Eddie and Mark Goldweber to work with her privately. They, in turn, would demonstrate the movements to the larger group. Eddie, in fact, was so intrigued by the ballet that he learned all the roles, not just his own, and would later demonstrate excerpts of *Sacre* to his friend Senta Driver. By the time Hodson began staging "Dance of the Earth," the ballet's seventh scene, Eddie was literally flinging himself into the tribal dance with the kind of frenzied abandon Nijinsky himself might have admired. At one point in the dance, the six Youths all perform the same chaotic solo, but in rotation, with each dancer beginning on a different movement. "Eddie danced like a madman," remembers Hodson. "He was almost reckless with his body."

Several days into his private sessions with Hodson, Eddie confided to her that he had been listening to the Stravinsky score in his room one evening and heard among the instruments the voice of a Youth calling to him. "Really, Millicent," he insisted, "I heard a *voice*." Hodson believed him. "Eddie had this clear spiritual awareness in him and was always looking to find that relevance in life. Maybe the intensity of his devotion as a dancer opened him to some other level of experience with this ballet," she would later acknowledge in a letter to Rose Stierle. "Maybe, after decades of waiting, Nijinsky in the higher realm recognized the dancer he needed for *Sacre*."

Two months after meeting her, Eddie sent Hodson a card, thanking her for the experience of *Sacre*. The card showed a Raoul Dufy drawing of a piano, with a Mozart score sitting above the keyboard. "Working with you these past few weeks," Eddie wrote, sounding more like mentor than student,

> has given me nothing but joy . . . your enthusiasm radiates such powerful energy . . . with each passing day and with all the progress on *Sacre* the excitement is building up inside of me. . . . I can't wait for the premiere!!! you are going to shock the world, and Nijinsky is going to be so proud. . . .

Nighttime diversions in Iowa City proved scarce, but one of the most popular spots during the company's month-long residency that June was 620, the only gay club in town. Six-Twenty was only a quarter of a mile from the university campus, and its main draw was its spacious dance floor at the end of a long bar. At 620, Eddie seemed as outgoing as he had been at every other club on tour. Indeed, the company's "man magnet" had no trouble attracting the men he desired and gave the other dancers little reason to suspect that anything had gone amiss in his life. Among Eddie's Joffrey friends in Iowa, only Ashley Wheater, Kyle Ahmed, and the company masseur knew that he was HIV-positive. During the tour, Eddie had started a relationship with the Joffrey's masseur, a handsome green-eyed blond named John who was "into New Age healing and crystals," remembers Kyle. "He was just crazy about Eddie and wanted to take care of him and heal him." Eddie, however, lost interest quickly. When Kyle arrived in Iowa, two weeks into the company's residency, Eddie was already trying to disentangle himself from the relationship. "Eddie wasn't really into him," says Kyle. "John was devastated when Eddie broke up with him."

The company was staying in a dorm on the campus of the University of Iowa and on his breaks from rehearsals, Eddie hung out by the pool with Ashley Wheater. "Eddie was still very horny and he and I discussed the dos and don'ts of sex," says Wheater. "I told him there was no reason why he shouldn't have an active sex life, but that if he slept with someone, he had a responsibility to tell him he was HIV-positive."

Eddie agreed with Wheater's counsel, but he wasn't sure how to put it into practice. What would he tell a man he had just met? Did he want to get into a discussion about his HIV status with everyone he wanted to sleep with? Would a sense of mortality have to invade every casual encounter? While he knew that most gay men embraced the idea of safe sex, he suspected that many of them would flee when face-to-face with an HIV-infected lover. Not wanting to risk either rejection or transmission of his infection, he decided that he would use condoms, but decided not to disclose his status automatically to every potential partner. The problem was, not every man he met wanted to bother with condoms. "Eddie told me he was fooling around one night with this guy he met at 620," remembers Kyle Ahmed. "He said when he saw where things were going he tried to resist, saying he didn't want to have unsafe sex, but the guy kind of took over and it just happened. They had sex anyway. He said he felt it was out of his control."*

A̲t the same time that they were learning *Le Sacre du Printemps*, the Joffrey dancers were also rehearsing the company's new production of *The Nutcracker*, the sounds of Tchaikovsky's Christmas classic seemingly at odds with the stifling summertime heat. Set in Victorian America, the Joffrey Ballet's *Nutcracker* was to be the first ballet Robert Joffrey had choreographed in seven years and many of the dancers were anxiously awaiting their first opportunity to work closely with their director. But Robert Joffrey didn't show up for the first week of rehearsal. Nor the second.

---

*Eddie's sister Rosemarie disputes this story, arguing that Eddie would not have agreed to have unprotected sex if he knew he was HIV-positive.

"We kept expecting Mr. Joffrey to come to Iowa and choreograph, but we were told he wasn't feeling well and wouldn't be coming right away," recalls Parrish Maynard. Then came the news that Joffrey's asthma was acting up and that Iowa's high pollen count would only exacerbate his problem. "We kept wondering, 'What's the problem?'" says dancer Victoria Pasquale, "but no one wanted to talk about it." Jodie Gates remembers "just waiting and waiting for him to come out to Iowa that summer to see *Sacre* and his *Nutcracker*—and he never came. That's when we all figured something must be really wrong."

In Joffrey's stead, Scott Barnard and George Verdak, a dance historian and former member of the Ballet Russe de Monte Carlo began staging *The Nutcracker*, while Gerald Arpino choreographed the dances for the Waltz of the Flowers and the Waltz of the Snowflakes. For his conception, Robert Joffrey drew on E.T.A. Hoffmann's 1816 fairy tale, as well as on the version of the ballet staged for the Ballet Russe de Monte Carlo in 1940—which, in turn, was based on the original Petipa/Ivanov version for the great Maryinsky Ballet in St. Petersburg. In Joffrey's *Nutcracker*, the child's home life becomes the stuff that her dreams are made of; family members become leading players in little Clara's wonderland fantasy. Eddie was cast in the roles of Fritz, Clara's pesky little brother; the Snow Prince; and Tea from China. In his rehearsals with Arpino, Eddie refined the choreography for the Snow Prince's whirling dervish of a solo, which made full use of his manic speed and airborne turns and jumps. Parrish Maynard was in the studio for those rehearsals and recalls how much fun he and Eddie had working with Arpino: "Eddie would do some steps and I'd be jetéing across the back of the studio and Jerry would say, 'Yes, babies, that's it! My kids, yes! C'mon. More, more. . . .'"

Inspired by his sessions with Arpino, Eddie decided to plunge into his own choreography. At the end of a seven-hour day of rehearsals, he began tinkering with *Lacrymosa* in the studio, and sometimes asked Lissette Salgado to work with him. Together, they sketched out the movement for a possible duet. Eddie also decided to teach the solo to Parrish Maynard because having only danced it himself, he wanted to see how it looked when performed by someone else. Before he taught it to him, however, he gave Maynard a pep talk about the ballet, making sure to impress upon his friend how important the ballet was to him.

"He told me it was about this angel who comes down to earth and is suffering and who pleads with God for having this problem," says Maynard. "He never told me what the problem was. He just said it could be anything.

"But then he said the strangest thing. He said, 'I want you to carry this on for me.' I had no idea what he meant."

Robert Joffrey surrounded by his ballerinas in *The Nutcracker*

14

CURTAIN CALL

In August, the dancers finally returned to the Joffrey's studios in New York. One day, while Millicent Hodson was in the midst of overseeing a *Sacre* rehearsal, the sound of clapping echoing down the corridor brought the dancers to a halt. Everyone in the room exchanged quizzical glances. The applause grew louder and louder, as if gathering momentum down the hallway. Suddenly, Robert Joffrey appeared in the doorway.

The dancers stared at him in shock for a moment before breaking into hearty applause. It was the first time they had seen him in two months. "Mr. Joffrey looked roly-poly as always," says Adam Sklute, "but his face looked ashen and he had to pause for breaths." The rehearsal resumed and any thoughts about Joffrey's illness were momentarily suspended by Joffrey himself, who seemed especially animated as he watched, transported, as *Sacre* came to life. When at one point during the run-through, several tall young ballerinas picked their way across the floor in their pointe shoes, Joffrey suddenly called out, "Storks! That's what she called them, storks!" Millicent Hodson was at a loss as to the reference. "Robert," she asked, "what are you referring to? Who is 'she'?" The "she" in question turned out to be Marie Rambert, Nijinsky's assistant, and later, one of the pioneers of modern British ballet, with whom Joffrey had stayed in London in the 1950s. Each night at dinner, Rambert would tell Joffrey stories about the Ballets Russes and the making of *Le Sacre du Printemps*. "We watched him remembering their conversation," says Hodson. "It was a very happy rehearsal."

Robert Joffrey was to make only four more public appearances.

The first came in Los Angeles, where the Joffrey company returned the next month for the West Coast premiere of *Sacre*. Looking tanned and still robust, Joffrey joined his dancers onstage for the closing bows, which were greeted not with catcalls, but with a standing ovation. Several of the gay men in the company, however, weren't convinced of Joffrey's good health. They wondered why their director was rapidly fading from view and only showing up now and then for premieres and important rehearsals. While he didn't *look* ill, there was clearly something amiss in his long absences. With no explanations forthcoming from management or the artistic staff, the dancers were left to come up with their own. In the dressing room, Eddie, Brent Phillips, and Tom Mossbrucker speculated it might be AIDS. "Nobody really talked about AIDS in the company except the gay men," recalls Phillips. "I doubt if it was talked about at all in the girls' dressing room."

Listening to the other dancers weigh the evidence about Joffrey's health only amplified Eddie's fears about his own. Though he was still as healthy and strong as ever, he was convinced that his colleagues would think him less capable were they to know that he was carrying the AIDS virus. Of course, he couldn't know for certain just how the other dancers might react, but he wasn't willing to put his career at risk in order to find out. Nobody in the company seemed able to broach the subject of AIDS comfortably and Eddie saw that it would be some time before he would be able to discuss his plight openly. But ex-lovers were another matter and there were several with whom he had still to settle accounts.

The week before *Le Sacre du Printemps* was to have its L.A. premiere, the Joffrey was in Costa Mesa and Eddie phoned Eric

Castellano, the young man he had met at the Little Shrimp a few months earlier. He and Eric had been sending each other postcards and had agreed to meet up again in Laguna Beach during the Joffrey's next Orange County stopover.

It was nearing midnight by the time Eddie and Eric took a stroll down the beach. "I have something to talk to you about," Eddie began. "I have something to tell you too," replied Eric Castellano, whose own news was double-barreled. "My father and I both got tested," he said. "I'm positive and my father already has AIDS."

For the next two hours, nineteen-year-old Eddie and twenty-six-year-old Eric talked about death and tried to help each other cope with a subject they had never had much reason to consider. "A close friend of mine had just died," recalls Castellano, "and I had gone through the process of his death. I told Eddie that the experience had changed my idea about death. I was trying to dismiss this idea that there is this dark hole you fall into. Eddie and I were both afraid. We both kept thinking, 'I'm not going to let this get me.' Neither of us was really educated about AIDS. We were just two kids trying to make it through the whole thing and trying to learn how to feel peaceful about it."

The conversation eventually turned to sex, the two subjects following each other in a devastating circle. Since they were both HIV-positive, "we figured we might as well go for it," recalls Castellano, and have unprotected sex. What good would protection do at this point, they wondered. Neither of them was aware that by not practicing safe sex, they ran the risk of reinfecting each other with different strains of the virus and further weakening their immune systems.

Eddie was planning to stay at the Santa Monica home of "Friends of the Joffrey" (F.O.J.s as they were known to the dancers) and invited Castellano to join him there when the Joffrey traveled to Los Angeles a few days later. He told Eric that in order to bring him "home," he would have to concoct a story for his hosts and tell them that Eric was a longtime Joffrey supporter who had just flown in from New York and needed a place to stay. The night of *Sacre*'s West Coast premiere, Eddie's L.A. hosts, a couple in their thirties, were only too eager to welcome a dance fan into their home and proceeded to solicit Castellano's opinions on a variety of Joffrey productions. Having never seen a ballet performance in his life, Eric Castellano did his best to fake his way through an answer before Eddie jumped to his rescue and answered for him.

The next morning things became all the stranger when they, along with most of greater Los Angeles, awoke to an earthquake that was serious enough to postpone the Joffrey's performance that evening.

With the ardor of an evangelist, Eddie hoped to convert Eric into a balletomane and invited him to the Dorothy Chandler Pavilion the next night to see him make his West Coast debut as Puck in Frederick Ashton's *The Dream*. Set in the Victorian era to music by Mendelssohn, the one-act ballet was based on Shakespeare's *A Midsummer Night's Dream* and suffused with the giddiness, romance, and high jinks of that comic tale of misadventure. Though transformations were Eric's stock-in-trade as a makeup artist, he couldn't get over the alchemy taking place in the moonlit glade onstage. As he sat in the theater for the first time, he watched his friend Eddie turn himself into Shakespeare's mischievous sprite, his gravity-defying leaps, suspended handstands, and quicksilver charm electrifying the entire house. He "seemed to split the sky with his jumps," *The Los Angeles Herald* would report the next day. Eric was impressed: "I had no idea that he was such a little starlet," he recalls. "Each time Eddie jumped, somebody would yell, 'Bravo! Bravo!' It was just like the movies." Eddie was back in the spotlight, but in landing the role of Puck, and with it first-cast billing, his rivalry with Parrish Maynard was put to a test it didn't—and perhaps couldn't—survive. Before the ballet had been cast, Eddie, Parrish, and Mark Goldweber had all been called to rehearsals with Alexander Grant to learn the role of Puck. Grant, who had danced the role of Bottom in the original Royal Ballet production, was staging *The Dream* at the Joffrey and seemed particularly pleased with the work of Eddie and Parrish. At least, that's what Parrish Maynard thought. "Alexander Grant was oozing all over Eddie and me," says Maynard of their early rehearsals at the Joffrey's New York studios in August, "and really working with both of us. At that point I was really sick of all the attention Eddie was getting. He was always mentioned in reviews and his picture was in the paper a lot. There was so much hoopla about Eddie and I was getting jealous and angry. I had just had enough. Well, in the middle of our rehearsals, I heard a rumor that Eddie had gone up to talk to Jerry [Arpino] and asked to be first cast. No one did that in the company, but Eddie did it all the time. He'd say to Jerry or Pennie [Curry, the company's executive director], 'I think I should be first cast.' And when the cast list went up and I saw that Eddie got first cast, Mark got second cast, and I got third cast, I was outraged. I felt that Mark should have had first cast because he was more senior, and I started being really evil to Eddie. We had a huge fight in the dressing room. I called him a conniving little weasel. I said, 'You can't deny that you went up there to ask for first cast. I heard you did. And I can't believe you would do that. I'm sick of the competition between us.' Eddie kept saying, 'I can't believe that you think I would do something that way.' And I told him, 'Eddie, I *know* how you work.' We had a huge falling-out and I totally cut him off."

There was little disagreement about just how Eddie operated. "If Eddie wanted something, nothing was going to stop him," says Jodie Gates. Kyle Ahmed remembers that Eddie would "fight, fight, fight for first cast. He did not want anything else." According to Scott Barnard, Eddie thought nothing of asking directly for what he wanted. "He would always ask, 'Am I going to be first cast?' and if the answer was 'no,' he'd want to know why. He was so aggressive and believed so much in what he could do that he didn't have much compassion for what other people got—or didn't get—or for the years that others had put in. He was only concerned with *his* career."

Whenever he didn't get the answer he wanted from Barnard, Eddie would take his request to Gerald Arpino or to Pennie Curry. Eddie, everyone agreed, could cut to the heart of an issue with an audacity and indifference to propriety that was at once startling and effective. "Eddie was always coming into my office, proposing something," recalls Arpino. "I'd think, 'He's precocious.' Eddie wanted to prove to everyone that he wasn't an underdog, and that he could dance taller than the tallest man and could fill that canvas of space faster than anyone else. He knew who he was and what he had to achieve."

Among the goals Eddie had set for himself was the role of company director, says Pennie Curry. "He was very up-front that he didn't just want to be a performer, he wanted to have his own company someday," she says. And he wasn't shy about saying it. "Eddie was going to hold to his agenda no matter what was happening around him."

Perhaps no one in the company was more rankled by the news that Eddie Stierle was to be the first-cast Puck than Mark Goldweber. Puck was the plum role he had long been waiting for. When the ballet had last been performed by the Joffrey in 1981, Goldweber was a junior company member and was thrilled to have landed the third cast of Puck; but this time, he felt sure that he would be given the opening-night performance of Puck, a reward for his eleven-year tenure.

The same night that Eric Castellano watched Eddie make his L.A. debut as Puck, Mark Goldweber stood in the wings, brooding. He knew the end of his carer was looming, whereas young Eddie Stierle seemed to have his still before him. As he waited his turn to dance in *Les Patineurs*, the last ballet on the program, his spirits flagged. "Here it was my eleventh year in the company and I'm waiting to go onstage to perform a ballet I've done thousands of times before," he says, "while Eddie, who's been in the company one year, is starring in the showpiece of the evening. *The Dream* was the ballet everybody was excited about, not *Les Patineurs*. I was feeling pretty bitter." Noticing how demoralized Goldweber was feeling, longtime Joffrey dancer Jerel Hilding tried to console him. "Don't fight it," he advised him. "Eddie is the new boy. Audiences want to see someone new. It doesn't have anything to do with you."

Indeed, in the so-called "all-star, no star" Joffrey, Eddie was soon generating an awful lot of ink. There were other prominent dancers to be sure, among them Glenn Edgerton, Dawn Caccamo, and Philip Jerry, but it was Eddie whose picture regularly graced Joffrey reviews and advertisements and it was Eddie who was often the focus of advance feature articles on the company.

On October 27, 1987, the opening night of the Joffrey's New York season, Eddie not only starred in all three ballets on the program, but made his New York debut in the two most anticipated works of that season: *La Vivandière* and *The Dream*. And most of the major New York critics were in attendance. While both Clive Barnes in *The New York Post* and Janice Berman in *New York Newsday* noted that Eddie's Puck "almost stole the show" in *The Dream*, Anna Kisselgoff gave Eddie and Tina LeBlanc the highest marks for their performances in *La Vivandière*, the kind of purely classical ballet that Eddie's teachers and colleagues had scoffed at the Razz Ma Jazz kid ever performing.

Having struggled against the limitations of his body, Eddie had finally become the dancer he had long envisioned himself to be.

Kisselgoff's review confirmed to Eddie that his performance onstage finally matched the one he was continually playing out in his mind. "Never have the clarity, virtuosity, and purity of the nineteenth-century French academic training come across the ages with such impact," she wrote in *The New York Times*. "Mr. Stierle, who appears mainly in character parts, proved himself the classical virtuoso he is at heart—with his clean line and noble partnering." In her 1987 retrospective of the year's highlights that December, Kisselgoff would recollect that "the superlative dancing in *La Vivandière*, including that of the gifted Edward Stierle, was one of the great pleasures of many a season."

Such unstinting praise did little to advance Eddie's popularity among the Joffrey men. Neither did his casting in back-to-back ballets on the same night. "We called those 'Ed Stierle nights,'" recalls Brent Phillips. "We'd think, 'Is Eddie through?'" After spending the entire night onstage, whipping off perfect pirouettes with split-second precision, Eddie would march into the dressing room, grumbling, "Oh, shit, I only did a triple, I meant to do four." It wasn't just that he showed his frustration at a performance many of them would have been only too proud to have pulled off, but that he talked about himself incessantly. A little self-involvement was de rigueur among dancers, but Eddie's narcissism was venturing out of bounds.

Highly ambitious even before he had tested HIV-positive, Eddie was now grabbing every opportunity he could, the awareness of his condition amplifying all aspects of his personality, including the grating ones. Behind his back, one of the dancers took to referring to him as "Me." "There goes 'Me' again," he'd say, and those within earshot would roll their eyes at having to listen to Eddie recount yet another story about his performance at the Jackson competition or his experiences at the Basel Ballet. Brent Phillips, whose locker was next to Eddie's at the Joffrey's New York studios, considered moving to another locker because he "couldn't stand to listen to him."

Eddie was hardly oblivious to their sneering; it troubled him that his success generated such hostility among his peers, as it once had among his siblings, and yet he did little to disguise his self-satisfaction. He felt that he had worked hard for everything he got and that he deserved the rewards he was now reaping. He was just beginning to learn that he couldn't persuade everyone he liked to see his point of view. That December, during the company's performances in Washington at the Kennedy Center, Eddie followed up on a promise to his mother to look up Robin Meredith, the family friend who had helped get him started on his modeling career as a child. "Eddie told me that the nasty atmosphere depressed him, but he never blamed anyone for it," recalls Meredith, who, though twenty years older than Eddie, soon struck up a close friendship with him. "Eddie preferred to see good in everything. He was always saying, 'I'll bring them around,' as if it was *his* responsibility to change their view of him."

He got his chance at Christmas when he pulled a name out of a hat for the Joffrey's Secret Santa lottery. It was a Joffrey tradition for the dancers to buy a gift for a specific company member, whose name they drew out of a hat. Eddie shook his head in disbelief when he saw the name he had drawn—Parrish Maynard. He and Parrish hadn't spoken in four months. Nevertheless, Eddie went ahead and bought Parrish a black hand towel with his initials monogrammed in white. At the company Christmas party, "everyone was waiting to see how I'd react when I saw who the gift was from," says Parrish. "Eddie had obviously gone to a lot of effort to make it special and it broke the ice. I thought it was very sweet." Ashley Wheater puts it more bluntly: "Parrish realized that he'd been an idiot and they made up."

The growing distress over Robert Joffrey's absences only exacerbated the hostility and envy encircling Eddie that fall. Joffrey had been on hand for the opening night of the New York season in October, and for the premiere of *Le Sacre du Printemps* the following night, and while he had looked more fatigued than he had in Los Angeles in September, he was still up to playing his role as "man of the hour," recalls Millicent Hodson. However, he hadn't been seen once during the remaining three weeks of the New York season, nor at any of the rehearsals that got under way on his *Nutcracker* in mid-November. It wasn't long before an uneasiness settled on the company. "Psychologically, the dancers suffered terribly during that time," says Scott Barnard. "Robert Joffrey was the father figure here and the strength of the company. He always made you feel that he knew you. He may not have been visible in the studio on a daily basis, but the dancers knew that he was always here, up in his office. If they needed to see him, they knew they could find him. So they realized that it had to be a most unusual situation for him not to be around. It was very difficult for them when they couldn't feel his spirit here, when they couldn't smell him here."

Just what was keeping their director sequestered at home was a question to which the dancers now demanded an answer. When they appealed to Pennie Curry, she told them that Joffrey was suffering from a respiratory ailment he couldn't seem to shake. "The rumors about his having AIDS," she remonstrated, "are completely unfounded." But the more the company denied the rumors, the more the dancers became convinced that Robert Joffrey had AIDS. "We were told he couldn't get over this terrible virus, it was like pneumonia," says Jodie Gates. "Then I heard that he had a degenerative muscle disease, but to me, it all had to do with AIDS."

Like many of the dancers in the company, Eddie assumed that Joffrey had AIDS and was ashamed to acknowledge it. But he shared his concern only with the gay men in the company. He never once discussed his frustration with his sister Rosemarie, even though he saw her regularly, because he didn't want to call her attention to the subject of AIDS. "I remember talking to Eddie and Tom Mossbrucker about Mr. Joffrey in the dressing room and we were all bothered by Mr. Joffrey's silence," says Adam Sklute. "We thought, 'Here is a man who has done so many incredible things for the ballet world and he seems so ashamed of his own sexuality that he has to hide the fact that he has AIDS, somehow thinking that people wouldn't respect him in the way they already did.' We were upset that he couldn't come out and do something for the AIDS cause. It was important to know that important people were dying of AIDS. That frustrated Eddie a great deal and he was more verbal about it, just because he was more verbal about everything."

Even members of the Joffrey's board of directors were thwarted in their efforts to learn the nature of Robert Joffrey's illness. "Bob wouldn't acknowledge to us that he had AIDS," says a New York board member. "We thought it was obvious from the symptoms, but we were constantly being told 'no.' We assumed that it was simply BS, that we weren't getting the story."

Though no one would confirm that Joffrey had AIDS, those among his inner circle had known since May of 1987 that he was dying from the disease. He had told them so himself, just before the company was due to begin rehearsals for *Sacre* and *The Nutcracker* in Iowa. Pennie Curry remembers being called to his town house, along with Richard Englund and Gerald Arpino. "I've been to the doctor and my tests have come back," Robert Joffrey announced. "I'm HIV-positive and I am going to start taking medication."

Joffrey's revelation confirmed what Pennie Curry had dimly suspected as far back as June of 1986, when she had spent two weeks in London with Joffrey working out the details of *Sacre*'s reconstruction with Millicent Hodson and Kenneth Archer. Though passionate about the project, Joffrey seemed to tire easily and had trouble keeping his focus. He wasn't feeling well, he said.

One morning he surprised Curry by asking her to take a look at some worrisome red bumps on the top of his head and at the back of his neck. "What do you think these are?" he wanted to know. "I couldn't admit to myself what it was," Curry acknowledges. "It crept into my mind and I just knocked it out." During their stay, Joffrey and Curry visited with Sir Frederick Ashton, who expressed concern at Joffrey's apparent poor health. "Maybe we both just need a rest," Joffrey remarked with a smile to the eighty-one-year-old Ashton.

By the time he was diagnosed a year later, Joffrey had his heart set on seeing his *Nutcracker* realized. Worried that the dancers wouldn't keep their focus on learning his ballet if they knew of his illness, Joffrey asked his associates to keep quiet about it. They agreed to say only that he was having asthma-related problems and needed to rest. Since he was relying on Scott Barnard to choreograph much of the ballet, Joffrey also stipulated that Barnard not be let in on the news for a while, a request that Curry was uncomfortable about honoring since Barnard worked directly with the dancers. "We were like this dysfunctional family," she says. "Our parent figure was asking us to keep secrets from each other and we all felt torn by our loyalty to him. We felt this was his company and this was how he wanted it played out."

As the months wore on and Joffrey failed to improve, Curry pressed him to let her tell Scott Barnard, the board, and the Joffrey dancers. "There's no need to talk about it," she remembers him saying. "He was a discreet man and he felt about his illness the way he felt about his homosexuality—it was a private matter," says Curry. "He feared that people wouldn't want to be associated with the company if they knew he had AIDS. He was worried it would hurt funding."

According to Val Golovitser, Joffrey's personal assistant at the time, Joffrey's illness was "never discussed directly" among his associates. Golovitser, who was never told that Joffrey had AIDS, says he assumed he had it and decided to keep it a secret. "I didn't want the dancers to panic," he says. Golovitser spent his days shuttling back and forth between *The Nutcracker* rehearsals at the Joffrey studios and Mr. Joffrey's town house, and whenever the dancers would ask him, "How is Mr. Joffrey today?" he would be sure to tell them that Joffrey was improving, when, in fact, he was growing dramatically worse. Pennie Curry was also providing optimistic updates that only further confused the dancers. One company member insists that Curry told the dancers that the asthma medication Joffrey was taking was adversely affecting his kidneys. Curry recalls feeling "horrible at having to lie to the dancers. I felt there was no reversal on this because Bob was going down too fast. I lived with the nightmare of knowing that I would one day have to face the dancers. I understood their bitterness. To go out on that stage night after night and not know whether or not their leader, the person with the vision, was ever going to be around again—what a void."

Tina LeBlanc, then the Joffrey's newest star, wasn't quite sure what or whom to believe at the time, but in hindsight believes that the company was trying to ensure its future without Mr. Joffrey. "They told us point-blank that the AIDS rumors weren't true and I think they were operating on the basis that since Mr. Joffrey's homosexuality wasn't acknowledged publicly, this sort of thing had to be denied to keep the people who gave money from running," she says. "They kept telling us, 'Deny, don't let the rumors spread,'" remembers Brent Phillips. "They would say, 'We are telling you it's asthma and if anybody asks, be sure to tell them it's asthma.'" Ashley Wheater offers another perspective: "Joffrey was a very proud man and in 1987 to be associated with the word AIDS meant something dirty, a sleazy life-style."

Even when the AIDS rumors were spreading outside the company, Joffrey's close circle of associates continued to issue denials both to their colleagues and among themselves. "We'd focus on Bob's specific problems," says Curry. "We'd think, 'If he could just get over this liver problem.' We never said AIDS. None of us used that word." Val Golovitser attended Joffrey night and day and never once remembers hearing Joffrey himself say the word AIDS. He didn't want people to treat him as if he were ill nor did he want to see in anyone's eyes the hopelessness of his situation. Since Joffrey was physically unable to choreograph the ballet he had envisioned, he called on Scott Barnard to oversee its staging.

Barnard took the dances Arpino created for the Snowflakes and the Flowers—as well as the variations that George Verdak had staged from the 1940 Ballet Russe de Monte Carlo version, the first American *Nutcracker*—and incorporated them into the full-length work Robert Joffrey had conceived. "Mr. Joffrey would say, 'This isn't done yet, will you help me?' The ballet was always done under that pretense," remembers Barnard, who conferred daily with Joffrey on the progress of *Nutcracker* rehearsals. "Mr. Joffrey was so overwhelmed by the idea that something like *that* could happen to him. He had an invincible quality about him. He had created a major company out of nothing, with no money, because he made sure that nothing was going to stand in his way. When he got sick, it was the first time in his life that something had all of a sudden stopped him. I bet more than anything, the fact that he was being stopped so devastated him, that he didn't know how to approach it." Gerald Arpino, too, was overwhelmed at the prospect of losing Joffrey. "That Bob would die was something we tried not to accept," he would later acknowledge.

The mystery surrounding Robert Joffrey's illness continued to fuel Eddie's own apprehensions and it was in that frame of mind that he paid his first visit to the lower–Fifth Avenue offices of Dr. John Oppenheimer in November. A thirty-two-year-old GP, John Oppenheimer was fast becoming a specialist in AIDS cases. He had come to New York City fresh from his medical studies at Tulane University in the summer of 1982, just as the new disease was being named and defined. He did his residency first at Harlem Hospital and then with HIV patients in the community medicine department of St. Vincent's Hospital in Greenwich Village, before opening his general practice in 1986. On weekends, he covered for two Manhattan AIDS specialists. By the time Eddie came to see him in November 1987, 50 percent of his patients were HIV-positive; of these, Eddie was the youngest.

"Eddie was hyperalert and wanted as much information as I could give him," recalls John Oppenheimer, a soft-spoken, laconic man, his dark beard flecked with gray. "He wanted to know what the incubation period was and how long ago he had become infected. At the beginning, they all focus on how they got it, but after a while, the means cease to matter." Eddie gave the doctor the results of his previous blood test in Los Angeles: His T-cell lymphocyte, he reported, had been 798. A normal T4 count ran anywhere from 500 to 1,000. (T4 or T cells, as they are called, are white blood cells that are key components of the immune system.) The doctor explained that some patients have normal T4 counts for up to ten years after they learn they've been infected, while others became sick right away with one of the distinctive infections that are markers for AIDS, a course that was then thought to have something to do with the patient's genetic makeup or with the particular strain of the virus. Some strains, it appeared, were more vigorous than others, but as statistics and percentages were constantly changing, the medical community hadn't yet established how long a person could be infected with HIV before showing any AIDS symptoms. "I told Eddie that he probably wasn't going to get sick with a T-cell count of 798. Ninety-five percent of the people who get PCP* have T-cell counts under 200, so I told him that if he got a cold, he shouldn't worry that it was a harbinger."

Given that several months had elapsed since Eddie's last round of tests, Dr. Oppenheimer decided to repeat the HIV test and to check Eddie's T-cell count. Once again his HIV test came back positive, but this time his T-cell count had fallen to 595 from 798, a drop that Dr. Oppenheimer considered faster than normal. The only anti-AIDS drug then on the market was AZT, which had just received FDA approval nine months earlier. While its merits remained controversial, AZT was shown to slow the replication of the AIDS-causing virus, though in late 1987, the drug was still not in widespread use and prevailing medical wisdom had it that patients should be treated with AZT only when their T-cell counts dropped below 200. (By the summer of 1991, in contrast, many doctors were starting their HIV patients on AZT when their counts dropped to the 500 level or plummeted sharply.)

There was nothing to be done, it seemed, but to hope that Eddie's counts would level off.

---

*PCP (*Pneumocystis carinii* pneumonia) is the most common life-threatening opportunistic infection in people with AIDS.

Five blocks south of John Oppenheimer's office, in the town house from which he now rarely ventured, Robert Joffrey continued to chart the progress of his *Nutcracker*. He was obsessed by the ballet, perhaps understanding that it was the last he was likely to do. He was born on Christmas Eve and had always taken particular delight in *The Nutcracker*, a ballet he hoped one day to fashion after his own childhood memories. For fifteen years, he had conceived every detail of the Joffrey's production—from its Victorian decor and costumes to its props and toys—and though unable to choreograph, his hand was still visible: Critics would later note that the staging looked unified "as if all its aspects flowed from a single imagination."

At home, he continued to pore over the Victorian prints, Christmas cards, and woodcuts he'd spent years collecting and met round-the-clock with his set, costume, and lighting designers about the textures and flavors of American Victoriana he hoped to convey. And each night, he scrutinized the videotapes of the day's rehearsal brought to him by Scott Barnard, with whom he discussed ideas for the ballet in his air-filtered study/bedroom on the second floor, the desk piled high with sketches, fabric swatches, and maquettes. One night, as Joffrey was reviewing a rehearsal of the First Act party scene, he advised Barnard that the exit of one of the guests seemed too rushed. "It's late in the evening," he pointed out. "She wouldn't be rushing off." Another night, Scott Barnard was in the midst of describing the steps he had devised for the Grandfather's dance in the party scene, when suddenly Joffrey announced excitedly, "You must do this step," and stood up to demonstrate. Grabbing Barnard, Joffrey began leading him in the polka around his room. "The two of us got to laughing and we ended up falling over the furniture," remembers Barnard. "We had the best time dancing in that little room. As sick as he was, he got so excited about *The Nutcracker*."

In December, *Dance Magazine* featured a robust and smiling Robert Joffrey on its cover, surrounded by five ballerinas in snowflaked white tulle. The picture had been taken that fall and the accompanying article quoted Joffrey as saying that he hoped this *Nutcracker* would prove "one of the most pleasant experiences

I've ever had in the theater." A few lines later, Gerald Arpino explained why the Joffrey had decided to mount its own version of *The Nutcracker*. "Well, I believe it's an important time in America," he commented. "We need to look at our values. We need to bring back the idea of the family, to restore some of the childlike qualities we've lost. . . . And, when I say *the family*, I include the family of friends, the family of community—family in a sense that you look after the other fellow for the sake of looking after him, not for what you can get out of it. That's what this *Nutcracker* is about."

By December 10, when his *Nutcracker* was to have its world premiere at the Hancher Auditorium in Iowa City, Robert Joffrey was too frail to make the trip. Instead, he watched a videotape of the final dress rehearsal from his bed at New York University Hospital. The tape had been made the day before and shipped overnight to New York so that Joffrey could watch his pop-up storybook of ballet at the same time that it was being unveiled in Iowa for the first time. Bedside were his assistant, Val Golovitser, and the Joffrey's longtime resident photographer, Herb Migdoll, and for the entire two-hour performance, they all imagined that they were 1,300 miles west of NYU Hospital, sitting in the orchestra of Hancher Auditorium.

Three weeks later, just hours before the New York premiere of *The Nutcracker* on December 30, Robert Joffrey was back at home, struggling to get into a tuxedo. Even with his assistant, Val, on hand to help him get dressed and down the stairs, the effort took hours. That morning, he had startled Pennie Curry by calling her at the Joffrey and announcing, "Penushka, I have a lovely surprise. I'm coming to the show tonight."

"Now the dancers will know," Curry said to herself.

Joffrey had made up his mind to attend the premiere at City Center and, while he knew his friends would advise against it, he was not about to be stopped. "He realized that it was his last chance to be part of the company," recalls Golovitser. Except for Pennie Curry, no one at the Joffrey Ballet had any idea that Robert Joffrey was on his way to the theater, not the critics, not the dancers, not Alexander Grant, who was guest-performing in the role of the magical Dr. Drosselmeyer—not even Gerald Arpino.

The houselights were dimming when Golovitser wheeled Robert Joffrey to the enclosed sound booth at the back of the orchestra, where he went unnoticed for almost the entire performance. Joffrey was so impressed with Eddie's performance that he would later notify Scott Barnard that he wanted Eddie to take a curtain call after both the first and second acts. They had earlier agreed that only those dancers who didn't continue on in the second act would be permitted to take a bow at the conclusion of the first act. However, Joffrey felt that Eddie had so distinguished himself in his Snow Prince solo that he deserved a special bow for his showstopping contribution to the first act. Eddie's performance also registered with the critics. During the company's appearance in Washington, D.C., earlier that month, *Washington Post* critic

Dancing "Tea from China" in *The Nutcracker*

Alan Kriegsman had written that his "breathtaking jumps and pirouettes as the Snow Prince [proved] the brilliant high point of the dancing" in the first act.

During the final divertissements of "The Kingdom of the Sweets," Joffrey turned to Pennie Curry, who was next to him in the sound booth. "I want to bow with my company," he said suddenly. "I don't think that's wise, Bob," Curry answered cautiously. "To go onstage just as the curtain is going up, with the dancers not knowing how ill you are—I'm not sure they can emotionally handle it." Joffrey just grinned back at her. "I want to bow with my company," he repeated.

Val Golovitser wheeled Joffrey backstage and waited with him in the second wing for the closing bows. Jodie Gates, who was standing in the wings awaiting the cue for her solo in "Waltz of the Flowers," froze the minute she spied Joffrey. "I couldn't believe it was Mr. Joffrey. He was in a wheelchair and he looked so sick." Gates was performing the Spanish Dance that night as well as filling in for an injured dancer as one of the flowers. "Mr. Joffrey looked at me and said, 'You're busy tonight, aren't you?' I started crying."

In the dark, Leslie Carothers almost tripped over Mr. Joffrey. She had danced the Snow Queen in the First Act and had come backstage to watch the end of the ballet. "I was completely stunned. Mr. Joffrey was such a vital man and here he was looking very, very ill. I went to the back of the wings and cried."

The shock of seeing their director so transformed registered at once on the dancers' faces, try though they did to mask their discomfort with smiles. "Mr. Joffrey looked close to death. He was just a ghost," says Victoria Pasquale, who had just come offstage when she caught a glimpse of Joffrey. "We were not at all prepared for the way he looked. We felt betrayed because we had no idea how sick he was."

As soon as the curtain came down, Joffrey was wheeled to center stage. "Hold me up, Alexander," he whispered urgently to Alexander Grant, making it clear that he had no intention of taking his final bow in a wheelchair. While Grant gripped him tightly on one side, Glenn Edgerton, the Nutcracker Prince, held him fast on the other. When the curtain went up, Robert Joffrey greeted his standing ovation with a childlike smile. Then he turned around and blew a kiss to his dancers.

"The whole company broke out in absolute hysterics," recalls Parrish Maynard. As soon as the curtain came down, the dancers gathered around Robert Joffrey. Cynthia Giannini, who had danced the Tea from China variation with Eddie that night, remembers the way they all stood around their director, crying as he praised them. "Thank you, company," he said, his voice barely audible. "It was a wonderful performance. You all danced beautifully."

"Then they whisked him off," says Maynard. "We all cried for hours after that."

On the way home in the van, Robert Joffrey was on a high from the night. He chatted happily with his assistant about how wonderful it had been to see his dancers, even though the effort had clearly drained him. "He had used up all his energy," remembers Val Golovitser, "trying to be the man he used to be."

Shaken by Robert Joffrey's rapid decline, Eddie went to see Dr. John Oppenheimer a week after Joffrey's charged return to the theater. In his notes, the doctor recorded that Eddie was suffering from "HIV anxiety." He had bouts of insomnia and was panicked every time he got a cold.

The Joffrey dancers were on tour in Chicago when they awoke to the news of Robert Joffrey's death. It was March 25, 1988, and nearly three months had elapsed since Joffrey had said good-bye to them on the stage at City Center. No one at the company had ever confirmed that Joffrey had AIDS. The reported cause of death was notable for its ambiguity. "Mr. Joffrey had been sick since April 1986, with an illness recently diagnosed by his doctor as an enlarged liver, asthma, and severe myositis, a disease that causes deterioration of the muscles," reported *The New York Times* in its front-page obituary, which went on to quote a statement from NYU Hospital's director of media relations. "We are simply saying," she said, "that he died of liver, renal, and respiratory failure."

15

LACRYMOSA
D'AMORE

Robert Joffrey's death left his dancers speculating
about their future and forced Eddie to confront his uncertain
present. He awoke many mornings feeling depressed and frightened and wondered how long it would be before he began developing symptoms of AIDS. He didn't want to wait until he was sick to
tell his family that he was carrying the HIV virus. With his life
now ticking away, Eddie wasn't ready to deal with his parents'
fears about his sexuality, much less their fears about losing him. As
far as they knew, he was sleeping only with women, the memory
of Richard Register and Basel having been dismissed as nothing
more than a moment of teenage confusion. He had tried to discour-
age his mother's dependence on him, but to little avail: He saw that
her life completely revolved around his own and he shuddered at
the prospect of telling her about his HIV status, knowing that the
news would destroy her.

Ever since testing positive in Los Angeles, Eddie had been
haunted by *Lacrymosa*, the prescient sadness of his solo making the
task of returning to it considerably difficult. And while he had put

189

it aside after working on it with Lissette Salgado in Iowa, he never doubted that one day he would pick up where he had left off. But between leaving off and picking up, his life had changed dramatically, for in the interim the ballet's once distant scenario had become soberingly real. Eddie was certain that only through making a ballet about loss and the transcendence of death would he find the language he needed to say good-bye.

His opportunity came in late March, when he was invited to make a work for the Joffrey II's upcoming Choreographers' Workshop, an experimental showcase for the Joffrey's aspiring dance-makers. Eddie knew at once that he wanted to expand *Lacrymosa* into a ballet for nine dancers and decided to set it to additional excerpts from Mozart's *Requiem*. He also expanded the ballet's title, calling it *Lacrymosa d'Amore* (or "Tears of Love," according to Eddie's translation.) Unlike composers or play-wrights, choreographers cannot pursue their craft in isolation. Only when face-to-face with dancers in the rehearsal studio can they begin to express the movement suggested by a piece of music. Since Eddie had never choreographed for anyone other than himself, he thought it best to begin enlarging the work with Lissette Salgado, the dancer whose movement qualities he knew nearly as well as his own. He and Lissette had taken their first steps in ballet together and she was the first ballerina he had learned to partner. From Liana Ballet to the Joffrey, they had followed each other's progress. But in Eddie's view, Lissette wasn't pushing hard enough to make herself known. She was too shy, he said, too insecure. If she wouldn't turn the spotlight on herself, he would do it for her. He cast her as the female lead in *Lacrymosa*, intent on showing others what he knew she could do.

Lissette quickly proved herself his ideal muse. In the same way that close friends can read each other's thoughts and finish each other's sentences, Lissette could anticipate Eddie's movement and complete the dance phrases he began. Together, they sketched the ballet's overall design and devised the movement for its central pas de deux, which showed a man and a woman struggling to say good-bye to each other. "It's about the loss of a loved one and the acceptance of death," Eddie informed Lissette, who wouldn't know for another year that Eddie was infected with HIV.

Several weeks into rehearsals, however, she pressed him for more details about the woman she was portraying. The woman, she observed, seemed to want to keep the man in her embrace. Whenever he would go off on his own, she always came after him. "Am I the man's lover or his mother?" she asked. "It's interesting you should ask that," Eddie replied. "The pas de deux is about my relationship with my mother." He elaborated no further, but that was all Lissette needed to know.

The making of *Lacrymosa d'Amore* happened to coincide with Rose and Bill Stierle's fortieth anniversary celebration in Miami on Easter weekend. (Though their actual anniversary was in December, April was the first month all eight children could clear their calendars.) The Christian symbolism could hardly have been lost on Eddie: Here he was in the midst of choreographing his farewell to his mother at the same time that he was about to celebrate her fortieth year of marriage—and on the weekend when Catholics were celebrating Christ's resurrection. To Eddie, life seemed perpetually to be intruding on art and blurring distinctions between the two.

On April 1, the Stierle clan converged on Miami to spend the weekend together at the Family Enrichment Center, a retreat run by the Archdiocese of Miami. As director of the Archdiocese's campus ministry, Eddie's brother Michael had booked it for the occasion. From Atlantic City came Rosemarie and her husband, Kit; from Kansas City came Bill, Jr., a high school football coach; and from Dayton, Ohio, came Tom, who was applying the financial know-how he had honed as manager of the family accounts to his new job as a marketing analyst for NCR. Closer to home, Patty had traveled down from Columbia, South Carolina, where she was in her last year of nursing at USC; while Kathy and her fiancé had driven from Florida, where her fiancé worked on his father's vegetable and cattle farm outside Gainesville. Closest to home were the two eldest Stierle children, Michael and Terri. Michael was married with two children and was in the process of adopting two more from the Dominican Republic; while Terri had four children and was hard at work at Respect Life.

The reunion was a noisy and happy affair. The following day, the entire party gathered in the chapel of the retreat center, where Bill and Rose Stierle renewed their wedding vows, surrounded by their children, assorted friends from Hollywood, and their coworkers from Chaminade High School and Madonna Academy. Bill was no longer the skinny guy with combed-back hair Rose had first danced with at Finnegan's. The years—and drink—had thickened him, his slender waist now obscured by a noticeable paunch. But though his face was worn and ruddy, his clear blue eyes were still bright and playful. Rose, too, had changed, but less discernibly. She still carried with her an old-country air. Pearl teardrops dangled from her earlobes and large glasses sat atop a prominent nose. Her hair was cropped short, brunette hair dye concealing threads of gray, and, as one might expect of Rose, her devotion to the Church was evident in the gold cross fastened around her neck.

The outdoor reception lasted well into the afternoon, and during the picnic lunch, Eddie and Rose sat on the grass catching up on Eddie's latest news from New York. "Mom, I'm using my *Lacrymosa* solo in a new ballet I'm doing," Eddie announced. "That's wonderful, Edward, what's it about?" Rose wanted to know. "It's about acceptance," Eddie replied, "but I want you to see for yourself." Rose remembered that when Eddie was making his solo for the Jackson competition, she had assumed that it was about "accepting the body God has given you," as she put it, and she saw no reason now to change her interpretation.

While in Miami, Eddie was to appear as a guest with Ballets Etudes, a local troupe that was presenting *Giselle* at the Jackie Gleason Theatre of the Performing Arts. The production was to star the legendary Russian dancer Rudolf Nureyev, and Eddie and Tina LeBlanc had been invited to perform the peasant pas de deux, a highlight of the First Act. Rose Stierle was delighted with the timing of the event, for it gave her a chance to fall into old, familiar patterns: She bought tickets for everyone in the family, assuming, as always, that everyone would go along with her plan. "Here was one more family excursion organized by my mother to see Ed dance," remembers Tom Stierle, who refused to play his assigned role. "I wasn't interested." Fifteen years earlier, Eddie's brothers and sisters had been only too happy to cheer on six-year-old Eddie as he tapped his way through his first dance routine during his parents' twenty-fifth anniversary party in the Chaminade cafeteria. But times had changed. "Everyone had had it by then with my mom going on about Eddie and his career," says Rosemarie, who accompanied her parents, her brother Michael, Michael's wife, Pam, and their two children to the performance. The other Stierle siblings went their own ways, so Rosemarie gave away the leftover tickets to friends.

Eager to prove himself in his new role of choreographer, Eddie arrived for his first day of rehearsal with the Joffrey II Dancers charged with ideas and enthusiasm. "Some fledgling choreographers need you to guide them," says Jeremy Blanton, a former Joffrey dancer who was then associate director of the Joffrey II Dancers.* "Eddie knew exactly what he wanted." The fact that Eddie was younger than most of the dancers was enough to give them pause, particularly when, instead of starting out with steps for them to do, he asked them to lie down on the floor, close their eyes, and "feel the music." Their apprehension quickly gave way to admiration, however, once they began to understand that Eddie wanted emotion to generate the movement he devised for them. His approach marked a welcome departure from the way movement was traditionally taught at the Joffrey, with its emphasis on counts ("step forward on one, move your head on two"), rather than on motivation. "Try to bring out a sense of urgency and longing in this step," he would explain, leaving it to the dancers to color the movement with the right emotional nuance. For the ballet's ensemble sequences, Eddie aimed to convey the turbulence of grief through the dancers' swirling, circular patterns and arched

---

*President Reagan's son, Ron, Jr., was a member of the Joffrey II Dancers from April 1980 through August 1982. He joined the Joffrey's main company, briefly, from August 1982 to January 1983.

arm and upper-body shapes. He had been influenced by the work of choreographer Jiří Kylián, the artistic director of the Netherlands Dance Theater, whose ballets were characterized by their fluent, whirling movements, high-speed ensemble crossings, and range of emotions.

Though Eddie was specific about the emotional qualities and steps he was after, he offered his dancers few clues about the subject matter of his ballet. He told them only that *Lacrymosa* was about separation and loss and asked them to discover in it a more personal meaning. "It seemed obvious to us that the lead male character was dying or leaving and that the woman was mourning his loss and reminiscing about the past," says dancer Joseph Brown, who met Eddie during the making of *Lacrymosa*.

By the time Eddie had finished setting the second movement, the ballet's themes had become apparent to all the dancers. Eddie positioned four men in a straight line facing into the wings and told them that they "represented time." He asked them to walk backward in an unbroken line, while Lissette Salgado wove through them trying to make her way to the other side. But each time she tried to break through the barrier of men, one of the men was to lift her high over his head and place her back behind the line. "We assumed he was trying to show that the woman was trying to return to the past," says Brown.

There was only one role in *Lacrymosa* that Eddie identified by name and that was the figure of Death. Eddie cast Adam Sklute in the role, an apt choice (though Eddie was never to know it), because Sklute suspected that Eddie was HIV-positive. Sklute had heard the rumor from another dancer and understood at once the deeper significance of both his role and the ballet.

"Eddie didn't want me to think of myself as Death," he recalls, "but more as a 'separating force.' But I found that idea confusing because Eddie never told me who I was separating from whom. Sometimes I took the man away, sometimes I took the woman away, and sometimes I comforted the woman, while at other times I comforted the man. I was very much a separate figure, but there were moments in the dance when I moved in and out among the cast, so I decided the point was that life goes on when someone dies, but that death is always hovering."

But Death was not to have the final word. Eddie intended to leave audiences feeling uplifted. "I want the last section to be happy," Eddie stressed to Jeremy Blanton, with whom he discussed his ideas for the ballet. "Eddie wanted to suggest a joyous celebration, the triumph over death," says Blanton.

Perhaps hoping to distance himself from *Lacrymosa* and mask the personal anguish it was meant to convey, Eddie began telling reporters that the ballet was made in response to Robert Joffrey's death. "Losing Mr. Joffrey has brought up a lot of emotions that I hadn't experienced before," he told *The Sun-Tattler* on his trip home to Florida, during an interview prearranged by his mother, not by the Joffrey's press office. "So I'm dedicating the ballet to Mr. Joffrey for all the inspiration he has given me."

Two years later, Eddie came closer to publicly revealing the ballet's source by telling *The Los Angeles Times* that *Lacrymosa* was his lament in a time of plague. "[*Lacrymosa*] came about," he said, "because I felt that young people these days are being confronted with issues concerning death, the loss of loved ones and friends, at an age when life is just beginning. It seems to be happening in the arts world, in the dance world, more than anywhere else. I wanted to bring some light and hope to my peers." Shortly before he died, Eddie would say, finally: "[*Lacrymosa*] paralleled all the pain I saw around me as everyone was dealing with Mr. Joffrey's death. It was a tribute, but also it was a lot about what I was going through at the time."

In the midst of his deepening obsession with *Lacrymosa d'Amore*, Eddie fell in love with Joseph Brown. Tall and boyish-looking with sandy brown hair and gray-blue eyes, Brown had a soft, sweet hometown-boy demeanor that contrasted sharply with Eddie's high-voltage style. Joe had, in fact, grown up in *very* small-town America, on a farm in a three-block town called Camas in Washington State. Several men in the company had noticed Joe before Eddie did and Eddie's infatuation did not escape their attention. "Joe was very cute," one of them recalls. "I remember overhearing Ashley Wheater say jokingly to Eddie, 'It figures you're the one who snatched him.'" Unlike Eddie, Joe had discovered dancing late, at the age of eighteen, and had none of the confidence that comes of being a child dancing star. By the time eighteen-year-old Eddie arrived at the Joffrey with his two international gold medals, Joe was twenty and still in the Joffrey School. The Joffrey students couldn't get over Eddie's phenomenal technique and after seeing Eddie perform, Joe understood why. But he had never found the opportunity to meet him until Eddie turned up to watch the Joffrey II dancers in class that spring, and cast Joe Brown in his first ballet.

Eddie liked Joe immediately, but thought it best to first establish his authority among all the dancers before pursuing a closer relationship with one of them. He relished his special status as choreographer and didn't want to let personal business mix with professional ambition. He focused on finishing *Lacrymosa*, which the dancers were not learning as quickly as he had hoped. Since both he and Lissette had a natural facility for picking up steps, Eddie had trouble understanding why the other dancers seemed to take longer to grasp the movement sequences he invented. There was one lift in particular that was proving especially difficult for Kyle Ahmed, who, while initially pleased that Eddie had cast him in his ballet, was beginning to regret the choice. "It was a one-count lift where you had to lift the girl under her shoulder blades and raise her over your head as she arched back slightly," he says. "It was very fast and I couldn't get it." One by one, the other male dancers got the hang of the lift, leaving only Kyle to master it. "Eddie got very frustrated with Kyle," remembers Joe Brown, who was then Kyle's good friend. "He said, 'I can't understand why you can't get this lift. I was doing it when I was a kid.'"

Despite his problems with Kyle, Eddie worked to create a collaborative atmosphere with the Joffrey II dancers. He knew that they considered themselves inferior to the dancers in the "main company," and he tried to encourage them to present themselves with all the aplomb they could muster. "Eddie made all the dancers

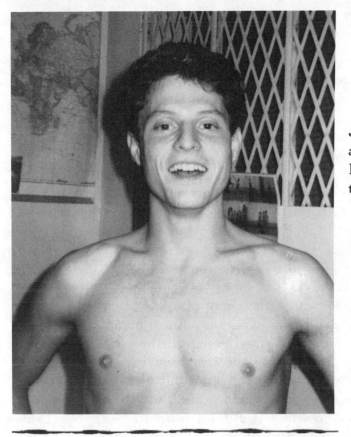

Joe Brown in the apartment he and Eddie shared. Eddie took the picture.

feel important," says Jeremy Blanton. "I've never met anyone who was more unselfish about giving of his art. Some dancers do tricks and don't want to tell anyone else how they do them. But if Eddie felt he could help them do a step better, he would show them how to do it."

Eddie waited until the Joffrey traveled to Los Angeles for its annual spring residency in May before deciding to ask Joe Brown out to dinner. "Kyle had told me that he thought Eddie had a crush on me," says Joe, "and I was flattered that he asked me out." When Kyle heard that Joe was planning to go on a date with Eddie, he warned him to be careful. "I've known Eddie for a while," he said, "and he might hurt you." Joe didn't understand Kyle's warning and assumed he was hinting that Eddie was much too focused on his career to have time for a relationship. But as Kyle would later explain, he didn't fully trust Eddie to tell Joe that he was HIV-positive because he knew that Eddie worried that he'd be rejected if he did. "Kyle was afraid that Eddie was just having a little fling with me and that if I did find out he was HIV-positive, I'd be freaked out," says Joe.

The day after he asked Joe out to dinner, Eddie picked him up in his rented car and took him to Chin Chin, a trendy Chinese restaurant in Santa Monica. Joe liked Eddie's "elflike looks." His reddish, sun-streaked hair was cut short on the sides and left long in the front so that it fell, coyly, into his eyes, and his face was tanned and freckled. Over dinner, they talked about their families and discovered they had a lot in common. Joe's father was a general contractor and, like Eddie, Joe had grown up in a large family of five children. He had not as yet "come out" to his parents either. Eddie told Joe about his family as well. "He tried to paint a picture of what it was like growing up with so many people in the house, with everyone coming and going all the time." Eventually the conversation moved on to their interest in each other. Joe confessed that he was stuck in a relationship that wasn't working and didn't know what to do about it. "Life is too short to go blindly through a relationship when you don't want to be there," Eddie told him. "I hadn't really looked at it that way," says Joe. "I was trying to make it work, just to make it work, no matter what."

After dinner, they strolled down Will Rogers Beach holding hands and talking. The next night, Eddie went to visit Joe at the house where he was staying and from then on, "we were inseparable," says Joe.

Eddie and Joe spent the remaining two weeks of the L.A. season together and by the time Joe returned to New York, he was convinced he was falling in love. But back in New York, he had another lover waiting at home for him and promptly ended that relationship. "Why don't you come and stay with me for a few days?" Eddie offered when Joe told him how strained things had become at home. He was naturally glad that Joe had ended his relationship and he liked the idea of having Joe come live with him for a while in the loft on Forty-seventh Street and Ninth Avenue that he shared with a waiter who worked for Glorious Foods, a tony catering company. It was so easy and relaxed between them and he was eager for more balance in his life. Never having been in a serious relationship, he was at a point where he wanted everything at once: He wanted more roles, he wanted a boyfriend, he wanted to be in love. Joe knew he couldn't stay on in his apartment and figured he'd stay with Eddie until he found a new place.

A few days later, he and Eddie were sitting in Eddie's living room when Eddie told him he had something important to tell him. "If it freaks you out in any way," he said calmly, "just know that you can walk away and I'll understand."

Then he told Joe that he was HIV-positive, his need for intimacy far outweighing his fear of rejection.

"I didn't really know what HIV-positive meant," says Joe. "I knew what AIDS was, but I didn't understand the difference between HIV and AIDS. So he explained it to me and I think he was really expecting me to leave. He was waiting for me to say, 'Oh, God, forget it.' But I wasn't shocked by it. We had been using condoms all along, and I told him I was more concerned about him and about what he was going to do."

Eddie talked late into the afternoon about how his HIV diagnosis had crystallized his sense of purpose and led him to filter out all the extraneous details of his life. Perhaps needing to see in it some divine plan, he told Joe that he regarded his diagnosis as a "blessing," for it had convinced him to stop trying to please everyone around him. Their relationship seemed to be getting serious, Eddie noted, and he didn't want to keep such an important part of himself from Joe. "I don't think I would have liked Eddie if I had met him just after he joined the company," says Brown. "But I met him after he'd been tested and after he'd done a lot of work on himself mentally. He was less aggressive and really wanted to balance out his life more."

Within a month of their first date, they were living together in the $1,500-a-month loft. "Doesn't this make you nervous? I mean, you've never lived with anyone before," Joe asked him one day as they were unpacking Joe's pots and pans. "I've never really stopped to think about it," Eddie replied. "I was scared at first and then got very comfortable," says Joe. "For Eddie it was the opposite." If the speed with which he and Joe set up housekeeping hardly fazed Eddie, it surprised his friends even less. "They met one day and the next day they were together," says Lissette. "That was Eddie—impulsive."

Eddie and Joe quickly settled into a domestic routine, and there was little that Joe found wanting in Eddie except in one area: his wardrobe. He tried to get Eddie to update his clothing, to replace the jogging suits and patterned polyester shirts that made him look like "a kid from 'The Brady Bunch.'" But it soon became apparent that in all other respects, Eddie set the pace. In the mornings, they would shower together before heading to City Center for a day of classes and rehearsals. Eight hours later, they'd meet in the lobby and walk home, sometimes stopping off at Westside Cottage for Chinese food. On most nights, however, Joe made dinner, after which he and Eddie played Scrabble before going to bed. Eddie usually won.

Then again, Eddie was always outdoing Joe in one way or another. While Joe preferred to relax at home or knit scarves and blankets on the bus during Joffrey II road trips, Eddie couldn't sit still, preferring instead to draft extensive lists, do the shopping, make phone calls, or reorganize his closets. And whereas Joe was quiet and indecisive, Eddie had strong opinions on everything from how hard Joe should work in class to the best dishes on the menu at Westside Cottage. "At the beginning, I was always trying to keep up," says Joe. "I thought, 'If I don't keep up, he won't want to be around me.'" But there was no way Joe could keep up, the discrepancy in their situations becoming only too apparent the minute they arrived each day at the Joffrey's studios. While Eddie, at twenty, was a star of the Joffrey's main company, Joe, at twenty-two, had yet to distinguish himself in the Joffrey's junior troupe. What's more, Eddie had already been invited to choreograph a ballet for the dancers of Joffrey II. Yet in the euphoria of their first months together, Eddie overlooked the things that separated him from Joe and delighted in showing off their new relationship to their friends. Joe remembers taking Eddie to meet a friend of his, who was "in the midst of a crisis" about whether or not he was gay, and recalls that Eddie "was all over me. He pulled me on his lap and started kissing my ear. I enjoyed it to a certain point, because I like being affectionate, but it was almost too much. It was as if Eddie was putting on a show."

Eddie took a similarly direct approach with Rosemarie. Just before Joe moved in, Eddie called to tell her that he had "found somebody he could share his life with," and that they were planning to live together. Over the previous few months, Eddie had called her to tell her about the latest man he had met, and always sounded exuberant. He seemed to be crazy about each one, she thought. Rosemarie wasn't so much surprised by Eddie's interest in Joe as she was by his hasty decision to live with him. "This is really fast, Eddie, how can you be so sure?" she asked. "I just *know*, Rosie, that's all," he said. "Joe cares about me and he likes to look after me. You should be happy I found someone." While Rosemarie didn't object to Eddie's choice on religious grounds, she was uncomfortable with the idea of Eddie settling into a serious relationship with a man, and particularly a man he hardly knew. She still hoped that he'd eventually get married and have a family and advised him to take his time.

But time was no longer his for the taking. He wanted a boyfriend and he wanted stability, and in Joe, he had both.

A few weeks later, Eddie and Joe visited Rosemarie in Atlantic City. Rosemarie pulled Eddie aside and told him that he and Joe couldn't spend the night in the same bedroom. Her in-laws were visiting at the time and she was uncomfortable about having to explain the situation to them. Adding to her concerns was the fact that Eddie was to occupy a bedroom that was being rented to a bass guitarist in her husband's band. She felt the guitarist would be angry if he knew that she allowed her brother and his boyfriend to stay in his bed while he was away. She tried to explain her position to Eddie, but to little avail. He felt that if she were truly accepting of him, she wouldn't care what the others thought. "She and Eddie had an argument about our sleeping together," recalls Joe, who went upstairs to let them talk. "It shed a new light on his sister for a while, because he felt she was tolerant of us, but not accepting."

Though realizing that the rest of his family was likely to be even less welcoming, Eddie insisted on telling his brothers and sisters about his relationship with Joe. In fact, the more resistant he suspected they might be, the more confrontational he became. "Would Joe and I be welcome in your home?" Eddie asked his sister Kathy shortly after she married and moved to a farming community outside Gainesville not known for its tolerant ways. (When busing went into effect in the local schools, the neighboring families got together and subsidized their own elementary school because they didn't want their children mixing with black children.) Kathy knew that Eddie was testing her when he asked if he could bring his boyfriend to visit and yet she felt her first loyalty was to her husband. "I knew he'd say, 'No, absolutely not,'" says Kathy, "and he did. We thought homosexuality was wrong. So I didn't invite Eddie. Instead I said, 'Well, I would really like for *you* to visit,' knowing that he wouldn't."

Terri was an even greater challenge: A by-the-Book Catholic and the most traditional member of the family, she disapproved of Eddie's sexual orientation and tried to remind him of his Catholic roots. (Though her brother Michael had served as a Marianist Brother and had earned his Ph.D. in Scripture, he took a broader view of Catholicism.) "Eddie had a take-it-or-leave-it, I-don't-care-what-you-think attitude about his sexuality at that point," says Rosemarie. "He had decided that this was right for him and if others didn't approve, well, too bad." Yet in openly declaring himself homosexual, he found he could no longer reconcile his differences with the Catholic Church. He knew the Church didn't accept him, so he, in turn, rejected the Church. "Eddie was very anti-organized Church when we first got together," says Joe. "He talked about how guilty the Catholic Church made him feel about being gay and how disappointed he was that the Church didn't allow everyone the chance to just be themselves."

Without the Church in his life, Eddie felt a spiritual void that he soon sought to fill. Unwilling to abandon his faith in a higher authority, he replaced his Catholic God with a nonjudgmental God.

He also began turning to New Age counselors like Louise Hay, whose books, *You Can Heal Your Life* and *The Power Within You*, and many cassette recordings encouraged followers to visualize their own good health. To Hay, who claims to have cured herself of cancer, the path to healing lay in loving and forgiving oneself. Having counseled many people with AIDS, she had arrived at the belief that by strengthening one's mental outlook, one could help heal the body of its physical ailments. More importantly, she placed the individual, and not some divine force, in control of his own destiny. "You are your own creative power and you can use your own power to help heal yourself," she tells the listener in her tape, "Self Healing." "Eddie was always reading some self-help book," says Tina LeBlanc. "He'd say, 'This is a great book, you've got to read it!' and I'd say, 'Another one, Eddie?'"

But the act of reading was solitary and Eddie thrived on interaction. He soon took at once to the relentlessly self-promoting Joyce Barrie, a stock broker–turned–motivational speaker and est graduate, who ran various workshops designed to help people overcome "the barriers to full self-expression." While it would seem that Eddie had already mastered the principles of Barrie's programs long before reaching New York, he somehow felt the need to pay $495 in the hopes of finding some higher truth in her "Humor Playshop," a weekend-long seminar. Participants were encouraged to lie on the floor and color with crayons, sing and dance in front of an audience, play charades, and stand up and talk about themselves. During the "sharing" portion of the weekend, Eddie introduced himself. He told the other twelve group members that he had been dancing since childhood and that he had managed to become a ballet dancer with the Joffrey Ballet when everyone said that he couldn't. "But last year a rock came crashing down on my head," he said. "I found out that I was HIV-positive."

It was the first time he had discussed his condition publicly, he told them. "I realized that I needed a support system. I want to keep myself healthy." Several people immediately volunteered to check up on him on a regular basis. One of them, a massage therapist and former dancer named Tina Awad, remembers thinking that Eddie had an "indestructible sense of himself." She couldn't get over how young and hopeful he was. "At first I thought, 'Is this just a big I'm-a-really-happy-guy routine?' But then I saw it was real. He had such inner radiance that it just poured out of him and you couldn't help but feel it. His message was, 'Look at the obstacles I've been able to overcome. There's no reason I can't beat this too.'"

Eddie unveiled *Lacrymosa d'Amore* at the Joffrey II Choreographers' Workshop that June. As Robert Joffrey had, Eddie sent the dancers a letter wishing them luck in their performance, but *his* was filled with the lingo he had recently acquired.

Dear Joffrey II,

I wanted to take this opportunity to thank each and every one of you for so many things. Firstly, thank you for taking the risk of this project with me and playing 110 percent. Secondly, thank you for walking across that rope last night and never once considering the safe "net" that could catch you. That "net" being that you're only "Joffrey II." Last night was not about being youth training for the *"main company."* It was about *being the main company!* You all were *"the"* main company last night and you have gained such great respect from each and every individual that was in that present moment. My only wish is that each of you continue to make your pictures of your capabilities better and better. You all are so special and continue to express that through your work and in your lives. We are always continuing to learn about our art, but more importantly we are always continuing to learn about our lives. So, promise me that no matter what lesson is thrown to each of you in your lives, you will learn and grow from it because those lessons can only come through in our work. I love you all and thank you for your patience, willingness, and hard work. Live and Learn from Now!

Eddie's ballet was one of three performed by Joffrey II for an audience of company supporters and friends in a studio at City Center. Veteran Joffrey dancers Carole Valleskey and Carl Corry also presented works, but it was "Eddie's ballet" that was "getting all the hype," remembers Brent Phillips. Then again, *Lacrymosa* "said something to everyone," explains Joffrey II's associate director Jeremy Blanton. "You either got heavily into its meaning or you saw it as beautiful, joyous movement. I don't know anyone who wasn't moved by it."

To Eddie, the showing couldn't have come at a worse time. He was privately hoping that his ballet would be taken into the Joffrey's repertoire and he wanted Gerald Arpino to have a look at his "first plantings," as Arpino would later call Eddie's earliest efforts. He wanted to show him what he could do. But the Joffrey was then on a layoff and Arpino was in Vienna. Determined to get a proper showcase for *Lacrymosa*, Eddie decided to arrange his own preview when the company resumed its tour in San Francisco a few weeks later.

En route to San Francisco, Eddie and Joe made a weekend detour to Ridgefield, Washington, to visit Joe's parents, but since Joe hadn't come out to them, he presented Eddie as a friend from the Joffrey. Joe's parents lived on a houseboat near the Columbia River, though not even the deer and blue herons roaming the wildlife preserve on the nearby embankment succeeded in distracting Eddie from *Lacrymosa*. On his first night on the boat, he awoke crying from a disturbing, sadly prophetic dream. "I saw myself lying in a coffin, dressed in a suit," he sobbed to Joe. "I was planning my own funeral." The line between life and art was momentarily obscured. "Eddie was trying to cope with the idea of dying and he was still afraid of it," says Joe. "*Lacrymosa* was the outlet for all his fear."

Joe could well understand his fears. He had been putting off the decision to get an AIDS test because he knew he wasn't ready to deal with the very issues Eddie was then facing. Eddie may have put on a brave face, but Joe saw how nervous he became before his checkups with Dr. Oppenheimer and had even offered to go along with him. At the doctor's office, he weighed the pros and cons of getting a test, and always came up with the same answer. As far as he knew, none of his previous lovers "were positive" and he and Eddie had been practicing "safer sex."* They weren't using condoms for oral sex, but most of the gay men he knew didn't either; he had heard that the likelihood of HIV infection from oral sex was slight as long as there was no exchange of body fluids. He figured testing could wait.

In the meantime, Joe joined the other Joffrey II dancers onstage at the War Memorial Opera House in San Francisco that month in a reprise of *Lacrymosa d'Amore* for the "main company." The ballet was dedicated to Robert Joffrey, "in memory of his everlasting vision," read the program note. Both its craft and depth took many in the audience by surprise. "The moment that Jerry and I saw Edward's work, we felt it was obvious he had a special gift," remembers Scott Barnard. "Both emotionally and structurally, it was very advanced for a first work," explains Millicent Hodson, who had just flown into San Francisco for the local premiere of *Le Sacre du Printemps*. Eddie was particularly anxious to have Hodson's encouragement and pressed her for feedback. "I was struck by the extreme motion and sudden stopping of the movement and the reverential visions of Lissette in Madonna poses," she told him. Even Val Caniparoli, the thirty-six-year-old resident choreographer of the San Francisco Ballet, and thirty-three-year-old James Kudelka, an internationally acclaimed choreographer whom *The New York Times* that year called "the most fertile mind in ballet," had to admit the kid showed promise. Afterward, Caniparoli took Eddie out for a coffee to discuss his work. "James and I were both impressed by how confident and well crafted it was," Caniparoli told Eddie, who was buoyed by the enthusiastic response to his first effort, especially one so personal.

The ballet also drew Gerald Arpino's attention to Lissette Salgado. While both he and Robert Joffrey had already glimpsed

---

*For "the safest sex," New York's Gay Men's Health Crisis advises the use of latex condoms for anal, vaginal, and oral sex and recommends against the exchange of blood, semen, vaginal, or cervical secretions and the use of recreational drugs and alcohol. However, personal definitions of "safe sex" vary. AIDS educators say that there are documented cases of HIV infection from oral sex; however, others say that condoms may not be necessary for oral sex if semen or blood is not exchanged.

Joe and Eddie visiting Joe's parents in Washington state

a special quality in Lissette, Arpino was struck by the newfound richness in her dancing that Eddie's ballet seemed to have brought alive. The following month, Arpino decided Lissette was ready for a promotion, and invited her to join the senior company. At the same time, Eddie learned that *Lacrymosa* had been accepted into the repertoire of the Joffrey II Dancers, the company's junior troupe. Its premiere was scheduled for October 14 in Aurora, Illinois.

Dancing the role of the Young Man in *Cotillon*

16

SELF-HELP

His career as a choreographer now set in motion, Eddie next cast his eye toward the roles that still eluded him. By the fall of 1988, he had an impressively diverse roster: His leading roles included Puck in *The Dream*; Fritz, the Snow Prince, and Tea from China in *The Nutcracker*; the Cavalier in *La Vivandière Pas de Six*; and the Cowboy in Red in Eugene Loring's 1938 American classic, *Billy the Kid*. He was also dancing important supporting roles, among them the Groom in *Petrouchka* and the Chinese Conjurer in *Parade*. Both *Petrouchka* and *Parade* were masterpieces from the Diaghilev era. The story of a puppet with a human heart, *Petrouchka* was first performed in 1911 and featured choreography by Michel Fokine, music by Stravinsky, and decor by Alexandre Benois. *Parade*, too, boasted a remarkable team of artistic collaborators, with a libretto by Jean Cocteau, music by Erik Satie, sets and costumes by Picasso,* and choreography by Léonide Massine, who danced the role of the Chinese Conjurer. It was also Massine who succeeded Nijinsky as chief choreographer of the Ballets Russes and, not incidentally, as Diaghilev's lover. Later that fall, Eddie would add one more starring role to his repertoire: that of the Young Man in *Cotillon*, yet another ballet retrieved from the past. Balanchine's "lost" ballet about a young woman's first coming-out ball, *Cotillon* was to be the centerpiece of the upcoming Robert

---

*With *Parade*, Picasso made his theatrical debut.

Joffrey Memorial Season at City Center that November and was considered among Balanchine's most sublime early pieces in its evocations of lost innocence and bittersweet romanticism. The ballet was made in 1932 for the Ballets Russes de Monte Carlo and remained in its repertory until 1946, when it literally disappeared from view—until Millicent Hodson and Kenneth Archer, the team that re-created *Le Sacre du Printemps*, set about assembling its missing pieces. The excavation took them to five different countries and through three generations of dancers who had performed in the ballet. It had been their success in reconstructing Nijinsky's *Sacre* that had convinced Robert Joffrey that the pair should next tackle *Cotillon*, a revival he never lived to see.

Tina LeBlanc was cast in the starring role of the Young Girl, and Eddie was cast as her escort, who, in one of the ballet's most fanciful moments, imagines himself a jockey riding to victory on a racehorse. In Eddie's view, the Young Man, like all of his roles, drew primarily on his bravura strengths and technical feats, while he now longed to demonstrate "that there was more inside of him, that he wasn't this hollow trickster," says Joe Brown. His agenda not only included dramatic roles such as Petrouchka, but the princely roles for which he was not physically suited. He refused to allow his body type to limit him, even though he knew that casting in ballet was determined primarily on that basis. But Eddie didn't define himself as a *demi-caractère* dancer the way everyone else did. As he saw it, he was a *danseur noble* trapped inside the body of a *demi-caractère* dancer. Indeed, he hadn't abandoned the hope that he would one day join American Ballet Theatre and dance the classics. "See you at ABT," he had informed Parrish Maynard, shortly before Maynard decamped for Ballet Theatre following the Joffrey's San Francisco engagement in August. "Once I'm done here, I'm going to come over."

While he had proven in *La Vivandière* that he could transform himself into the very picture of academic excellence, Eddie was the only male in *Vivandière* and the ballet demanded technical perfection, not a tall, princely presence, to achieve its full effect. Eddie constantly worked to pull long lines out of his body, to lengthen his stocky thighs and improve the arch in his foot, in the hope that

Arpino and Barnard would reward him with the two roles they knew he desperately wanted to dance: the Sugar Plum Fairy's Cavalier, which he had danced at the School of the Arts, and the lead male in Arpino's *L'Air d'Esprit*. But neither role would be his, for both required tall dancers with better ballet proportions. A celebration of Romantic ballet, *L'Air d'Esprit* involved intricate airborne partnering and was made "with the idea of the girl being high in the air and flying," says Scott Barnard, who was surprised to hear Eddie tell him that he was holding out for the role. "You can only push a body like his so far," he explains, "but he would ask to do some of the most *ungodly* roles. He had reached a point in his career where he felt he had the clout to start advancing the idea that he could do the lead male roles, not the *demi-caractère* roles."

Discouraged by Barnard, Eddie went directly to Arpino to ask for a crack at his *L'Air d'Esprit*. "I said, 'I don't know, you're not physically right for it,'" recalls Arpino, "and Eddie said, 'Let me show you, let me try.' When Scott heard that Eddie was proposing himself for the ballet, he said, 'Edward doesn't do the casting here.'"

As Arpino had become preoccupied with assuming his new duties as artistic director, Scott Barnard had become much more powerful: He now did virtually all the casting and oversaw most rehearsals in addition to his day-to-day management of the repertoire and dancers as the company's associate artistic director. His day usually began with company class, which he oversaw with an iron hand. It was in morning class, he felt, that the dancers not only tuned their bodies, but learned the art of discipline: "Discipline," he would say, "is learning a step and doing it even when the body doesn't feel like doing it." He expected the dancers to execute each step with the kind of academic precision he demanded and rarely suffered disruptions lightly. Eddie, however, frequently disregarded Barnard's rules without giving thought to the possible repercussions. The moment of reckoning finally came during morning class in Los Angeles at the Dorothy Chandler Pavilion. Barnard had interrupted class one morning to demonstrate a movement combination when he noticed Eddie chatting with Ashley Wheater at the barre.

Scott Barnard teaching company class at the Herod Atticus Theatre in Athens, the setting that inspired Eddie's *Empyrean Dances*

"Edward, if you'll demonstrate the combination to the company, please."

Eddie's back stiffened at once. He knew he'd been caught.

"I don't know it," replied Eddie.

"I just did it," insisted Barnard.

"I don't know it. I was talking."

"Then get out of my class," snapped Barnard.

"This is my time, Scott. I need to jump tonight."

Eddie was dancing *La Vivandière* that night and depended on morning class to loosen his muscles for the evening performance.

"Get out!" repeated Barnard, his face flushed with anger.

Eddie picked up his dance bag and stalked out of the room, as the other dancers looked on in astonishment. No one tested Barnard's authority. "We couldn't believe it," recalls Brent Phillips, who was standing next to Eddie. "It seemed as if Scott was saying,

'This boy is getting too much power. I need to teach him that he isn't everything to the Joffrey.'"

Eddie was angry and embarrassed. He hated losing ground to Scott this way, and he was convinced that Scott was giving him a deliberate dressing-down in front of the company. Suddenly, he seemed to have lost his diplomatic immunity at the Joffrey.

In his sixteen years of teaching, Barnard had never thrown a dancer out of class and his act mortified him as much as it did Eddie. "After Bob [Joffrey] died, I became more demanding than ever, because I was determined that his legacy was not going to falter," he says. "I thought if we faltered in the first couple of years, we would never get it back. All through that period of time, class was so valuable that I would never have thrown anyone out of class. Edward was the only one who ever provoked me to that point."

What particularly irked Eddie about Barnard was the way he treated the dancers like children and insisted on teaching class "by-the-numbers and breaking everything down," says a Joffrey dancer.

"Eddie felt my kind of discipline numbed the artist in one," acknowledges Barnard. "And in class he had a tendency to talk over me while I was explaining something. I had warned him several times. I said, 'Edward, if you're going to take my class, it's my class, try to get out of it what I'm trying to teach you.' But Edward was like a kid. You had to slap him on the back of the hand and say, 'No.' So finally there came the day when I told him to get out of my class. He flew out of the room. He was very angry. Afterward, he came to my dressing room in tears. 'You didn't need to throw me out,' he said. And I said, 'Edward, let me just tell you something: If you ever do it again, I will throw you out again. You can cry, you can carry on, you can act any way you want to in front of me, but if you don't have manners in my class, you will be thrown out.' He thought about it for a minute and then said, 'Do you really think that kind of training is necessary?' And I said, 'Edward, it's training you haven't learned and it's going to hold you back.' He took offense that I was slowing down the class for him mentally by helping someone who didn't have his facility. I said, 'Edward, if you don't trust and see the vision here, you shouldn't be here.'"

Scott won the round, but Eddie "unnerved" him, just the same. By the fall of 1988, they were regarding each other warily. "Eddie questioned *everything*," says Barnard. "There wasn't a stone left unturned."

Given his turbulent relationship with Barnard, Eddie felt much more at ease in class when it was led by the Joffrey's new ballet mistress, Barbara Forbes, a soft-spoken teacher, who had an entirely different impression of Eddie. "Eddie seemed to me to be this energetic sponge. I don't think he expected things from his teachers. He seemed to have this reciprocal feeling that we could help each other. It was if he was saying, 'I have this talent—it's so exciting; how far can we go together?'"

The closer Eddie moved toward his ambitions, the further he moved away from Joe. Where Eddie was making ballets, planning new ones, and pushing for roles, Joe preferred to sit and wait for opportunities he felt would come to him in due course. To Eddie, Joe's "wait and see" approach suggested a lack of ambition and he hoped that with proper encouragement, he could bridge the gap between them. He was still in love with Joe and didn't want to leave him behind. To that end, he tried to help him become more aggressive. When Joe would leave it to him to choose a movie, Eddie would retort, "Don't say you don't care which movie we see. Make decisions." In class together at David Howard's studio during company layoffs, Eddie would praise Joe's improvement and offer tips on technique. But well-meaning as it was, his strategy was bound to fail because it only succeeded in making Joe feel inferior. Brent Phillips remembers finding Joe "in tears because Eddie was mean to him. Eddie would say, 'If you want to get into the Joffrey, you have to do this and that better.' Joe was so nice. I felt a little badly for him. Not everybody had 'Eddie's kind of talent."

As Joe saw it, Eddie's criticisms were unfounded. He felt that his approach was no less valid than Eddie's. "Our ideas of 'drive' were different," he says. "I wasn't the kind of person who's always pushing for the things I want. But Eddie looked at me as being weaker." Eddie began to get irritated with what he saw as Joe's complacency. Didn't he realize that he had to go after the things he wanted? he would demand of Joe. "I was afraid of taking the big steps," Joe remembers. When Eddie would mention a celebrated dancer whom Joe didn't know, Eddie would upbraid him: "You should know who these people are."

Lissette Salgado, who would soon come to regard Eddie as her own Svengali, believes in retrospect that Eddie didn't know how to let those he loved be themselves if he saw how he could improve them. And yet his life with Joe gave him the stability he needed and he hoped it could work out between them. "Eddie wanted Joe to be more like him," says Lissette. "And Joe tried to please him because he loved him." But the more Joe tried to please, the more Eddie became convinced that Joe—like his mother—gave so much more to him than he would ever be able to give in return.

Convinced that he had a problem with accepting Joe's love, Eddie was soon back in one of Joyce Barrie's workshops, this time a one-day $175 course entitled "Relationships: Play to Win!" Barrie asked her participants to write letters to someone they cared about, acknowledging sentiments they felt could not go unsaid. In the letter he mailed to Joe in August, four months after their first date, Eddie struggled to clarify his inchoate feelings.

That fall, after passing by a jewelry store near City Center on his way home from rehearsal, Eddie proposed to Joe that they exchange gold rings. Their relationship was then in its sunniest phase and Eddie wanted to give Joe a symbol of his commitment. Since he was then making $890 a week to Joe's weekly salary of $200, he offered to pay for both 18K-gold bands with the understanding that Joe would pay him back in installments. "It's like we're married," Eddie declared happily to Joffrey dancer Cynthia Giannini as he showed her his gold band one day. "I feel like Joe and I could live together forever." Eddie even described his domestic bliss to Eric Castellano, his Costa Mesa boyfriend. "I've been seeing someone for some time now and we are living together," he wrote to Eric in June. "It has been absolutely perfect."

Five months into their relationship, Joe had yet to meet Rose Stierle, but already she had made her presence felt through the packages she regularly sent Eddie. He would only have to sniffle on the phone and a supply of cold medicine would arrive in the post; a glowing review of Eddie had only to run in a newspaper somewhere and Rose would find it and send it, plastic-coated, for Eddie's personal scrapbook.

Eddie had put off the inevitable phone call to his parents, but with the Joffrey II Dancers' premiere of *Lacrymosa d'Amore* approaching in October and his parents due to show up for it, he decided he ought to give them some advance warning. "My friend Joe is living with me, Mom," he told Rose over the phone. "I can't wait for you to meet him. He's really nice." Rose said little and telephoned Rosemarie for a reading.

"Eddie is serious about a guy and I'm not happy," she told her daughter.

"He's trying to find out what's right for him," Rosemarie explained. "Give him time."

Lacrymosa was to have its premiere at the Paramount Arts Centre, a small theater in Aurora, Illinois, on the outskirts of Chicago. Rose and Bill flew in for opening night and Eddie assumed they'd be staying on for a day to spend time with him. (While they had scrimped for years to feed their family, they no longer had any children at home, so the extra money now went into plane tickets.) But the moment they arrived, they announced they were leaving early the next morning to visit their son Bill in Kansas City. "I guess it's because of Joe that you're not staying," Eddie said.

"Oh, no," Rose protested. "We're so close to Kansas, we couldn't come all the way here and not stop off to see him." At dinner following the performance, Rose and Bill had few opportunities to speak to Joe, because Liana Navarro had also flown up from Florida to see "Lissette dance in Eddie's ballet" and had brought ten of her students with her. That night, they all stayed in the same hotel, where Rose and Bill were given a room directly below the room Eddie shared with Joe. "I felt so terrible all night," remembers Rose Stierle. "I kept thinking, 'Maybe this will pass.'" Unlike his wife, Bill Stierle didn't go in for wishful thinking: "I was unhappy that Eddie was choosing that direction," he remembers, "and I was uncomfortable about it, but I felt it was his business."

Approve or not, Rose was not going to cut herself off from her son while waiting for "it" to pass. Any break with Eddie was inconceivable to her. "Eddie told me that his mother lived for him," says Joe, "and that even if she didn't accept us, she would pretend that she did."

Two weeks after her trip to Aurora, Illinois, Rose flew to New York for the opening night of the Robert Joffrey Memorial Season, bringing her daughter Kathy's mother-in-law with her. Eddie invited them to stay with him and Joe, but Rose demurred. She had managed to get a great deal on a room at the Sheraton, she said, and she wanted to enjoy the luxury of a hotel. Eddie dismissed her rationale at once. "I know you're really uncomfortable with Joe," Eddie said quietly. Rose hoped to sidestep the discussion. "I'm really more uncomfortable about *her* being with me," she said evasively, nonetheless making it clear that she was not about to invite her in-law to spend a weekend with her gay son and his lover. But she did stop by their apartment on her own, long enough, in fact, to leave her mark. Not only did she clean the kitchen, but she completely rearranged Joe's cooking utensils, organizing them in the fashion she found most handy. Over Chinese food with Eddie and Joe at Westside Cottage the night following the gala, Rose appeared distracted. Eddie felt she wasn't listening to anything they said. "She was lovey-dovey to me," says Joe, "but it didn't seem genuine." Back in their apartment that night, Eddie confessed his disappointment to Joe. He saw that his mother was uncomfortable. She had been affectionate with Joe only to please Eddie, not because she supported their relationship.

Years later, she still refused to see what Eddie had tried to show her: that his life with Joe had brought him some happiness. "The one thing that turned against Eddie," she would insist, "was the fact that he really liked men."

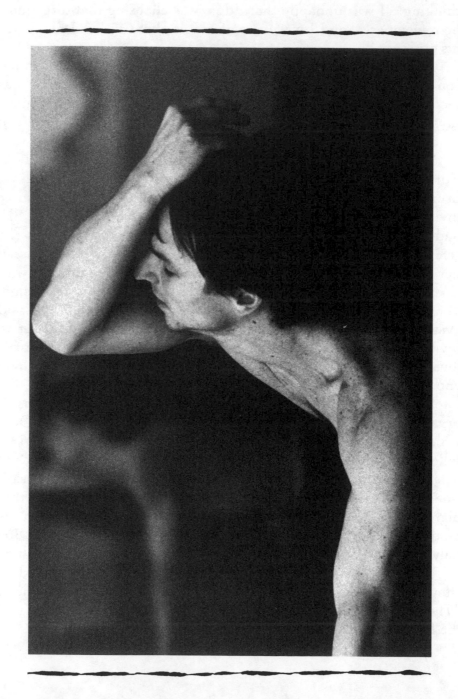

17

ENDLESS SIREN

The Robert Joffrey Memorial Season marked another turning point in Eddie's career. In role after role, he continued to outpace himself, the knowledge of his infection having introduced a new momentum to his dancing. He had begun to approach his roles by drawing on his own experience and outlook, which came to combine the insouciance of youth with the sobering maturity that accompanied the acceptance of his mortality. "I want to express something about life, about how I'm feeling," he told a reporter. "If you can convey something about your life across the proscenium, then ultimately you're going to reach people."

And reach people he did, impressing everyone from first-time ballet-goers like Eric Castellano to veteran dance observers like Anna Kisselgoff of *The New York Times* and Laurie Horn of *The Miami Herald*. "Twin Pleasures: Cotillon and Stierle," ran the headline on Horn's review of the Joffrey's 1988 New York season. Horn had watched Eddie "bouncing, rebounding, and luxuriating in three roles in a marathon evening's program" that featured *The Dream*, *La Vivandière*, and *Cotillon*. "Such versatility—not to mention stamina—is a marvel." Kisselgoff, too, was struck by Eddie's remarkable powers of transformation. During the Joffrey's City Center engagement, she singled out Eddie and Tina LeBlanc for special mention. "Suddenly the Joffrey—more than other American companies—is blessed with dancers of brilliant technique and great individuality—namely Mr. Stierle and Miss LeBlanc." In her annual "Best-of-the-Season" roundup that year, Kisselgoff called Eddie one of the country's finest dancers, one who "made a breakthrough with his virtuosity and depth." She went on to say:

> Mr. Stierle, stocky and exuberant, is a *demi-caractère* dancer by type, but through inexorable discipline he can assume the nobility that makes his dancing in *La Vivandière* so classical and pure. His versatility is a given, but the quality of his movement in each role is amazingly varied. [His] Puck . . . brought out Frederick Ashton's wit with bravura and drama; he was inimitable as the dashing young man in *Cotillon*, his energy shaping the mix of classical and character styles so difficult to grasp today. We see Mr. Stierle transformed in every role, magnificent in each.

Eddie also made *The Los Angeles Herald Examiner*'s list of the year's Top Ten dance events, his star turns as Puck in *The Dream* and as Fritz and the Snow Prince in *The Nutcracker* singled out for special mention. As 1988 drew to a close, Eddie made a breakthrough on another front: His brother Tom finally asked him for a ticket to see him dance. On his way to visit Rosemarie in Atlantic City, Tom made a special detour to New York to catch Eddie's performance in *The Nutcracker*. Sitting in the balcony at City Center during a Saturday matinee, he watched his younger brother take over the family Christmas party onstage in his role as Fritz, the bratty younger brother of little Clara, whose Nutcracker doll he breaks in a fit of jealousy. Eddie's portrayal, *The New York Times* would observe that season, seemed "a distillation of childhood emotions." Following a quick costume change, Eddie became the Snow Prince, and Tom watched, spellbound, as Eddie flew through high-velocity turns and jumps, his body spinning in the midst of a winter storm. It was not only the first time Tom had seen Eddie dance since his days with Razz Ma Jazz. But his first glimpse of a professional dance company, and he couldn't get over the "athletic talent" of the dancers. It had simply never occurred to him that dancers and basketball players could have "so much in common."

Afterward, he and Eddie walked down Broadway toward Eddie's Forty-seventh Street apartment and stopped in for tea at the Howard Johnson off Times Square. "Eddie wanted to get on a better track with me," recalls Tom. "He had started calling me a few months before to ask for financial advice." Unlikely as it was for a twenty-year-old dancer, Eddie was planning to buy a co-op in Manhattan and had been consulting Tom and Rosemarie about how to go about it. Just as he had for his parents, Tom drew up financial plans and budgeting projections for Eddie. Tom figured that with the money left over from Eddie's earnings as a child model, and the thousands of dollars he had managed to save from his paycheck, Eddie could put $20,000 toward a down payment. Tom also helped Eddie negotiate with the Joffrey for a better contract. Although only in his third year, Eddie had argued persuasively that since he was dancing so many leading roles, his workload and stature were more commensurate with those of dancers in their sixth year with the company. By January of 1989, Eddie was making $908 a week for a forty-week season (or $36,320 annually), a sixth-year dancer's salary.

It had taken months, but gradually, Eddie and Tom had discovered a comfortable meeting ground on which to build a friendship. As they sat talking in Howard Johnson, Eddie now steered their conversation from finance to family ties. "He told me that he resented me when we were growing up because of all the attention I got at the dinner table," says Tom. "He said he hated going to my basketball games and didn't understand why I tried to force him to work with me on the house. I told him I was frustrated at not being able to connect and build a relationship. It was the first time we'd ever talked about these things."

Emboldened by their frank discussion, Eddie went a step further. He asked Tom how things were going with his girlfriend and when Tom complained that she seemed "passive," Eddie seized the opportunity to draw Joe's name into the conversation. "She sounds a lot like my boyfriend," Eddie said. Tom didn't want to hear about Eddie's boyfriend, but decided not to cut him off. "I wouldn't have asked about Joe," says Tom. "I thought the relationship was ridiculous and would have preferred to ignore it. I wasn't interested in discussing that part of Eddie's life."

Yet it was precisely that part of Eddie's life that was giving Eddie the support he most needed. Joe was still one of a handful of people who knew about Eddie's medical condition, and the fact that he treated it as just another component of their relationship helped Eddie to get on with the business of living, even in the face of death. The dailiness of their domestic routine gave Eddie a sense of permanence and calm, and a brief respite from the enormity of the issues confronting him.

In January 1989, he and Joe finally settled into the apartment that Eddie had spent months looking for: the duplex penthouse of a seven-story building on West Thirty-fifth Street between Fifth and Sixth avenues. The $120,000 co-op was a stone's throw from Macy's and had a brick-walled living room, a small kitchen, and a winding staircase leading to a second-floor bedroom with a skylight. It was the skylight and the large terrace just off the bedroom that had most appealed to Eddie, and soon after moving in they made plans to put down a deck and build closets and shelves, his father's construction tenets stamped indelibly on Eddie's memory. They also took on a roommate to help them pay the mortgage, a young pianist with the Metropolitan Opera named Kamal, who didn't mind sleeping on the pullout sofa in the living room. Eddie saw that he could benefit from Kamal's expertise and quickly enlisted him as his personal music teacher. Before long, Eddie was able to read and count complex musical scores.

That same month, Joe accompanied Eddie to his checkup with John Oppenheimer, the doctor's visits having become an integral part of their life together. They were barely out of their teens and just approaching their prime as dancers, yet their routine of doctor's visits, with its heightened focus on staving off imminent death, resembled that of the geriatric couples who lived out their days in the Miami Beach condos of Eddie's youth.

Dr. Oppenheimer did not have good news. Eddie's T-cell count had taken a precipitous dive from 451 of the previous June to 285 in September and now further still, to 153. Though Eddie was still asymptomatic, his counts announced the probable arrival of AIDS-related illnesses, the forerunners to full-blown AIDS. The permanence Eddie so eagerly sought seemed to be slipping away from him faster than he could have imagined; he told the doctor he no longer wanted to know his counts. "Eddie began to get very anxious about getting the results," says Dr. Oppenheimer. "From then on, we had an understanding that if it wasn't going to change what we were going to do, he really didn't want to know. He was just going on an emotional roller coaster."

By then, he was using an aerosol pentamidine inhaler every other week to reduce the risk of PCP. He had also started on dextran sulphate, an experimental drug thought to inhibit the HIV virus, though later studies revealed that it was not effective. Dextran sulphate had not won FDA approval (in fact, it was never approved) and could be obtained only from contacts in the AIDS underground. During Eddie's visit, Dr. Oppenheimer did a skin test with antigens to further measure the strength of his immune system. When injected into people with healthy immune systems, the antigens produced swelling; when injected into Eddie, there was barely any swelling at all.

Eddie's was hardly an isolated case. At the time of his HIV diagnosis in May of 1987, 31,405 people had died of AIDS since the beginning of the epidemic. In early January 1989, only a year and a half later, 28,019 additional AIDS deaths were reported to the Centers for Disease Control, almost the same number as the total for the first six years of the AIDS crisis. Between Eddie's January 1989 visit to Dr. Oppenheimer and June of 1989, 19,268 more people in the United States would learn that they were carrying the AIDS virus.

With Eddie's immune system in such a potentially precarious state, Dr. Oppenheimer put him on AZT, a highly toxic drug that in some studies had been proven capable of delaying the onset of symptoms. "I told him that there wasn't anything that was proven to work, but that there was evidence that something *might* work," says Dr. Oppenheimer. "I tried to be encouraging." Eddie had put off taking AZT because one of its many possible side effects was muscle weakness, a setback he could ill afford. But now the full weight of his situation fell over him and he saw that he had little choice but to try any therapy that would give him more time.

To fortify himself against a downward spiral, Eddie was to take two capsules every four hours, then the standard dose. He would have to get up at evenly spaced intervals during the night, waking to his alarm clock to take his medication.* The night Eddie was to begin taking AZT, Joe was out of town with the Joffrey II, so Eddie waited until after Joe's performance to call him. He wanted to hear his voice when he swallowed his first pill, a pill that might make reaching thirty a plausible hope. He hated taking the drug because, in his mind, it meant that he already had AIDS. He couldn't see it as a therapy against AIDS; to him, it was the disease itself.

---

*Doctors no longer recommend that their HIV patients wake up in the middle of the night to take AZT.

18

RITES OF PASSAGE

An assignment from the North Carolina School of the Arts put his thoughts of mortality temporarily on hold. One week before his twenty-first birthday, Eddie flew to Winston-Salem to put the final touches on a new ballet he had choreographed for the school's Winter Concert. In a departure from *Lacrymosa*, his *Concerto con Brio*, an ensemble piece for fourteen dancers to music by Prokofiev, was lively and energetic and fueled by the driving force that infused his own dancing. During his visit, he caught up with his former teachers Duncan Noble and Melissa Hayden and spent time with his sister Patty, who had driven from South Carolina to see him, just as she had when Eddie was enrolled at the school. Patty had just earned her nursing degree from the University of South Carolina, "the first Stierle girl to graduate college," she would proudly point out, and she was working in the critical care unit of a hospital in Columbia, South Carolina. As part of her training, she had to study a specific health issue and Patty had chosen sexually transmitted diseases. Though it hadn't touched anyone she knew, AIDS piqued her interest because so little was known about it. When she spoke to Eddie on the phone, she would bring him up to date on her research and remind him to use condoms, unaware that he was already HIV-positive. In the critical care unit, she began caring for people with AIDS and had seen firsthand the way AIDS patients were often deserted by their families and stigmatized by the disease. She made sure to use gloves only when necessary so as not to deny patients the reassuring feel of human touch.

As her visit with Eddie drew near, she thought about how much she was looking forward to escaping from the pressing concerns of the hospital into his world, the world of the arts. She hoped she could have time alone with him without interruption from their mother. But when Patty announced her plans to spend Eddie's twenty-first birthday with him at the school, Rose Stierle decided she would come up for the premiere of Eddie's new ballet.

After the performance, the school threw a birthday party for Eddie in the lobby of the Stevens Center. "Eddie wanted to go off with me and a few of his friends after the party and he didn't want my mom to come along," recalls Patty. "But my mom really wanted to come. I liked being recognized as Eddie's sister, but that wasn't my whole goal in life. I didn't want to be a focal point, because it was my brother's time to shine. Whereas my mom wanted to be a big, big part of his world. She wanted to share in his glory."

Two weeks after Eddie celebrated his twenty-first birthday, Joe turned twenty-three on St. Patrick's Day and decided that he was ready to get his first AIDS test. But was it such a good idea? Eddie asked him. "If you're positive, you might blame me, and if you're negative, then you may want to end our relationship or be afraid to take any chances with your life." Joe ignored Eddie's warnings and went ahead and had his blood drawn. When he went back to learn his test results, it was Eddie who now accompanied him to Dr. Oppenheimer's office.

As the doctor sifted through the papers on his desk, Eddie took Joe's hand and squeezed it tightly.

Joe was HIV-positive, the doctor told them.

Eddie tightened his grip and looked at Joe. "I'm so sorry," he whispered, half expecting Joe to break down or show signs of going into shock. Joe, however, appeared to take the news calmly. He felt numb and suddenly found himself thinking about how unreal the whole moment seemed.

Eddie, meanwhile, felt "so guilty about Joe's diagnosis," as he would later confide to Lissette, even though Joe himself wasn't pointing any fingers. While Joe could not have known when he had first been exposed to the virus, he preferred to believe that he had been infected by Eddie. "Eddie didn't understand why I hoped I got it from him," he says, explaining the rationale that allowed him to cope with his diagnosis. "Since my immune system was in good shape, I figured that if the infection had been recent, it meant that I'd have that much more time."

How much time did he think he had? "I have several friends who are HIV-positive," he said, three years after his diagnosis, "and most of us accept the fact that we probably won't see thirty."

19

BEING POSITIVE

In March 1989, one year after the death of its founder and namesake, the Joffrey Ballet was back in Chicago, the very city where the company had been performing the day Robert Joffrey died. Nineteen-year-old Lissette Salgado was among the company's newest recruits, and on her first tour, Eddie invited her to be his roommate. Of Eddie's handful of close friends, Lissette was the only one who didn't know about his HIV status and while he'd considered telling her when they were working on *Lacrymosa*, he figured she probably wouldn't be able to handle it. "She's such a baby, she'll freak out," he told Joe. But now that they were spending every day together in Chicago, the burden of keeping his secret was sapping his energy. He no longer wanted to coast along, smiling at her, the way he did at everyone else, as if to say life couldn't be better. Besides, she would notice his pills soon enough and wonder why he was getting up in the middle of the night to take them.

"What's wrong?" she asked him as they were leaving their hotel room at the Palmer House. It wasn't like him to act withdrawn and she hoped she hadn't provoked this sudden shift in mood. "I don't know if I should tell you," he replied. "I don't want to alarm you."

"C'mon, tell me, what is it? Is something wrong?" Eddie waited until they sat down to lunch at the Irish pub across the street. What he said was the last thing Lissette expected to hear. She knew HIV was a virus that people died from and that was about all she knew. "Eddie has HIV and I don't know how to react," she said to herself, unsure of what to do. Eddie recounted his whole story, how Dr. Stone had given him the news abruptly just before he went on to do *The Clowns*, how he'd tried to deal with it himself, how Joe had known all along, and how *Lacrymosa* was his farewell to his mother. All through lunch, he tried to reassure her. "Eddie kept saying, 'I'm fine, don't worry. I'm taking these pills and I have a great doctor,'" remembers Lissette. "But he seemed so upbeat that I couldn't help thinking, 'I hope he's not going to die soon.' Eddie was good at keeping stuff inside. He was such a performer."

Encouraged by the way Lissette calmly handled the news, Eddie decided to let Gerald Arpino in on his secret. He hoped that if Arpino knew why he was in such a hurry, he might agree to make special allowances for him when necessary. He had always felt a strong rapport with Arpino and he assumed that Arpino would be particularly understanding after having experienced the devastating loss of Robert Joffrey. Awaking from a fitful sleep one night while still in Chicago, Eddie took a walk down the hotel corridor and noticed that Arpino's light was still on. He knocked on the door.

"Mr. A," he announced when the door opened, "I just want to tell you something I don't think you're aware of."

Arpino studied Eddie's face. "Oh no," he thought, "Eddie wants to leave the company."

Eddie sat on the couch and, for the second time that week, repeated his story.

"I didn't show any shock because I am a man of faith and hope," recalls Gerald Arpino. "'You are dancing at a great peak and you have my support and prayers,' I told him. 'I will do everything to help you. Since you have taken me into your confidence, I won't let you down. If there is anything you need, without

With Gerald Arpino

anybody knowing why, I will arrange programs for you so that you can maintain your health and your standards. It's going to cause me trouble, because they are going to say that I'm favoring you, but I don't give a damn. I treasure you and I'll do everything I can.'"

With reassurances from Arpino that he wouldn't lose any ground as a result of his HIV status, Eddie resolved to accelerate his agenda. If he couldn't accomplish all he wanted with his life, then at least he would accomplish what he could in his art. His relationship with Joe was taking up too much of his time, he thought, time that he needed for his dancing and his dances. Joe already relied on him for financial support, housing, and career boosting, and he feared that Joe would increasingly look to him to provide strength now that he, too, had tested positive. "He had so much to deal with on his own," says Joe. "He didn't want to have to deal with someone else's problems too."

In the process of retreating into his own worries, Eddie dealt much more bluntly with everyone else around him. Joe was the understudy for the young man in *Lacrymosa* and he still remembers the day that Eddie told him that he wouldn't personally rehearse him in the role because he didn't think he could "pull it off." One morning before they were about to hop into the shower, Joe confessed that he was hoping to make it into the main company.

"You'll probably never get into Joffrey," came Eddie's reply. "The best you can hope for is a regional company."

Joe was stunned. "Eddie had been fighting against remarks like that his whole life," he says, "and he was living proof that if you want something badly enough and work hard enough, it can eventually happen."

But in this case, Eddie was right. In April, Joe learned that he had been turned down by the main company and that the Joffrey II was about to fold due to a financial squeeze. He suddenly found himself without a job, without medical insurance, and in danger of losing Eddie, with whom he was still in love. He had also begun to feel an uneasiness the first few days Eddie was back from tour, whereas before "we were all over each other immediately," he recalls. "Eddie wanted more time to himself and I began to get uncomfortable. I didn't know how much or how little to give." Their one-year anniversary was coming up in May and Joe hoped the occasion would reignite their fading romance. Decidedly low on cash, he splurged anyway, buying Eddie a $150 designer watch and flying out to L.A., where the Joffrey was on tour, to give it to him on their anniversary.

But when Joe arrived in L.A., he found Eddie to be cool and distant. On the day of their anniversary, he gave Eddie his present, but Eddie refused to open it because he didn't have anything to give to Joe in return. He hadn't had time to buy him a present, he said. A few days later, they finally went out to celebrate. Eddie gave Joe a teddy bear. Opening Joe's present to him, Eddie smiled nervously, unsure of what he should say. He knew he was ready to end the relationship, but he didn't want to hurt Joe, especially not after Joe had flown all the way out to the West Coast to see him. He broached the subject tentatively, suggesting to Joe that he didn't feel he was giving him the kind of time Joe wanted or needed. "I don't know about our relationship anymore," he said, finally.

Sensing Joe's despair, Eddie said he needed to think about it. By then, though, he had already strayed and resumed his affair with Eric Castellano. He was now more infatuated with Castellano than he had ever been, his fierce sexual attraction to him only compounding his confusion about Joe. Not only did they have great chemistry, but they had shared their experience with AIDS from the very beginning. Yet not even Eddie's closest friends knew about his dilemma, because Eddie kept his life so compartmentalized that there was rarely any overlap between one friend and the next. He could create an instant intimacy with people he'd just met and make them feel that they were not only uniquely special, but that they understood him in a way no one else could. Since he preferred to focus on one person at a time, his friends could only guess at what was really going on in the areas of his life in which they were not directly involved.

"Eddie always painted a wonderful picture of his relationship with Joe," remembers Jan Epstein, a masseur who became friendly with both Eddie and Joe after Eddie helped him to find work at the Joffrey. "It wasn't until just before they broke up that I finally got some truth out of him. He really wanted to see other men. They had their fling and then it was like there was other candy in the candy store. He was too young to make that kind of commitment." Eddie reminded Epstein of Huckleberry Finn, especially in the way he regularly bounded into his apartment and jumped up on the massage table. Eddie's voice, like his manner, was equally boyish and animated; the first time Eddie called him to make an appointment, Epstein assumed he was speaking to a girl.

While in Los Angeles that May, Eddie honored a promise he had made to his friend Bruce Kahl, a psychiatrist and ballet fan he had met that year at a Joffrey gala. At forty-three, Kahl was six feet two inches tall and good-looking, a warmhearted, easygoing man who in addition to running a private practice was the director of counseling at the California Institute of Technology. By the time he was introduced to Eddie in 1989, Kahl had known for three years that he was HIV-positive and had already been hospitalized once for recurring PCP. Dancer Patrick Corbin brought Kahl and Eddie together after Eddie had broken down in the dressing room at the Dorothy Chandler Pavilion and confided in Corbin that he was positive. Soon after, Eddie went to visit Kahl at his home in Pasadena and spent the afternoon listening to him describe how he had learned to live with HIV. He had accepted the situation, he told Eddie, by staying as active as possible. Kahl's philosophy struck a familiar chord, prompting Eddie to give Kahl a full accounting of his myriad plans for the future. "Eddie's a little spark plug," Kahl reported to his lover, Simon Pastucha, after Eddie had gone home. Still, the visit had filled him with sadness. He couldn't believe that a man half his age was confronting the dilemmas he himself had trouble comprehending. "I'm in my early forties and I never expected to be thinking about these things," he told Pastucha. "Eddie's way too young to be dealing with this." Kahl would be dead in three years; he would outlive Eddie.

A firm believer in traditional Western medicine, Kahl was concerned about Eddie's falling T-cell counts and convinced him to solicit a second medical opinion. "I've been through a lot of doctors," he counseled Eddie, "and I finally found one I really like. He's become a good friend and I want you to promise you'll go see him."

And so it happened that on May 9, 1989, eight years after he had reported the first AIDS cases to the Centers for Disease Control and three years after the death of Rock Hudson, his most famous patient, Dr. Michael Gottlieb added the name Edward Stierle to his burgeoning caseload.

As he examined Eddie at his office in Sherman Oaks, Michael Gottlieb marveled at his physique and tone. "I'd never examined a dancer before and I thought his body was just remarkable," he remembers. Gottlieb also marveled at the discrepancy between Eddie's superb level of fitness and his T-cell count. It was unusual for someone with Eddie's low count to be feeling "at his peak" the way Eddie then did and Gottlieb was concerned that Eddie's infection had picked up pace rather rapidly in the last year. Ninety-five percent of his practice was devoted to HIV patients and Eddie was as young as he'd seen them. The fact that Eddie had become infected with HIV as a teenager confirmed what Gottlieb had long suspected: that the safer-sex prevention message was not getting out to younger people.

"Edward's having HIV at all represents an unconscionable error of omission on the part of the educators and the government, grounded in homophobia," he says. But despite having spent the past eight years looking at the disease from every possible angle and leading the fight for federal funding and research, Dr. Gottlieb still had no answers as to why some people with the virus progressed rapidly over a three- or four-year period to an AIDS diagnosis whereas others could go twelve to fifteen years without showing any AIDS symptoms. As the first physician in California to conduct studies of AZT, Gottlieb had more experience with the drug than any other West Coast physician and was disturbed that Eddie hadn't started on AZT before his count dropped to 200. At the time, "New York physicians were more conservative than West Coast physicians with respect to the early use of AZT," explains Dr. Gottlieb. "We had information that early intervention could make a difference and here was Eddie starting AZT when the horses were already out of the barn."

Asking Eddie to slow down, however, was out of the question. There was no proof that exercise damaged the immune system and, besides, "Eddie had such a glow and talked with such enthusiasm about his work, that I would never have considered restricting him," says the doctor, who was intrigued by the way Eddie described *Lacrymosa d'Amore*. "He told me about the death of Robert Joffrey and how other people he knew had AIDS. He said he was beginning to realize that he, too, would not survive AIDS and that he had wanted to express that sadness in some way."

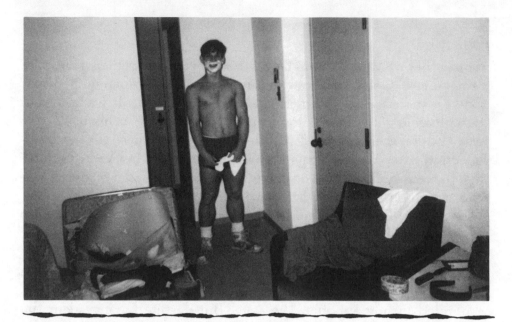

On tour in Florida, 1989

Despite now having doctors on two coasts, Eddie refused to let his medical worries dominate his life. He was determined to keep moving in every conceivable direction, convinced that his unflagging determination was his only shield against encroaching illness. There was always something else to discover, something *more* awaiting him.

Returning home to New York, Eddie told Joe about his affair with Eric Castellano and confessed he still hadn't made up his mind about their relationship. "Let's just see how it goes," he said. A week later, he and Joe went to see *Dead Poets Society*, a film about a teacher (played by Robin Williams) and the group of students he inspires. Over and over again, the teacher exhorts his pupils to take chances with their lives. "*Carpe diem*," he tells them. "Seize the day." Eddie took the film's message to heart and broke up with Joe at once. But he was in no hurry to get rid of him and, instead, invited Joe to stay on in the apartment, with the understanding that they could both pursue other relationships.

Which Eddie did. It wasn't long after their breakup that Eddie invited his ex-boyfriend Richard Register over to the apartment to watch a videotape of *Lacrymosa d'Amore*. Register was trying to get his acting career started and was working as a waiter to pay the rent. One afternoon in the Thirty-fourth Street subway station, he and Eddie had happened to catch sight of each other, just as the doors of Richard's train were closing. Eddie called Richard the next day. "Eddie couldn't fathom the idea that I had to work in a restaurant because I couldn't make enough money as an actor," recalls Register. After watching *Lacrymosa*, Eddie and Richard "started kissing madly," says Register. "I stopped it from going any further because I didn't just want it to be a fluke. He hinted at getting back together, but nothing ever came of it."

As if he didn't have enough to occupy him that summer, Eddie agreed in June to accept his nomination as Dancers Union representative, a position he shared with Tina LeBlanc. It was not a popular job: The dancers' rep had to represent the dancers to management, which meant ferrying complaints back and forth between hostile parties. Among their numerous AGMA (American Guild of Musical Artists) duties, they were to ensure that the dancers got a five-minute break every hour and got paid their $30-an-hour overtime if rehearsals ran too long. Given that Scott Barnard was pretty much running the show at that point and that most of the dancers were intimidated by him, outspoken Eddie Stierle was seen as the ideal candidate for the job. "It took me ten to twelve years to get up the nerve to take issue with Scott," says Joffrey veteran Carl Corry. "Eddie would just march upstairs and spell it out. It was just amazing to me." Indeed, Eddie soon marched upstairs and told Barnard that the Joffrey members were so intimidated by him that they were "dancing out of fear." "Good," Barnard is said to have replied. "They should."

In June, the Joffrey traveled to Granada and Hamburg, where Eddie seemed to be testing his physical limits. In Granada, the company's performances didn't begin until 11 P.M., after which Eddie would stay up all night dancing at a club with Joffrey friends. Tom Mossbrucker remembers wandering the streets of Granada with Eddie in the early morning hours waiting for a café to open. Eddie was limping around "because he had danced all night in these pointy-toed cowboy boots," says Mossbrucker. "He was wild when he went out. He was totally uninhibited and loved to be the center of attention."

The next month, Eddie visited with his brothers Tom and Bill at Rosemarie's house in Atlantic City over a July Fourth weekend. One afternoon they all went canoeing and, while drifting on the water, Eddie asked them whether they would have changed anything about their lives if they could live them over again. Tom was the first to answer. "I wouldn't really change anything," he said. Bill and Rosemarie paused to consider the question for several minutes. "I wouldn't have changed anything either," Rosemarie said. Eddie, however, felt otherwise. "I would have changed a lot of things," he told them. "I would have tried to be part of the family more. I would have gone fishing with you guys and worked on building projects with you when you told me to." They thought he had finished when suddenly he blurted out: "And I wouldn't have let Mom influence me as much as she did."

Back in his New York apartment after weeks on the road, Eddie quickly began to feel stifled by his living arrangement with Joe. Despite their mutual understanding, the situation had become awkward for both of them, particularly as they were sharing the same bed and Joe was still in love with Eddie. Since Joe had found a job dancing with the Feld Ballets/NY, they both agreed it was time for him to find his own apartment. But while Eddie wanted more time for himself, he didn't want to live alone.

The same week Joe moved out, Lissette Salgado moved in — and never left.

20

PETROUCHKA'S CRY

Darkling I listen; and, for many a time
   I have been half in love with easeful Death,
Called him soft names in many a mused rhyme,
   To take into the air my quiet breath;
Now more than ever seems it rich to die,
   To cease upon the midnight with no pain,
     While thou art pouring forth thy soul abroad
     In such an ecstasy!

            John Keats
            "Ode to a Nightingale"

"Do you think when somebody dies young they've finished all their work?" Eddie asked.

Millicent Hodson and Kenneth Archer assumed Eddie was referring to Mozart. Or was it to Keats? On that October day they were discussing artists whose creative lives had been cut short. Eddie had tried to imagine what more Mozart might have composed, and Archer happened to mention that the poet John Keats had once lived in Hampstead, the London neighborhood where he and Hodson owned a house.

"Yes, I think it's sometimes true," Hodson answered Eddie after a moment's reflection. "Look at Keats. He died at twenty-six and achieved more than most people do in a whole lifetime."

Unfinished work was much on Eddie's mind that autumn as he set about campaigning to get *Lacrymosa d'Amore* into the repertory of the Joffrey and struggled to learn two new taxing roles: the lead male in *Trinity* and the title character in *Petrouchka*. As he had discovered during his work on *The Clowns* and *Lacrymosa*, the ballets that most absorbed him drew their power from the social or personal concerns they reflected. In *Trinity* and *Petrouchka*, Eddie saw not only strong parallels to his own situation, but reflections of the tenuous temper of the times. While he didn't want to let the specter of AIDS haunt his life, it invariably colored the way he approached his art; as a result, he continued to borrow from his offstage experience in bringing his characters to life.

A rock ballet celebrating the youthful energy and idealism of the 1960s, Gerald Arpino's *Trinity* featured explosive, frenetic movement that intermingled virtuosic classical feats with pelvic thrusts, high kicks, and powerhouse pirouettes. By contrast, the ballet's closing section was contemplative: Forming a processional, the dancers placed votive candles on the stage and then exited, leaving the stage empty save for the dancing lights. "I use *Clowns* with its theme of nuclear holocaust and its survivors as a metaphor for AIDS," Eddie told a reporter that month. "And in *Trinity*, when I come out with one of those candles, it's for someone we've lost. That's what *Trinity* is about now to me."

Galvanized by real-life drama, Eddie's performances provided an outlet for his despondency and frustration, emotions he could put to better advantage on the stage rather than off it. "A lot of people I know use AIDS to act out their anger," says the masseur Jan Epstein, who was also HIV-positive and had then been living symptom-free with the virus for seven years. "Eddie put his anger into his dancing and transformed it into something creative."

While radically different in style, *Petrouchka* also led Eddie to ruminate on death and the invincibility of the spirit. First per-

Rehearsing *Trinity* with Gerald Arpino, 1990

formed by the Ballets Russes in 1911, *Petrouchka* tells the story of a puppet with a human heart and soul who aspires to human love without a human form to support him. The ballet opens on a street fair in 1830s St. Petersburg, where a magician is presenting a puppet show. After the show, the magician drops the curtain of his booth and the puppets are left to their own devices. Petrouchka curses his fate when the frivolous and beautiful ballerina puppet he loves turns her charms on the Moor puppet. In a contemptuous rage, the Moor kills Petrouchka with his scimitar. Yet in the ballet's final moment, Petrouchka's ghost mysteriously reappears on the roof of the puppet booth and frightens away the magician. "Petrouchka must live—that is the mystery of him!" Diaghilev is said to have remarked of the ending he invented. As *Petrouchka*'s librettist and designer Alexandre Benois envisioned him, the tragic puppet was "the personification of the spiritual and suffering side of humanity. . . ." Benois had arrived at his interpretation after hearing "Petrouchka's Cry," a fragment of music that Igor Stravinsky had composed for the ballet. As he listened to Stravinsky's score, Benois "began to discern in it grief, and rage, and love, as well as the helpless despair that dominated it."

Eddie was drawn not only to the pathos of Petrouchka's character, but to the fact that Nijinsky had originated the role of this immortal Pierrot, "a Hamlet among puppets," as Nijinsky biographer Richard Buckle has observed. Nijinsky's grasp of the character was said to be so profound that Alexandre Benois was moved to write of his debut:

> The metamorphosis took place when he put on his costume and covered his face with makeup. . . . The great difficulty of Petrouchka's part is to express his pitiful oppression and his hopeless efforts to achieve personal dignity without ceasing to be a *puppet*.

Fascinated by the Nijinsky legend, Eddie undertook to get to the heart of Nijinsky's interpretation. He threw himself into his research, reading everything he could find about the making of the ballet, poring over photographs of Nijinsky as Petrouchka, and even going as far as to reproduce his putty-faced style of makeup.

He closely studied Nijinsky's diary, a moving record of a broken mind careering between lucidity and delusion. In it, Nijinsky espouses his views on life, death, art, religion, and love. At one point, he writes:

> Many people will say: "Why does Nijinsky always speak of God? He has gone mad—he is a dancer and nothing else." I understand all these sneers and they do not make me angry. I weep and weep. Many people will say that Nijinsky is always weeping. I am not. I am alive and therefore suffer, but I rarely shed tears. My soul is weeping. . . . Life is difficult, because men do not know the importance of it. Life is short . . . I love life. I love death. Death can be lovely when it is God's wish, dreadful when it is without God. . . .

Not surprisingly, Eddie would later say of his work on the ballet: "I did a lot of soul-searching when I was getting ready for *Petrouchka.*"

To help him get ready, Eddie hired another celebrated Petrouchka* to coach him privately during a layoff. Gary Chryst, a Joffrey star in the 1960s and 1970s, had been the company's most singular and best known performer, distinguishing himself in many roles, including ones in *Clowns*, *Trinity*, and *Parade*, that Eddie later inherited. Chryst had starred in the first performances of the Joffrey's *Petrouchka*, and had been taught the ballet by Léonide Massine, the dancer who took over the lead role from Nijinsky. Wiry and intense with curly black hair and soulful eyes, Chryst first met Eddie at a party in 1986, shortly after Eddie joined the Joffrey. He liked Eddie's aplomb, the way he strode up to him at the party and simply announced, "I'm doing your role in *Clowns*." He soon discovered there was also a competitive edge to Eddie ("How old were you when you did this role," he wanted to know) and yet at the same time, a beguiling sensuality and maturity. Eddie, Chryst said to himself, "is an old soul in a little body."

---

*Other well-known interpreters of the role include Alexander Grant, Jerome Robbins, and Rudolf Nureyev.

To get that little body to move as if he were a puppet trying to be like a person—and not a person imitating a puppet—Chryst insisted that Eddie rehearse with large flat mittens. In this way, he would learn to convey the choreography's jerky, confined movements and gestures without articulating his hands and fingers. Chryst also wanted Eddie to work on expressing the gamut of Petrouchka's emotions and to avoid what he saw as "the trap" of presenting a one-dimensional, self-pitying Petrouchka. "Petrouchka isn't weak, he's not put together well," Chryst advised him. "Yes, he can feel pain, but he can also feel love and anger. Look at how angry Nijinsky looks in the photographs taken of him in the role." Chryst was impressed by Eddie's attention to detail and by his indefatigable interest in exploring every facet of the role. It was unusual for dancers of "Eddie's generation," as Chryst thought of them, to do their homework with such diligence.

Chryst had just finished a road tour of *A Chorus Line* and was in between Broadway assignments when Eddie asked him to come in and coach him on *Petrouchka*. Knowing that Chryst would be too proud to ask for wages, Eddie quietly slipped a check into his bag at the end of the week.

At the same time Eddie was expanding his repertoire, he was fast becoming the focus of a good deal of press attention. In September 1989, a month before the Joffrey opened its New York season, he landed on the cover of *The New Season*, a special magazine supplement of *The New York Times* devoted to highlights of the cultural calendar. Eddie found himself in good company: Among the thirteen figures drawn on the cover by renowned caricaturist Al Hirschfeld were actors Marlon Brando, Vanessa Redgrave, and Shirley MacLaine, choreographer Tommy Tune, and comedian Jackie Mason. Several weeks later, Eddie was back in *The New York Times*, this time in a profile for the Sunday "Arts & Leisure" section, which ran with the headline: "The Joffrey Returns, Spotlighting a Virtuoso." The virtuoso in question was to try on several new roles that season, which in addition to *Trinity* and *Petrouchka* included a Spanish dancer in a new work by Arpino entitled *The Pantages and the Palace Present Two-a-Day*, a tribute to vaudeville.

Though *Two-a-Day* was dismissed as an entertaining trifle, Eddie was singled out for his brilliant recovery during the ballet's New York premiere, when the sash of his costume began to unwind as he was dancing. In *The New York Times*, Anna Kisselgoff noted that Eddie "rewound the fabric around his waist without a rhythmic hitch," adding, "Mr. Arpino might consider inserting the mishap into the piece."

Eddie's first performances as Petrouchka met with mixed reviews. While *Newsday*'s Janice Berman called his Petrouchka "poignant, yet indomitable," and Barbara Forbes, the Joffrey's ballet mistress, felt that he movingly conveyed "the triumph of Petrouchka's spirit," other critics and observers considered his interpretation overly energetic. Carl Corry, the Joffrey's first-cast Petrouchka, remembers discussing his approach to the role with Eddie during rehearsals for the season, and believes they each came to the role from decidedly different starting points. "I approached Petrouchka very intimately as though I was truly alone with myself," says Corry. "My characterization was focused inward, whereas Eddie's was projected outward. He was a natural performer and I don't think he could help himself when it came to an audience. He had to perform for them." For her part, Anna Kisselgoff felt that while Eddie made a strong impression, he was "an always angry puppet, snarling and gritting his teeth, never poignant."

Choreographer Senta Driver recalls bumping into Kisselgoff at intermission the night of Eddie's debut. "He's too angry," she remembers Kisselgoff telling her. "But, Anna," Driver protested, "he has a concept. How many dancers have a concept? This is an artist on his way. He's not just trying to show off." Yet even while defending Eddie, Driver saw that Kisselgoff had a point. She, too, felt that his characterization was too forceful. "Eddie had so much physical power that he had trouble curbing it and going dead into it to get to the puppet. His performance had a little too much of the prizefighter in it."

But it was just a beginning and, in retrospect, Driver wonders what Eddie might have done had he had the time to develop in the role. He had occasion to perform it only twice and was still working on his characterization. As Hamlet is to the actor, so Petrouchka is one of those rich, dramatic roles that takes the measure of a dancer's artistry and continues to present new challenges as that artistry gains nuance and depth.

At the age of twenty-one and in his fourth year with the Joffrey, Eddie was at a point in his career where he was starting to learn how to put his energy at the service of his art and use it for accent and color. "Edward found it difficult to channel his energy because he was afraid he would lose it," says Scott Barnard. "He felt his energy had gotten him to where he was."

That fall, Dr. John Oppenheimer also turned up at City Center to see Eddie dance, but his evaluation of the performance was determined by an entirely different set of criteria. He had by then cut Eddie's AZT dose from twelve to eight pills a day and even though Eddie was asymptomatic, he worried about the drug's potential side effects, particularly the muscle weakness it was known sometimes to cause.* In Eddie's case, such a development would mean the end of his career. "I didn't enjoy the performance," Dr. Oppenheimer admits, "because I was worrying about what to advise him to do." He decided to measure the enzyme activity in Eddie's muscles, which turned out to be high and, thus, potentially career-threatening. "That was a bit scary," recalls Dr. Oppenheimer, who did his best to reassure Eddie that the tests often fluctuated. Eddie was relieved only after a follow-up test showed his muscle strength to be in the normal range. "Eddie didn't let his HIV infection paralyze him," says Dr. Oppenheimer. "Some people fall apart, but he did everything he wanted to do. I was amazed by his energy and concentration and by the way he managed to do all these things even though he was so young. I really admired the way he got up there and danced."

---

*The potential side effects of AZT include headaches, anemia, muscle weakness, vomiting and diarrhea, and bone-marrow suppression.

Ever since he had first shown *Lacrymosa* to Gerald Arpino in July 1988, Eddie had been trying to persuade him to take the ballet into the repertory of the main company. "Don't you think it would be a wonderful tribute to Mr. Joffrey?" Eddie would suggest to Arpino, showing the instincts of the born impresario. "He knew it was a good hitch and that Arpino would go for it that way," remembers Joe Brown.

Arpino thought Eddie showed great promise, and privately hoped to groom him for the post of resident choreographer. In November, he told Eddie that the Joffrey would begin dancing *Lacrymosa* the following March. For the Joffrey performances, Eddie was to dance the autobiographical role of the young man. There were to be other changes as well: Since Lissette Salgado was a junior company member, she would be relegated to the corps and the starring role would be assumed by a more established ballerina.

Lissette may not have been cast as Eddie's leading lady at the Joffrey, but offstage, she was already performing the part to perfection. She had picked up where Joe Brown had left off: She shopped for groceries, she refilled Eddie's prescriptions for him when he was too busy to do it himself, and she accompanied him to his doctor's visits. She quickly made herself indispensable to Eddie, placing herself emotionally, artistically, and domestically at his service. In return, she looked to Eddie to guide her, trying, as Joe did, to meet whatever challenges he gave her. Shy and sensitive, Lissette preferred to hide behind Eddie's bravura. "Eddie really cheered her on and gave her confidence," says her friend, the dancer Cynthia Giannini. It had taken her years to master English, her second language, and as a result, she spoke hesitatingly and came off sounding inarticulate. "You shouldn't be so insecure," Eddie liked to advise her before class, "stand at the front." At meals, he supervised her caloric intake. "Should you be eating that?" he'd ask the diet-weary Lissette, who was perpetually in pursuit of a more sylphlike shape.

While acknowledging that she "always felt in Eddie's shadow," Lissette was still happy just to be at his side. Whether on the road or off, they were inseparable, their days soon falling into a familiar routine: They walked to morning class together and back home at night, they made dinner, played Scrabble, and then sent each other off to bed with a good-night kiss, Eddie climbing the stairs to his room with the skylight, and Lissette taking to the pullout couch in the living room.

It wasn't long before Lissette found herself falling in love with Eddie. She liked to tell their friends that they lived "like a married couple," though with Liana Navarro she took things a step further. "Sometimes I pretend we are," she said. According to Cynthia Giannini, "Lissette knew that Eddie was gay, but thought maybe he would change and love her. She kept waiting for him to come around and wouldn't make herself available to anyone else." Refusing to believe that their relationship couldn't evolve into a love affair, Lissette continued to rehearse her part in it, hoping that, in time, Edde would reciprocate the passion she felt for him. At the same time, his virus frightened her. "I had this other picture in my mind," she says. "I tried not to see what was going on."

But the nights Eddie went to bars and didn't come home served as painful reminders. Liana Navarro recalls the tearful phone calls she would get from New York on those nights. "Lissette would call me crying when Eddie would go out. She suffered a lot because she was in love with him. I'd try to tell her, 'You have to get Eddie out of your mind because you know it's not possible. You have to go out and meet someone else.' The harder it became, the more headstrong she got."

Upon returning home the next morning, Eddie had to deal with a terse and angry Lissette, who would spend the rest of the day punishing him as if he were a philandering husband. As irrational as it may have seemed, she felt that if she couldn't have him for herself, she didn't want anyone else to have him either. "Did you have a good time?" she would ask him, her voice filled with accusation. Ignoring her disdain, Eddie would fill her in on the details of his date. "He'd tell me where they went and what they talked about and if they had sex or not," she says. "He'd say, 'I went out to this bar and I met a really cute guy there and he made a pass at me.' I was trying to listen as a friend, but I was mad and really jealous. I wanted it to be me." That Christmas, Eddie bought her a golden cocker spaniel puppy they named Missy Joe. "The dog was our baby," she says, looking back.

Lissette was not alone in hoping that Eddie would fall in love with her. Eddie's father, Bill, had always had a special affection for Lissette ever since photographing her at Liana's. Now that she was his son's roommate, he took the liberty of introducing her as his daughter-in-law, or simply as "Ed's girl." Rose Stierle was relieved to see that Lissette had at least replaced Joe Brown as Eddie's roommate, while Tom Stierle was convinced that "if Eddie gets over the guy thing, he'll eventually come around to Lissette." Indeed, Eddie spoke so effusively about Lissette that he frequently led nonfamily members, as well as Lissette herself, to a similar conclusion. In front of the other Joffrey dancers, Eddie would point at Lissette and say, "Wow, look at her, she's gorgeous. Isn't she beautiful?" Yet his compliments only further confounded her. She remembers thinking, "What's wrong with me? Why is he saying those things if he's not attracted to me? Am I not sexual enough for him?"

When Eddie called on Liana Navarro in Hialeah during a visit home to Florida, Liana decided to find out for herself just how Eddie felt about Lissette. "Do you think that maybe you and Lissette will get married someday?" she asked him. "You never know," replied Eddie, whose vague answer led Liana to assume that he hadn't ruled out the possibility. "Eddie would go on and on about Lissette and her dancing," says Liana. "I thought he had confused feelings for her, but I never told Lissette because I didn't want to give her any encouragement and maybe make things worse for her." Even Kyle Ahmed thought that Eddie might have looked at Lissette differently had he not been dealing with HIV. "Eddie and Lissette really loved each other," he says. "Their relationship was platonic, but I can't help thinking that if Eddie hadn't tested positive, it might not have remained that way."

Only Lissette's parents, it seemed, were troubled by Lissette's apparent intimacy with Eddie. Having raised her in a sheltered

Cuban-Catholic household, they looked disapprovingly on their nineteen-year-old daughter's living arrangements in New York City. They called her frequently and tried to talk her into getting a female roommate. Finally, they gave up and in December flew to New York to see for themselves how she was doing. On the day they came by the apartment, Lissette's father happened to notice one of Eddie's AZT containers in the bathroom. Unfamiliar with the name of the drug, he proceded to write it down and went home to Miami to ask his doctor what it was. No sooner did he find out that it was an antiviral drug prescribed to people with HIV than he was on the phone to Lissette demanding that she move out.

But Lissette would hear none of it. She did her best to assuage their panic by reassuring them that she couldn't possibly contract the virus by casual contact with Eddie. Since she spoke to them in Spanish, Eddie had no idea that he was the subject of their heated exchanges nor that he was the cause of Lissette's sudden rupture with her parents. And Lissette never told him, for she didn't want to give him anything more to worry about.

The chill in the air that announced December in New York signaled the start of the Joffrey's Christmas season in Los Angeles, where the only snow in town was to be found onstage at the Dorothy Chandler Pavilion during performances of the Joffrey's *Nutcracker*. Presiding over the company's winter storm was Eddie Stierle's Snow Prince; and as Dr. Michael Gottlieb sat watching Eddie perform for the first time, he suddenly remembered a remark that a colleague had made to him at a recent AIDS conference. All lives are irreplaceable, the doctor had told him, but when we lose an artist, we're really losing two people: the person and the artist the person has become. Watching Eddie now, he couldn't help thinking of the dancing years he was likely to lose, the ballets he would never get to choreograph, and the incalculable contributions that would likely go unrealized.

During his weeks in Los Angeles, Eddie resumed his relationship with Eric Castellano, who had moved to nearby Pomona to take care of his dying father. Faced with the prospect of his own early death, Eric was also trying to cope with the experience of watching his father waste away from AIDS, the same disease that he knew would eventually claim his own life. The strain of grief had left him depleted. He needed support and a friend suggested he check out the services at the Unitarian Community Church in Santa Monica, where every Sunday night a smart, snappy, beautiful woman named Marianne Williamson dispensed her special brand of "spiritual psychotherapy."

A self-styled New Age healer, Williamson dressed in Armani knockoffs, joked about her own checkered past, and spoke in the argot of the thirty-something generation. No Mother Teresa, the thirty-six-year-old Williamson brought people into the fold by reason of her accessibility. She was funny and flawed and had a knack for making the holy seem hip. Her subject matter was remarkably wide-ranging: To packed houses on both coasts, she preached on everything from Jesus, Cinderella, and AIDS, to intimacy, agents, and careers, her lectures a patchwork of philosophies and religions. Peppered with references to Buddhism, Christianity, pop psychology, technology, and 12-step recovery programs, Williamson's lectures were based on the principles of *A Course in Miracles*, a three-volume tome published in the 1960s, which has since spawned thousands of study groups across the country. The book was written by a Columbia University psychology professor named Helen Schucman, who felt compelled to write down what a "voice" told her to write, although she later rejected what she had written. "The Course," as it's referred to by devotees, advocates, among other things, a return to spirituality, the turning away from materialism, the power of a positive perspective, and not least, the Golden Rule. The change in perception that results from approaching life in this loving, nonjudgmental way is said to produce miracles.

Raised in Houston, the daughter of left-wing Jewish parents, Williamson had worked as a waitress, lounge singer, tarot card reader, and seller of books on metaphysics before stumbling on her calling as a teacher of "the Course."* En route, she had suffered a nervous breakdown, the effects of which had led her to seriously reshuffle her priorities.

By 1989, in addition to preaching her message of love and forgiveness, Williamson was deeply involved in the fight against AIDS. She had recently founded the Manhattan and L.A. Centers for Living, two organizations offering meals, meditation, and counseling to people dealing with "life-challenging" illnesses. Her Project Angel Food, also founded that year, provided hot meals daily for homebound AIDS patients in L.A. Having rallied some of the entertainment industry's biggest names to her lectures and causes, Williamson was fast becoming a spiritual trainer to the stars. Actors Kim Basinger, Anthony Perkins, and Cher, as well as moguls David Geffen and Barry Diller, counted themselves among her supporters. (In 1991, her visibility was markedly enhanced when she officiated at the much-ballyhooed wedding of Elizabeth Taylor and Larry Fortensky at Michael Jackson's ranch in California.)

Gay men dealing with AIDS comprised a large percentage of Williamson's most loyal following. Like Eddie, many of them felt excluded from more established religions, with their intolerance of homosexuality and their emphasis on sin. "You are not your virus," Williamson would counsel, stressing the separation of body and soul. "It is not a reflection of who you are. Don't let it define you. The spirit is impervious to illness."

Eric took Eddie to see Williamson. The moment Eddie set eyes on her, he recognized a kindred spirit. It wasn't just what she said that struck a chord, but the way she said it with such conviction and earthy humor. Her philosophy was not all that dissimilar from that of Louise Hay, the spiritual guru Eddie had first turned to following his rejection of Catholicism. Hay also based her teachings

---

*Just how persuasive a spokeswoman Williamson is for "the Course" is reflected in the sales of her book: Since 1976, *A Course in Miracles* has sold about 800,000 copies, while Williamson's bestseller, *A Return to Love: Reflections on the Principles of A Course in Miracles*, has sold more than 1.5 million copies.

Marianne Williamson

on *A Course in Miracles*, but it was Williamson, with her bravura performing style, who managed to make the principles meaningful to him in a new way. When one woman in the audience asked why she seemed to attract unavailable men, Williamson retorted: "It's not that you attract them, it's that you give them your number." Eddie appreciated Williamson's rapid-fire delivery and her abiding sense of showmanship, but above all, he welcomed her emphasis on the enduring life force of the soul, which resonated with his Catholic beliefs. And yet, Williamson's philosophy avoided those judgments that had pushed Eddie away from his Catholic roots. Jesus also popped up in Williamson's sermons, although she was careful to explain that His name was used metaphorically to convey "the unconditionally loving essence of every person." As far as Williamson was concerned, sin had no place in discussions about death, a word she generally avoided. To her, death was not an end, but a transition to another plane, "like taking off a suit of clothes," she'd say.

After the lecture, Eddie and Eric spent most of the night talking about Williamson. "It was as if Eddie had seen the light," recalls Castellano. "He was completely emotional about Marianne. Her message about replacing fear with love clicked with him. That lecture changed everything for him because it made him less fearful of the disease. He loved the idea that there is a spiritual life that continues after the body is not here."

Eric loaned Eddie one of Williamson's lectures-on-tape, which Eddie practically memorized in a week after listening to it daily in his car and on his Walkman. "You've got to come with me to hear this woman," he insisted to Lissette as they were listening to Williamson's "Being Positive" in his car on the way to rehearsal. The next Sunday, Eddie and Eric took Lissette with them to Williamson's lecture. "Eddie absolutely believed in Marianne," says Lissette. "She made him think everything was possible as long as he thought positively."

Buoyed by his faith in Williamson, Eddie started attending her monthly lectures when he returned to New York in January. As her popularity had grown, Williamson had moved from the small churches in which she began to Town Hall, a 1,500-seat theater on West Forty-third Street. Later on, Williamson would preach to millions more from the televised pulpits of Oprah and Larry King.

On his first visit to Town Hall, Eddie took his friend Tina Awad, the reflexologist he had met in Joyce Barrie's "Humor Playshop." Before the lecture got started, Williamson had invited several actors and singers to give a little performance. That was all the prompting Eddie needed. After listening raptly to Williamson's ninety-minute lecture, which she delivered without notes, and the question-and-answer period that followed, Eddie turned to Awad and said, "You know, I'd really like to dance for her. I'm going to tell her." Awad, who at that point had been going to Williamson's lectures for two years, had never thought of introducing herself to Williamson because she assumed that since "people were in awe of Marianne, everybody in the hall would want to ask her a personal question," she says. "But Eddie had no limits at all. He just marched up to the stage. A few minutes later, he came back to the seat looking ten feet tall and said, 'It was great. I talked to her.'"

There were at least thirty people waiting in line to ask Williamson's advice that night and Eddie was the one she still remembers. "There was such a radiance that came from him," she says. "He was one of those really bright lights, one of those people with whom you fell in love at first sight. He reminded me of an elegant leprechaun. I didn't know who he was and the first thing he said to me was, 'I love your lectures and I want to do a special ballet for New Year's Eve or Easter about resurrection.' He was someone you realized was major the minute you met him. He had amazing charisma, so it didn't surprise me to find out that he was on the stage. I lecture to many, many people and there are only a few in every group who think to give back to me. And he was one of them. He said, 'Thank you so much. I just love what you do.'"

Just as his mother turned to priests and nuns to clarify her course in life, so Eddie now turned to Williamson to guide him in the principles of dying. Before leaving Town Hall, he stopped in the lobby to buy more lecture cassettes ("Death Does Not Exist," "All Things Are Lessons") as well as *A Course in Miracles*, Williamson's workbook. He would prepare for dying with the same spirit and tenacity that had always propelled him: The model son and star dancer would become Williamson's valedictorian.

At the same time he was exploring matters of the spirit with Williamson, Eddie began teaching *Lacrymosa* to the Joffrey dancers. By putting them through their paces, he would take them through the stages of grief as he had experienced them. In preparation for that process, Eddie decided to break his silence on his HIV status. Before talking about it with his peers, he thought it best to open the dialogue with his sister Rosemarie, whom he trusted to ease his way with the rest of the family.

Rosemarie was then starring in *Wildfire*, a new cabaret revue at Merv Griffin's Resorts casino in Atlantic City, and one weekend in January 1990, Eddie caught her act. Afterward, they went to hear her husband Kit's band play at a nearby lounge club and sat talking over drinks. Eddie had asked Rosemarie to make the costumes for *Lacrymosa* and they discussed ideas. When Rosemarie happened to mention in passing that one of the singers had become accidentally pregnant during a brief affair, Eddie scoffed at her willingness to have unprotected sex with someone she barely knew.

They were two hours into their conversation and finally he'd found the segue he was looking for. An odd silence hung between them.

"I've waited a long time to tell you this and now I think it's time," he said. "I'm HIV-positive, but I'm absolutely fine. I'm taking really good care of myself."

Rosemarie was stunned. "How long have you known?"

"Almost three years," he replied.

She started counting backward in her mind, rewinding the moments as she searched for missed clues. "I can't believe you've kept this to yourself for so long," she said, at once hurt that he hadn't told her and awed by his strength.

"*Lacrymosa*, that's my story, Rosie," Eddie explained gently. "What did you think when you saw it? I thought you would have figured it out then."

So that was the clue she had missed. Now when she thought of *Lacrymosa*, it seemed so obvious. But at the moment, little else seemed clear. What could she do for him? she asked.

His biggest fear, he told her, was that the news would kill their parents. "He was worried about the judgments everyone would make and that they'd want him to stop dancing," remembers Rosemarie. "He didn't want to have to carry everyone else emotionally. He only wanted to be surrounded by people who thought positively. He kept saying, 'I don't want to ruin your life.' So I did my crying privately and kept really positive for him."

Eddie was the first person Rosemarie knew who had the virus. To her, AIDS had been something distant and remote, an abstract concept. The day Eddie took the bus back to Manhattan, Rosemarie started making calls. She phoned the National Institutes of Health in Washington and the Gay Men's Health Crisis in Manhattan and asked them to put her name on their mailing lists. From then on, there wasn't a promising development, therapy, or drug that Rosemarie didn't know about.

Midway through rehearsals on *Lacrymosa* (he had decided to shorten the title), Eddie invited Jodie Gates out for a drink at the Alpine Tavern, one of the dancers' favorite hangouts near the Joffrey's studios. Work on the ballet had been going much more slowly than it had at Joffrey II because Scott Barnard was overseeing rehearsals and wanted each step to be precisely counted and each dancer to perform the steps the same way. Eddie, on the other hand, was trying to avoid dictating to the dancers. "Dig into yourself," he would tell them. "Show me what you want to do." Gates, one of the company's finest dramatic dancers, was dancing Lissette Salgado's role and she and Eddie had spent the day rehearsing their "farewell" pas de deux. "There's something I need to tell you that may help you with the role," Eddie said. "This piece means a lot to me. I made it for Mr. Joffrey and because I'm HIV-positive."

Gates, a sleek, dark-haired ballerina, slumped in her chair. She'd known four other men who had died of AIDS by then, but none of them was as close to her as Eddie was. She kept thinking, "This person who I adore is going to die."

"You can look at the role two different ways," Eddie continued over her silent soliloquy. "You are my lover or my mother. During our pas de deux, I am about to die and you want to say good-bye for the last time or you're grieving my death and you imagine that I've come back. You want to touch my face and caress me and you don't want to let me go."

The information could not help but color her approach to the ballet. "It brought a whole new emotional dimension to performing the work," she says. "I knew the story behind it."

On March 9, 1990, one week after Eddie's twenty-second birthday, a revised *Lacrymosa* was given its world premiere by the Joffrey Ballet in Lincoln, Nebraska, with Eddie in the starring role of the dying man.

Three hundred and sixty-four days later, he would be dead.

Rehearsing *Lacrymosa d'Amore* with Tina LeBlanc

21

COUP DE THÉÂTRE

Two months after the premiere of *Lacrymosa*, another drama was unfolding on a not-too-distant stage. At its center was the conflict between Gerald Arpino and the Joffrey board, which potentially threatened the existence of the Joffrey company. The day before the Joffrey was to open its month-long season at the L.A. Music Center, Arpino showed up at a company board meeting in New York to read the following statement: "I refuse to participate in an organization which I believe has lost its moral and ethical foundation," he said, adding:

> After much thought and in great despair and anguish, I have concluded that because of this situation, I have been left no alternative but to sever my relationship with this management, and sever from the company that part of the repertory that Robert Joffrey and I created together and independently out of our hearts, for many generations of Joffrey dancers and audiences.

And with that, he resigned as artistic director from the company he helped found with Robert Joffrey in 1956 and took his own and Robert Joffrey's ballets with him.*

---

*Arpino owned the performance rights to Joffrey's ballets.

The trouble had started soon after Robert Joffrey's death in March of 1988, when disagreement erupted on the Joffrey board about Arpino's qualifications to succeed Robert Joffrey as head of the company. Although Arpino's ballets made up about a third of the Joffrey's repertoire, Robert Joffrey had always been in charge of running the company, setting its vision, and maneuvering among its bicoastal board. Naturally there was concern about whether Arpino could ever fill Joffrey's shoes. With Joffrey at the helm, the company's diverse personalities maintained an often uneasy alliance—one held in check by a mutual respect and admiration for the man who had brought them together. While, as resident choreographer, Arpino could be relied on to supply new dances each season, he had little experience as a manager or in making the kinds of broad-gauge, savvy decisions that the urbane Robert Joffrey made daily.

Sensing a growing concern about how well the company was functioning, the board formed a committee in the fall of 1989 to assess its well-being. As the dancers' representatives, Eddie and Tina LeBlanc were soon called to a meeting to report on the dancers' state of mind. Eddie wanted to represent the dancers' best interests, but he also had his own future to think about. The Joffrey had been invited to perform *Lacrymosa* at the International Ballet Competition in Jackson, Mississippi, that summer, with the understanding that the dancers would have to be paid less than union scale. Eddie found himself in the self-serving position of trying to convince the dancers to accept less money than they were entitled to for an opportunity from which he would be the chief beneficiary. Not wanting to compromise himself further or become ensnared in company conflicts, Eddie resigned from his post as union rep shortly after the meeting.

Meanwhile, two camps began forming among the Joffrey's bicoastal board. On one side was Arpino and his supporters, while on the other was Anthony Bliss, the Joffrey's longtime New York board chairman, his wife, Sally, an ex-ballerina who had once headed the Joffrey II Dancers, David Murdock, the multimillionaire chairman of the Joffrey's L.A. board, and Pennie Curry, the company's executive director.

Arpino smelled a plot to usurp him and began to insulate himself from the Bliss camp. "Jerry felt that it was his and Bob's company and he wanted ownership," says a board member. "So when anybody strong came in, he was paranoid that they were trying to take control."

The backroom machinations took center stage on May 1, 1990, after the Joffrey's board voted to establish a nine-member operating committee to run the company in place of Arpino and the full fifty-five-member board. Upon reading his statement, Arpino promptly bowed out as director and ten board members quit in protest. The embattled Joffrey was suddenly front-page news. The vote for the committee virtually stripped Arpino of all his powers as artistic director and was seen by some board members as the only way to ensure continued financial support for the company, which then faced close to a $2 million deficit, nearly half of which was owed to the IRS in unpaid federal taxes.*

The dilemma facing the board was clear-cut: The people who wanted Arpino out were the same people willing to keep the company solvent. But without Arpino, many on the board feared the company could no longer continue.

Arpino's resignation wreaked havoc on the L.A. season and put the entire future of the company in question. "The odds are that today will see the end of the thirty-five-year history of the Joffrey Ballet," read the opening line of a memo circulated among the Joffrey's board on the day that Arpino quit. Hoping to smooth over the conflict, the board refused to accept his resignation and publicly expressed hope that the matter could be resolved.

In the meantime, however, Arpino had sequestered himself in his L.A. hotel room and was refusing to talk to anyone or attend the negotiations, which succeeded only in alienating several more

---

*The Joffrey's fiscal chaos—apparently hidden by Joffrey executives from the board—had come to light only at the previous month's board meeting in April. It was then that the board discovered that someone periodically over the past two years held back at least $820,000 in federal payroll taxes to pay salaries to keep the dance company in business.

board members. "By that point, no one was feeling reasonable," says a former trustee, "which made the scars a lot deeper."

Amid the turmoil and confusion, the Joffrey dancers began casting about for answers. From one day to the next, the company's fate hung in the balance and they struggled to adjust to program changes, missed paychecks, and unforeseen anxieties about their already short-lived careers. As they were aware, employment opportunities in the hard-pressed dance world were scarce indeed. The day after Arpino resigned, the dancers met at the Music Center and tried to make sense of the situation. "We felt abandoned by our director," says a leading dancer, voicing the sentiments of many of her colleagues. "We heard bits and pieces, but no one seemed to know what the deal was." While Eddie, like most of the dancers, remained loyal to Arpino, a few expressed their intention to stay with the company regardless of who was in charge.

With the rights to Arpino's ballets still up in the air, the Joffrey had decided to withdraw two scheduled works by Arpino just hours before the dancers were to perform them at the Dorothy Chandler Pavilion on May 6. One of the ballets substituted was Eddie's *Lacrymosa*, which wasn't supposed to debut in L.A. until three days later. The reviews for *Lacrymosa*, like everything else that season, were mixed: The critic for *The Los Angeles Times* felt the work didn't "measure up to the stately glories of Mozart's final work. And yet Stierle's emotional honesty and noble ambition suggest a choreographic sensibility worth future attention."

Despite the excitement Eddie felt at seeing his ballet premiered in L.A., the Joffrey's crisis had plunged him into a crisis of his own. The next month, *Lacrymosa* was due to kick off the Fourth U.S.A. International Ballet Competition in Jackson, the dancers having agreed to lower wages. The 1990 competition ws dedicated to Robert Joffrey, who had been cochairman of the IBC's jury for its first three seasons, including the year Eddie had won the junior gold medal. The Jackson competition drew many of the ballet world's most distinguished teachers, coaches, and company directors and Eddie recognized its PR value, especially where *Lacrymosa* was concerned. After all, the ballet had its beginnings at Jackson as a solo in 1986, and Robert Joffrey had invited Eddie to join his company shortly after watching him perform it. Eddie now wanted to complete the circle by returning to Jackson not only as a star with Robert Joffrey's company, but as the lead dancer in a ballet he had made to commemorate the late director.

Adding to his distress was the fear that he would never get another chance to choreograph, his health an unknown quantity in future equations. "I don't consider myself a choreographer yet, that's a craft that takes years to develop," Eddie told *The Los Angeles Times* that month when asked how he felt about seeing his name in the program alongside those of such venerated choreographers as George Balanchine and Nijinsky. "I consider myself a dancer who's being creative. In ten years, if I'm still creating and crafting, *then* I'll call myself a choreographer."

Before the L.A. board showdown, Gerald Arpino had mentioned to Eddie that he was thinking of asking him to make a second ballet for the company. Now Eddie worried that the company wouldn't survive long enough for him to get started on it. Soon, he would have cause to worry that *he* wouldn't survive long enough to see the company perform his new ballet.

Negotiations between Arpino and the board continued through most of the L.A. season. "This is like losing Bob Joffrey all over again," Arpino told *The Los Angeles Times* that month, making a pointed reference to the attempted coup d'état. "It is as if my whole life is wiped out in one tyrannical stroke."

On the stage of the Dorothy Chandler, the Joffrey performed *The Green Table*, a ballet about the ravages of war, in which Eddie danced the role of the sleazy Profiteer. The 1932 ballet by Kurt Jooss is set around a conference table, as corrupt diplomats try in vain to negotiate peace. All the while, the figure of Death dances in the foreground. *Romeo and Juliet* was also on the bill that season, the ballet's battle-scarred landscape and woeful finale yet two more apt reflections of the Joffrey itself that month. Eddie danced the role of Mercutio, Romeo's loyal friend, who is killed in a duel with

As Mercutio in *Romeo and Juliet*

Juliet's cousin Tybalt. Mercutio's prolonged death scene is one of the key dramatic moments in the ballet and Barbara Forbes recalls that Eddie's performance came across as instinctive. "You felt he was experiencing the feeling of saying good-bye to this world," she says.

As the L.A. season drew to a close, the behind-the-scenes dueling by the Joffrey's warring factions finally arrived at its own denouement. After much bloodletting, secret negotiating, and dissension, Arpino came back to lead the company and Anthony Bliss, David Murdock, and Pennie Curry resigned. Arpino's victory was not without sacrifice, however: The company had lost its executive director, both its board chairmen, and its biggest patron at a time when it faced a $2 million deficit. Strapped for cash, the company decided to cancel its summer tour, which included its performances in Jackson, leaving Eddie relieved at the company's survival yet upset and frustrated at losing such an influential showcase.

One week later, the trip was back on, saved by a last-minute infusion of cash from corporate and foundation sources. The company had come back from the brink, just when all looked lost.

On Mykonos

22

GHOSTS AND RUINS

The art of dancing stands at the source of all the
arts that express themselves first in the human
person. The art of building, or architecture, is the
beginning of all the arts that lie outside the person;
and in the end they unite.

Havelock Ellis
The Dance of Life

He felt a catch in his chest each time he drew a deep
breath and he was dogged by pounding in his head that would
strike without warning. Eddie and Lissette had been busy painting
their apartment all week and Eddie figured he'd better stop inhaling
paint fumes in the middle of a July heat wave and get some fresh
air. Jan Epstein had invited him out to the house he was renting
on Fire Island and Eddie was looking forward to spending a few
days at the beach. But the day of his trip, he awoke to a fever.
Instead of riding the ferry to Fire Island, Eddie hopped a cab to
John Oppenheimer's office.

The doctor put him on the antibiotic erythromycin to treat a
possible bacterial lung infection, and told him to return for a chest
X-ray if he didn't feel better in a day or two.

Eddie's chest X-ray revealed that he had swollen lymph nodes in his left lung. Worried that Eddie might have lymphoma, tuberculosis, or PCP in his lungs, John Oppenheimer ordered a TB test, which proved to be negative, as well as a Gallium scan,* which showed that an infection or tumor was developing. At the same time, the doctor tested for cryptococcus, a fungal infection rarely seen in people with healthy immune systems. Cryptococcal disease was not commonly the first AIDS infection, nor did it tend to strike only the lungs, but the doctor wanted to rule it out as a possible problem.

To his surprise, the test came back positive that week. The sudden downward turn frightened Eddie, especially as its significance was so uncertain. He had further reason to worry when Dr. Oppenheimer sent him off to see a pulmonary specialist named Muthiah Sukumaran for a more detailed analysis. A keen-witted, genial man in his early forties, Sukumaran had a soothing bedside manner and managed momentarily to calm Eddie. Born in southern India, Sukumaran had gone to medical school at the University of Madras and had done his residency at New York's Mount Sinai Hospital before opening a private practice in Manhattan in 1978. He had been involved in the staggering fight against AIDS ever since the fall of 1979, when clusters of several rarely seen maladies began popping up in New York City without any apparent cause.

Sukumaran took one look at Eddie's X-rays and suspected that he had cryptoccocal disease not only in his lungs, but possibly in his brain. Cryptococcus usually showed up first as meningitis, an extremely serious brain disease: Treatment was tough, prolonged, and produced terrible side effects, and even with treatment the patient's prognosis was generally poor. After consulting with John Oppenheimer, Sukumaran told Eddie that he would have to undergo a spinal tap in order for them to determine whether or not the disease was affecting his brain. Eddie would be admitted to St. Vincent's Hospital that afternoon. At the mention of the word *hospital,* Eddie panicked.

---

*A Gallium scan shows whether white blood cells are accumulating in a part of the body.

"I did only one thing wrong," he suddenly said to Sukumaran. "I'm so young. Why am I getting this so young?"

Over the years, Sukumaran had treated babies and children with AIDS; however, Eddie was the youngest "adult" AIDS patient he'd seen. The doctor had just been thinking about Eddie's relative youth when Eddie, as if reading his thoughts, broke the silence with his question. There was only one answer and Sukumaran preferred to focus on remedies, not conjecture. He offered a compassionate smile by way of a reply. Later, Eddie would come to call the Indian doctor "Sukey," a nickname his colleagues had given him. A formal man, he rarely, if ever, allowed patients to address him as his friends did, but as he recalls, there was nothing in Eddie's assumption of familiarity that irked him.

The spinal tap was painful, but at least there was some good news at the end of the day. Eddie didn't have cryptococcal meningitis after all. He was diagnosed with cryptococcal disease affecting the lung only, a much more treatable problem, and admitted to the AIDS ward of St. Vincent's, where he was put on Fluconazole, a promising new antifungal drug.

Rosemarie was in her kitchen when Eddie called from the hospital.

"Rosie, it's official. I have AIDS and I'm in the hospital."

Rosemarie heard the panic in Eddie's voice and tried to calm him down. Her brother had never sounded so upset before. Then again, he had never called her with such bad news.

"Eddie," she said slowly, "they can call it whatever they like, but you're going to be fine. You're gonna beat this, okay?"

For the next several minutes, she gave him a pep talk, borrowing phrases she'd picked up in Marianne Williamson's lectures, which she'd been attending with Eddie at Town Hall. "Keep positive," she told him. "I'm sure the drugs are going to work. Just focus on getting better." Still, she was afraid for him. She knew that Eddie was seeing for the first time that he wasn't immune to AIDS. She hoped he would tell their parents soon and not wait until he was too sick to make the trip home. It made her uncomfortable to keep his AIDS diagnosis from the rest of the family. She felt they had a right to know and worried that the burden of carrying his secret would drain Eddie of the energy he needed to get well.

Meanwhile, at St. Vincent's, Lissette was keeping vigil by Eddie's bed in the room he was sharing with another AIDS patient. "The AIDS diagnosis really shook him up," she says. "He was so worried about what it all meant." At the same time, he was relieved that he didn't have KS or PCP, AIDS-related illnesses that Eddie considered much graver. The man in the next bed had been in and out of the hospital several times and "believed in self-healing," remembers Lissette. The man convinced Eddie that he would pull through, be cured, and be back dancing in no time. "Keep fighting," he urged Eddie.

The medicine took effect almost immediately. Within two days, Eddie's energy started rebounding and he was allowed to go home. By the time Rosemarie got to Manhattan, Eddie's anxiety of the day before had all but disappeared. He was on a high about how well the drug was working, believing in part that his buoyant mind-set had helped the healing process.

Convalescing, however, was out of the question as far as Eddie was concerned. Instead of languishing on the living room sofa in air-conditioned comfort, Eddie was soon pushing the furniture back against the walls to make room for dancing. Gerald Arpino had just given him the go-ahead to make his second ballet for the Joffrey and he wanted to have it set in his mind before he started working with the dancers in October. Since the Joffrey's tour to Athens and Paris was coming up in September, his plan was to have the ballet sketched out before he left town.

After listening to more than twenty recordings recommended to him by the Joffrey's music director, Allan Lewis, Eddie chose Howard Hanson's Concerto in G Major for Piano and Orchestra, a stirring four-movement work made in 1948, as the music for his new piece. He spent the next several weeks reading the score of the Hanson concerto, while simultaneously listening to it on the CD player in the living room. He would try to pick out various sounds in the music that he wanted to translate into movement. "Doesn't that sound like a bird getting ready to fly?" he asked Lissette one day while listening to the third movement, a section he would later dub "The Perch" after devising a sequence meant to convey the feeling of dancers preparing to take flight.

Each day, he and Lissette worked on ideas, phrases, and combinations, improvising and inventing until Eddie found just the movement qualities he was looking for. He had been impressed with Millicent Hodson's stories of Nijinsky's drawings and with Hodson's own detailed colored drawings of each dance step in *Le Sacre du Printemps*, and decided to adopt their method. He jotted everything down in his notebook, filling pages and pages with brilliantly colored swirls of shape, line, and pattern. Then he enclosed each page in a clear plastic sleeve together with the scored music that would accompany each of the steps drawn. In this way, he could see at a glance the exact note on which a particular movement would begin.

By mid-August 1990, in the dead heat of summer, Eddie was obsessed with finishing the blueprint for his ballet. He was taking ballet classes every morning and choreographing his ballet in a studio at City Center for three hours each afternoon. He was also working out with weights and pulleys at the White Cloud Studios, where he also ran through a series of yoga-based exercises designed for dancers to enhance flexibility, strength, and coordination. Lissette and Rosemarie worried that Eddie was overdoing it. "He wasn't taking care of himself," says Lissette. But any attempts to slow him down were met with resistance. "I don't have much time," he'd say over and over, a refrain that pained Lissette and Rosemarie every time they heard it. Like the White Rabbit in *Alice in Wonderland* who runs around exclaiming "I'm late! I'm late!" Eddie rushed around complaining of having "so little time," whenever anyone asked how his ballet was coming along. When pressed, he'd explain that the Joffrey wasn't giving him much rehearsal time with the dancers, but for anyone who knew he was sick, the implications loomed larger. "Eddie was not obsessed with AIDS, he was obsessed with his ballet," says Jan Epstein, whom Eddie saw regularly for massage therapy. "To him, it was all a matter of time."

To supplement the drugs he was taking, Eddie looked for spiritual comfort in the free HIV/AIDS support group that Marianne Williamson led once a month at the Manhattan Center for Living, a plant-filled loft space in SoHo. The meetings were held on the Wednesday night preceding her Town Hall lecture and drew about 150 people, most of them gay men, who sat in folding metal chairs listening to one another's stories. Their hopefulness faltering, some people sought reassurance and guidance from Williamson; others more practiced in Williamson's philosophy offered upbeat testimonials about recent successes in their lives: Someone had overcome a recent bout of illness with flying colors, another had faced down his worst fear and triumphed. The emotions in the room ran the gamut from the despair of a young man whose lover had just left him after learning he was HIV-positive, to the rage of a woman who didn't want to leave her young children without a mother, to the panic of another man who had lost the lease to his apartment and had little money and no place to live.

Williamson met each query head-on with compassion, humor, and tough practical counsel, refusing to indulge those she felt were being weak, or worse, dishonest. To those who voiced their fears of dying she would say, "You have more faith in the power of AIDS than in the power of God to heal you." When Eddie stood up to tell his story one night in August, Williamson had little to do but listen, for she saw that Eddie understood her lessons perfectly. He had certainly been applying himself to his homework: Each day he reviewed one of the thirty-five affirmations taken from *A Course in Miracles* that he'd copied onto yellow slips of paper. ("I Love myself, therefore I am thankful for healing myself," was one of them, while another read: "I Love myself, therefore I release resentment, guilt, and the burdens of the past.")

Eddie told the group that he had been in the hospital with cryptococcus and had just been diagnosed with AIDS, but had beaten the illness quickly and was already back dancing and choreographing. "Eddie seemed to personify the teachings of *A Course in Miracles*," says Williamson. "The teachings are: Love other people, love yourself, and feel the peace that all that brings. The only thing that was new to Eddie about my work was how it all applied to AIDS, but the spiritual essence of it he already understood before he came to me. I saw his metaphysical studies laced throughout everything he said. This boy was a leader. When somebody is great in any area, there's bleed-through. It wasn't that Eddie was just a great ballet dancer, he had a greatness to him and ballet was his primary vehicle. He was so sweet that he made it easy for others to accept that they were in the presence of someone further along than themselves."

The aggressive, willful layers of his personality had fallen away in the preceding months, revealing a softer, more altruistic Eddie at its core. Eddie now spoke with a warmth and humility that deeply affected the others in his group. Where the men sharing his Joffrey dressing room had grown tired of Eddie's "me" focus, the men and women facing death in his AIDS support group enjoyed listening to Eddie talk about himself, because he sounded at once both grounded and hopeful. For perhaps the first time in his life, Eddie was singled out without inviting rancor or envy from his peers.

"Whenever Eddie spoke he really moved me," recalls Doug Ireland, an aspiring actor in the group. "He spoke from a deep spiritual place and seemed to be looking at the whole thing in the most uplifting way possible. He wasn't willing to hold anything back." Kyle Ahmed went along with Eddie to several meetings and recalls that the glamour of their profession impressed the others in the room. "Eddie got a reputation really quickly," says Kyle. "He would talk a lot and people liked him. He was a star dancer and yet he also had this virus. People would use him as an example. They'd say, 'If Eddie can do it, so can I.'"

Away from his meetings, Eddie resumed his life as a hardworking dancer and only the most discerning eyes noticed anything amiss about him that summer. Watching Eddie one day in the professional dancers' class he led at his Manhattan studio, ballet coach David Howard saw Eddie's coordination falter ever so slightly. For barely a second, his body lost its perfect pitch and went off key. The moment came in a flash and was over just as quickly; no one but a master teacher would have caught it or detected anything portentous in it. "There's something wrong here," Howard said to himself. "This shouldn't be happening."

Over the years, Howard had grown accustomed to seeing his

middle-aged students experience sudden changes in their bodies as they hit upon "a change of life," as he delicately referred to it. But he was having trouble coming to grips with the sudden changes in body patterns that he was seeing in some of his youngest and most promising dancers. "When you work closely with dancers, you get to know their physical patterns of behavior," he says. "I knew something was going on with Eddie because by then I'd already lost twenty-five dancers to AIDS. You can't help but think, 'All of that work and all of those dreams—gone.' It's been devastating and the only conclusion I've come to is: You can't judge a life by its length."

By the end of August, the cryptococcus had completely cleared from Eddie's lungs, leading Eddie to conclude that he could overcome any medical challenge. "Eddie was much more positive than most people in his situation," says Dr. Oppenheimer. "Sometimes I was a little concerned about that. I tried to sober him by telling him his condition was serious. He said he knew, but he was still very positive about it." The doctor saw that Eddie's immune system was impaired to such a critical degree that new infections were expected. His T4-cell count had dipped below 100. While the doctor kept his worries to himself, he decided to take Eddie off AZT since Eddie seemed to be developing a resistance to it, and put him on a new antiviral drug called dideoxyinosine, or ddI, which was dissolved in water and taken twice a day.

Before meeting up with the Joffrey in Athens for a week of performances in September, Eddie, Lissette, and Kyle decided to take a brief vacation together on Mykonos, a starkly beautiful Greek island popular with gay men. Kyle had just been promoted to the Joffrey's main company. "The three of us felt really close to each other that week," remembers Lissette. "We were having so much fun." They hit the beach during the day and the island's nightclubs after sundown, dancing late into the night and then sleeping till noon in their hotel high up on a hill overlooking the Aegean Sea. Their room had only two single beds, so they took turns doubling up.

Whether on the beach or at the clubs, Eddie was still the Joffrey's "man magnet," drawing attention the moment he showed up. Each afternoon, he and Kyle would set off for the nude gay beach, leaving Lissette off at the "mixed" beach, where she felt more comfortable. Kyle and Eddie were a study in contrasts: While Eddie was fair-skinned and freckled, his nose a little big for his boyish face, his reddish-brown hair streaked blond by the sun, Kyle was exotically handsome, his dark Mediterranean coloring set off by vivid green eyes and jet-black eyebrows and hair. Lying on the beach one afternoon, Kyle looked up to see Eddie running out of the water screaming that he'd stepped on a sea urchin. "Suddenly there were ten naked men rushing at Eddie to help him," recalls Kyle. "One of them was a doctor named Cesare, who happened to have a doctor's kit with him, so he took out the needles from Eddie's foot."

The next day, Eddie and Kyle decided to take pictures of each other posing on rocks in the turquoise Aegean. Modesty prevailed and they slipped on their skimpy suits. As they tried to one-up each other with tricky ballet poses, standing on one leg, arms reaching up toward the sky, a crowd of young men began to gather around them. "Bravo! American boys," they cheered, their enthusiasm mounting each time the boys with the sinewy ballet bodies completed a pose and leapt into the sea. "Eddie and I were on such a high after that," says Kyle, remembering their summer idyll. "Eddie was really on the prowl. He was so sex starved. He had a fling with a Frenchman he met on the beach."

He was hardly rested by the time he got to Athens, dashing to rehearsal directly from the ferry terminal. The company was dancing out-of-doors amid the ruined splendor of the Herod Atticus Theatre, the amphitheater at the city's famed Acropolis. During rehearsal one day, Eddie asked Lissette and Kyle to pose for him on collapsed columns scattered on the ground. As he watched them horse around, striking poses, Eddie got the idea to set his new ballet in the midst of architectural ruins. He shot a roll of film with the intention of asking Campbell Baird, the set designer, to re-create the 1,800-year-old Herod Atticus Theatre on the stage of City Center.

Flexing on the beach on *Mykonos*

In Athens with Lissette and Kyle

Intoxicated by the ideas that came so fluidly in Athens, Eddie seemed to abandon himself to a Dionysian frenzy. "He listened to his Walkman all the time, in airports, at meals, everywhere. He couldn't stop," remembers Kyle. Despite the cool night temperatures in Athens, Eddie insisted on filling in for an injured dancer and ended up dancing two roles in Paul Taylor's strenuous *Arden Court*—out-of-doors. After performances, he stayed up half the night in his hotel room, furiously mapping out his new ballet. Lissette could see he was wearing himself out, but when she urged him to go to bed, he'd only nod his head and continue drawing in his notebook. His first few rehearsals were coming up in Paris and he wanted to be ready.

The Paris engagement held a particular significance for the Joffrey dancers; *Le Sacre du Printemps* was to be danced for the first time since its premiere performances by Diaghilev's Ballets Russes in 1913—and on the very stage on which it had provoked that notorious opening-night scandal. The Diaghilev troupe gave only five performances of *Sacre* at the Théâtre des Champs-Elysées in Paris, followed by a few more in London before dropping the ballet from its repertory that same year. On September 19, 1990, history was remade — and *Sacre* reborn — during the Joffrey's own opening-night performance at the Théâtre des Champs-Elysées. Instead of catcalls, fistfights, and shouts of outrage, this reconstructed *Sacre* was greeted with thunderous applause, repeated curtain calls, and shouts of approval. Both audience and dancers alike were caught up in the excitement of the occasion, its mystic pull as powerful as the force of the earth in *Sacre*. "Nijinsky's spirit must be in this theater," Eddie said to Millicent Hodson before going onstage that night. In fact, all the dancers "were convinced that Nijinsky's ghost was going to turn up at the premiere," remembers Hodson. "We had a joke going around that everyone should be on the lookout for a little Polish man."

Nijinsky's ghost never materialized backstage at the Théâtre des Champs-Elysées, nor even at Nijinsky's grave, which Eddie visited and photographed that week at the cemetery of Sacré Coeur. But Nijinsky's presence was felt nonetheless, especially on September 22, the night the Joffrey bid adieu to Paris with a final performance of *Sacre*.

It was the last time Eddie would dance onstage.

That same night, Eddie had a dinner date with Hodson and her husband, Kenneth Archer, who had been feted all week for their sixteen-year labor of love in reassembling the lost *Sacre*. Before taking Eddie to their favorite brasserie in the Marais, Hodson suggested they say good-bye to Nijinsky, who was dancing in stone relief on the facade of the Théâtre des Champs-Elysées. Pausing in front of the art nouveau theater, the three of them looked up at the illuminated figure of Nijinsky, carved into the theater's pediment. After a moment, Hodson felt the chill in the air and buttoned up her camel-hair coat. Unseasonably cold temperatures and a major flu epidemic had just hit Paris and she wondered how Eddie could be dressed in nothing more than shorts and a T-shirt. "You really should be wearing warmer clothes," she cautioned him.

By the time they arrived at Le Dôme St. Paul, it was past midnight and the restaurant had stopped serving. However, the headwaiter knew Hodson and Archer and had taken an interest in the dance they were reviving. When he was told that Eddie had danced that night in *Sacre* and was hungry, he yelled to the chef, "We have a dancer here who has just been dancing. He is empty and we must fill him up!" Over supper, Eddie talked excitedly about the new ballet he was making and the thrill of leading his first rehearsals earlier that day in the theater where Nijinsky had worked. He showed them the detailed notebooks that Hodson had inspired him to make, both by her own examples and through her stories of Nijinsky's drawings. In turn, Hodson and Archer described a future Nijinsky project they hoped to tackle: the reconstruction of a solo Nijinsky performed in 1919 in Saint Moritz. Eddie told them he hoped to make a ballet about the life of Nijinsky. "Wouldn't it be great if we could all present our Nijinsky ballets on the same program?" Eddie suggested, full of optimism.

The next morning, illness interrupted his plans. Awakening with a bad cold, he decided to cut short his visit. He had hoped to stay on and do some sightseeing with Lissette, but the cold worried him and he wanted to get back to New York to have it checked out. He also had another pressing matter to address.

The moment he was back in his apartment, he called Rosemarie.

"Rosie, I've decided to do it. I'm going to go home and tell Mom and Dad."

Guanacos

DECEMBER

Sunday	Monday	Tuesday	Wednesday	Thursday	Friday	Saturday
		Markhor		*Mountain goat*		**1**
2	**3**	**4** Patty leaves Town 4:30 Massage w/Jan 8:30-9:00 Dinner w/Bill	**5** 10:00 White Cloud 12:00 App. Campbell 3:00 App. for X-Ray 5:00 App. Dr. Astro 8:30 Tom Arrives from Dayton	**6** 3:00 App. with John Oppenheimer	**7** 1:30 App w/Tina	**8**
9 Tom leaves New York	**10** 10:00 White Cloud 1:00 Dr. Dinari	**11** 10:00 Ban 6:00 Tom Massage	**12** Hanukkah (begins sundown) 10:00 White Cloud App. Michael Naso	**13** 10:00 Class Lisette back from Iowa ←	**14** 8:00 White Cloud 10:00 Class Kathy to visit in New York	**15** *Bighorn lambs*
16 Kathy leaves New York	**17** White Cloud App. Dr. Astro Class Co. leaves for L.A.	**18** Class	**19** White Cloud Class	**20** Class	**21** White Cloud Class	**22**
23 / **30**	**24** / **31**	**25** Christmas Day	**26** Boxing Day (Canada) 2nd Week of Performances I.A. Season	**27**	**28**	**29**

Eddie's calendar, December 1990

23

HITTING HOME

On the flight home to Florida, Eddie reviewed his expectations of the coming weekend. He assumed that his father would react calmly and rationally and that his mother would fall apart. "It's her Italian emotion coming out," he remembered hearing his father say whenever Rose got especially upset. Eddie thought about all the difficult conversations he'd had to get through ever since his HIV diagnosis in 1987, and it now struck him that they were all dress rehearsals for the coming announcement, the moment he'd put off for as long as he could.

A few days earlier, he'd flown to Dayton to tell Tom that he had AIDS and was surprised by the way his brother had seemed to take the news in stride. But Eddie didn't realize that Tom had only the vaguest idea of what AIDS meant. Tom assumed that AIDS was "a sickness like the flu, something that was treatable." He figured a cure was imminent. In any event, he had been supportive and caring, and had promised to back him up if he ran into problems with their parents.

Eddie had a full agenda that October weekend. He was hoping to persuade his parents to come to New York for a weekend-long

AIDS workshop Marianne Williamson was planning to lead at the end of the month. He wondered what the odds were that his parents would agree to join him. Slight, he thought, but worth a try all the same.

His parents were there to meet him at the airport. "You look so thin, Edward," said Rose on the drive home to the Hollywood apartment she and Bill had just moved into. "You've always wanted to be thin." She assumed he was pleased and tried to sound encouraging.

"I've been working really hard on my new ballet," Eddie explained, misreading her enthusiasm over his lost weight. "I have to start rehearsing as soon as I get back."

Eddie waited until he was alone with his father the next afternoon to get the discussion rolling. He told his father he had AIDS. Tears slipped from the corners of Bill's blue eyes. He read the papers enough to know what AIDS was and what AIDS meant as far as his twenty-two-year-old son's long-term prospects were concerned. Bill thought of AIDS as a gay disease and had "semi-expected that Eddie would get it" ever since he realized that Eddie "liked the guys." Eddie's preference made him unhappy and one night in 1985, after learning about Eddie's affair with Richard, he had grumbled to his daughter Kathy, "If Eddie gets sick, I won't be there for him." Now he looked over at Eddie and told him he'd be there for him whenever he needed him. "Just tell me what you need me to do," he said. When Eddie promised him that he was taking good care of himself and was feeling fine, Bill felt better. "I figured he was probably going to be okay for a while," Bill recalls. "I didn't know a lot about how AIDS worked."

But later that afternoon, while Eddie and Rose were sitting outside by the pool of the apartment house, Bill was suddenly overcome by the weight of Eddie's news. He called Tom in Dayton, the first of many such calls. "My dad was a total wreck," says Tom. "He called me in tears. I was still totally positive about it all. I said, 'Dad, Eddie's doing okay. He's healthy.'"

That evening, after Bill had gone to bed, Eddie and Rose stayed up late talking. "Mom," Eddie said gravely, "I need to talk to you about something."

"Great! Tell me all the exciting news," Rose replied, patting the spot on the sofa next to her where she wanted Eddie to sit. On the end table were two framed photos of Eddie in motion. In one, Eddie was leaping to prominence at the Prix de Lausanne, while in the other, he was dancing the solo he made for *Lacrymosa:* the bookends of a brief career.

"Remember when I called you from L.A. three and a half years ago and I sounded upset? Well, that day I went to get tested for the AIDS virus and I found out that I was HIV-positive."

Rose remembered their conversation, but had no idea what Eddie was talking about. What did HIV-positive mean? She sat in silence for a moment, waiting for him to fill her in.

"You know, Mom," Eddie said, startled by Rose's placid expression, "you can ask me questions."

So Rose asked a few questions. What did HIV-positive mean? Was he taking care of himself? Had he been to the doctor? Was the doctor giving him something for the virus?

Eddie reassured her that he had great medical care and was doing fine. Rosemarie had been checking up on him, he said, and Tom knew about it, too, if she had any questions. He'd tell the other kids when he had a chance. "You really don't need to worry, Mom," Eddie told her. "My friend Bruce Kahl in L.A. has had the virus for ten years and he's still okay." Rose searched Eddie's face for signs of illness. It was true he looked tired and thinner, but he didn't exactly look *sick*. "Well then," Rose said to herself, "obviously there's a cure for this virus Eddie has. I'll have to call Rosemarie when Eddie leaves and find out what we need to do."

The next night, Saturday night, Eddie stopped by to see his sister Terri and her kids Frank, Mike, Juliette, and Andrea, who were always excited when their "Uncle Ed" was in town. The minute he walked in the door, they would start fighting over him. While Eddie rarely had much time to spare on his trips home, he never failed to squeeze in a visit with his nephews and nieces. This particular visit, however, filled him with sadness and apprehension, for he imagined that his sister might ban him from her house and from seeing her children once she found out he had AIDS.

After Terri's kids and her husband, Mike, had gone to bed, she and Eddie caught up on each other in the living room, a brown-paneled room decorated with religious plaques, framed Christian inspirational sayings, and a Joffrey poster of Eddie as the Snow Prince. A thin, nervous woman with long brown hair, Terri stubbed out her cigarette as she listened to Eddie recount his experience with the AIDS virus and his philosophy about dealing with the disease. Unlike her parents and brother Tom, Terri was well versed in the literature about AIDS. Her work in the pro-life movement had kept her up-to-date on thorny medical and moral issues and, as a former librarian, she was an avid reader. Eddie's maturity astonished her. Terri couldn't get over his profound sense of spirituality. "I was impressed by his strength," she remembers. "He didn't sound scared and he must have been. I just listened, because I didn't want to seem preachy. I was extremely hurt that he didn't tell me earlier, but I appreciated his honesty. The family put me in an ultra-right position. Being pro-life doesn't make me stupid."

According to Rosemarie, "that was the healing moment of their relationship. Before that, they had always had a grinding debate about religion. Terri assumed that Eddie was misguided and that his life and sexuality lacked any spiritual focus." During their conversation, Terri "shared with Eddie that AIDS was one way of God getting society's attention and that some ultimate good comes from tragedy."

An hour before flying back to New York, Eddie asked his parents to come to Williamson's AIDS workshop. "She's great. You'll really like her," he told them as he made his pitch and filled them in on Williamson, *A Course in Miracles,* and the HIV support group he had joined. "You can learn a lot about AIDS at the weekend workshop and you'll meet other people who have it." Rose agreed to come at once and Bill promised to think it over. But both were equally apprehensive about just what awaited them at that weekend workshop. "My mother was thinking, 'Oh, no, is it some kind of religious meeting?' " recalls Rosemarie, "whereas my father was thinking, 'Oh, my God, there's going to be a room full of gay men talking about sex.' "

As soon as Eddie's plane left the ground, Rose rushed home to call Rosemarie, who had already fielded calls from Terri and her father. "It took me a while to realize how little my mother knew about AIDS," Rosemarie acknowledges. "She wanted to know what it meant when someone had AIDS. Her approach to any problem was to fix it, so she thought here was another problem that she could fix. I told her that Eddie had really good care and that the best thing we could do for him was to support him in a positive way."

The last call of the night came from Eddie himself.

"It was so strange, Rosie. Mom and Dad didn't act at all the way I expected," he said, both relieved and confused. "Mom was totally calm and Dad was the one who cried."

Eddie had little time to think about the events of the past weekend. The day after he got back to New York, he started working with the Joffrey dancers on his new ballet. The ballet was to premiere the night of the Joffrey's thirty-fifth-anniversary gala on March 5 during the second week of the company's New York season. Absolut Vodka was sponsoring the gala and had agreed to mark the occasion by underwriting three new works in celebration of new American choreography. The New York season promised to be a major showcase for Eddie: The Joffrey was booked into the New York State Theater at Lincoln Center, a more prestigious house than City Center, and *Lacrymosa* would have its New York premiere.

In the days leading up to rehearsals on his new ballet, Eddie had finally come up with a title, after thumbing through the thesaurus in the Joffrey's press office. Hoping to find a word that evoked a sense of heavenly heights or hopefulness, he had started with the word *sky*. Under *sky* was the word *empyrean*, and when Eddie checked out its meaning in *The American Heritage Dictionary*, he saw how perfectly the word summed up the themes he hoped to express:

em·py·rean *n.* **1. a.** The highest reaches of heaven, believed by the ancients to be a realm of pure fire or light. **b.** The abode of God and the angels; paradise. **2.** The sky. —*adj.* Of or pertaining to the empyrean of ancient belief.

Whereas *Lacrymosa* was about the anguish of loss, *Empyrean Dances* was meant to suggest hope and renewal. As the choreographer Senta Driver has observed: "How do you top yourself after you've choreographed a ballet about your own death? You tell us what heaven is." Eddie envisioned a stage littered with the fragments of a crumbling wall. "The dancers complete these sculptures and create new shapes from the shapes that are already there," Eddie explained to a reporter prior to the ballet's premiere. "These people are in this destroyed place, and they are rebuilding it with their spirit." Of course, such lofty ambitions were difficult to realize in a two-week rehearsal period, which was all Eddie had to transfer the patterns in his notebook to the bodies in the studio. He'd had a long time to develop *Lacrymosa,* first in a workshop setting, then in rehearsals with Joffrey II, and later in rehearsals with the main company. With *Empyrean Dances*, he was starting from scratch — and time, money, and resources were tight, given that the company was mounting three other new ballets that season.

Faced with his first big commission from the main company, eighteen dancers awaiting his instruction, and twenty-two minutes of music to set to movement, Eddie was naturally nervous on his first day of rehearsal. To offset tensions, he began by asking Lissette to demonstrate a dance phrase he had choreographed. Then, he asked each dancer, one by one, to perform his or her version of the same phrase for the rest of the cast. "Eddie wanted us all to dance in the way that was most natural to each of us," recalls Tom Mossbrucker, who was one of only a handful of dancers with whom Eddie had discussed his having AIDS. "He wanted *Empyrean Dances* to be a celebration of life and of us as dancers." Brent Phillips remembers that Eddie was determined to encourage a creative dialogue between himself and the dancers, "which wasn't the Joffrey way. He wanted to push a whole other way of doing things. Some people got irritated with him because they thought he was rebelling against the system."

Set to Hanson's lushly romantic score, *Empyrean Dances* was to feature two leading couples and a chorus of fourteen dancers.

Eddie had hoped to cast Lissette in one of the principal roles, but the Joffrey's directors had overruled him on the grounds that Lissette was overweight. Instead, Eddie had to settle for choreographing a brief solo for Lissette, who was frequently called on to demonstrate the movement sequences that she and Eddie had tried out in their living room. Lissette's solo looked deceptively simple: She was only to step forward toward the audience, swivel, and kneel on one knee, her upturned palm cradling her face. Yet in that brief moment, she was to convey the whole point of the ballet. "I was opening my soul," she says.

During the first week, Eddie discarded bits and pieces as he began to pinpoint the images that most satisfied his eye. In a recurring motif suggesting joy or hope, the dancers curled forward and then arched their torsos skyward at the exact moment that they were hoisted high into the air. Since choreographers are not given to long discussions about their intentions, Eddie told the women only that the ballet was about relationships between people. He told the men that he wanted their group dance to convey the feeling of "guys hanging out on the street" and asked them to wear jeans and sneakers to rehearsal because he liked the stop-start momentum sneakers afforded. When Eddie demonstrated a movement he wanted, one of the dancers jokingly mentioned that it looked like something from the Jets dance in *West Side Story,* and from then on, the men thought of *West Side Story* whenever they danced the second movement of *Empyrean.*

In transferring two-dimensional drawings onto bodies in motion, Eddie discovered that certain ideas just didn't pan out. He had no trouble envisioning in his head the dancers moving in a surging, diagonal sweep, but his patterns were often so intricate and involved that he had difficulty communicating his ideas to the dancers. He'd ask one group to run across the stage in one direction and a second group to run across in another, look at the pattern that emerged, reject it, and start anew. Making their job more complicated still was Eddie's interest in having them leap off plaster fragments, which the set designer had made to look like the broken columns and pedestals Eddie had seen in Athens at the Herod Atticus Theatre. When a pattern didn't work, "Eddie kept going

Eddie's choreographic sketches for *Empyrean Dances*

back to his notebook to find other patterns," remembers ballet mistress Barbara Forbes, who supervised those rehearsals. "He could get very impatient with the dancers. He'd say, 'C'mon, just do it!' and I could see their hackles rise. But he spoke on an equal level. One day he said to them, 'We're all here to work together to create and I'm not asking anything of you that I wouldn't ask of myself.'"

The trouble was, Eddie always asked plenty of himself. The steps he created for Tom Mossbrucker in the ballet's swift second movement were marked by the surging drive and athleticism of Eddie's own dancing, because Eddie fully intended to dance the role in the third cast. The central male figure threads his way in and out of a group of men, initiating the movement and using the pedestals as springboards. "It was extremely energetic," recalls Mossbrucker of the solo. "Eddie was envisioning himself doing it. I had about eight counts to get from one side of the stage to the other."

On a break from rehearsals one weekend, Eddie took Lissette to see Mark Morris' company perform at the Brooklyn Academy of Music. Morris was considered the most inventive young choreographer of his generation, and Eddie was hoping to pick up some ideas or at least inspiration. In the lobby, Eddie ran into Senta Driver, and for most of the intermission they remained locked in a firm embrace. Driver was going through a wrenching time: Randy Wickstrom, a prized dancer in her troupe, was dying of AIDS and she'd been spending long hours by his hospital bed. She hadn't seen Eddie in a year and was angry at him for falling out of touch. She saw that he looked worn-out and suddenly intuited that something was amiss, even before Eddie himself supplied any clues. Like David Howard, she was attuned to the body's mute cries of distress. "There was something tight about him," she remembers. "I was embracing him and babbling out of control, saying, 'You shouldn't have done that to me. I've never stopped loving you,' and he said, 'I know I've hurt you. I should have called you, I'm sorry,' and I told him, 'You know, Eddie, you really can't fall out of contact with people these days, you just can't. People don't see each other again. I've got a dancer now who's dying of AIDS.' That's when he told me about the Manhattan Center for Living. He said I ought to know about it. And I was thinking, 'Why does he know about that?' but I couldn't ask him. I could only deal with Randy, and Randy was dying."

Worried that *Empyrean Dances* was falling behind schedule—and worse, that his creative momentum had hit a snag—Eddie went without sleep, night after night, as he tinkered with his drawings and reworked his blueprint. Plugged into his CD Walkman so as not to bother Lissette, he would listen to the Hanson score while he sketched, hoping to hear something in the music that might awaken a new idea. It wasn't long before he was skipping meals and his daily doses of ddI and Zovirax, drugs intended to protect him against the infections to which he was now so vulnerable, given that his T4-cell count was a precarious 27. As he grew increasingly fatigued, his shallow cough worsened. Stirring from her own fitful sleep in the middle of the night, Lissette would hear Eddie coughing and see his light on at the top of the stairs and wonder how he could be so reckless with his health. When she'd plead with him to rest, he would take his headphones off long enough to answer, "Just a few more minutes," and then stick them back on his ears for the rest of the night. It seemed to her as if he had decided that since he couldn't nurture both his body and his creativity, he would sacrifice one to the other. "Eddie put all his energy into what he knew would probably be his last project," she says. Just as the Chosen One in *Sacre* sacrifices herself to the god of light and creativity in order to make the spring come, Eddie abandoned the care of his body in order to make *Empyrean Dances*.

Each day, he arrived at the Joffrey's studios with a totally revised plan. "He would come in all excited," says Barbara Forbes, "because he had reworked everything we'd done the previous day. He'd say, 'I'm exhaused. It took me all night to figure it out.'"

The news hardly cheered the dancers, who were putting in six hours a day on Eddie's ballet.

"It was getting ridiculous," says Adam Sklute, for whom Eddie originally made the role of Death in the Joffrey II workshop production of *Lacrymosa d'Amore*. "Every hour and every day, something was changed. It was giving everybody a headache and we were all getting grouchy. We would think, 'Which version does he want now?' You could sense that Eddie felt he was running out of time. He had so many things that he wanted to express and he wanted to put them all in that one ballet. It got to be too much."*

At the end of his allotted two weeks of rehearsal in October, Eddie was only three-quarters of the way through the ballet. Scott Barnard and Jerry Arpino agreed to find an extra week of rehearsal for him sometime in January, although "they were a little annoyed that Eddie kept changing things," says Barbara Forbes. On the other hand, they both recognized that Eddie's ballet was ambitious and complex and they could well understand his need for more time. Arpino was still the only member of the Joffrey's artistic staff to know of Eddie's HIV status. Eddie was visibly exhausted, but there was to be no break in between assignments. On October 26, the same day *Empyrean* rehearsals came to a standstill, Rose and

---

*Dance critic Allan Ulrich of *The San Francisco Chronicle* would later remark that *Empyrean Dances* was one of the saddest ballets he'd ever seen because it left him with the sense that in it was every idea Eddie wanted to explore.

Bill Stierle arrived in New York to join Eddie the next morning at Marianne Williamson's AIDS workshop.

In the intervening two weeks since Eddie's pivotal visit home, Rose had already joined a support group for parents of AIDS patients at Center One, an AIDS outreach organization in Fort Lauderdale. She was trying to learn what she could about the disease, but the litany of medical terms, drugs, and opportunistic infections confused her. As soon as she got home at night from her meetings, she'd ask Rosemarie to translate. Since Rose knew nothing about AIDS, she couldn't give the others in the group any firm information about what stage Eddie was at or which drugs he was taking. When she told them that Eddie was still healthy, she was comforted to learn that he could remain healthy for a long time. That was all she needed to know.

To make up for the days of work she was going to miss by going to Manhattan, Rose had been putting in extra time making lunches for the students at St. Elizabeth's, a Catholic grade school in Pompano (Madonna Academy had merged with Chaminade College Preparatory), and cooking supper for the Brothers who lived at the nearby Marianist retirement home.

She was ashamed that Eddie had AIDS, seeing in his diagnosis her failings as a mother, and she asked Bill not to tell the Brothers about Eddie. By the time she arrived for the weekend seminar, Rose, like Eddie, was exhausted from her round-the-clock preparations.

The next morning, Eddie, Rose, and Bill walked the six blocks from Eddie's Thirty-fifth Street apartment to Manhattan Center Studios, a conference center and banquet hall, where two hundred people, primarily men in their thirties and forties, sat on metal chairs awaiting Marianne Williamson. Most of them looked healthy, although a few had begun to manifest the gaunt pallor of advancing illness. Many had brought along friends, lovers, brothers, and sisters. Rose and Bill Stierle were the only parents in the room. The minute they arrived, Eddie introduced Rose and Bill to Williamson, proudly showing off each to the other. "It doesn't happen very often that both parents show up," observes Williamson. "Everybody in the group is always so impressed when a parent is there. On some level, they wish it was their own."

Williamson began the session with her signature opening prayer, a prayer Eddie often recited to calm himself.

"We see in the middle of our minds a little ball of golden light," she intoned. "We watch this light as it begins to grow larger and larger until it covers the entire inner vision of our mind. We see within this light a beautiful temple. We see a garden that surrounds the temple and a body of water that flows through the garden. We see that the temple is lit by the same beautiful golden light and we are here for we have been drawn together by the power and in the presence of God. We devote our time here together and our relationships with one another to Him."

For the next few hours, Williamson led them in discussion and meditation. She encouraged them to define health in terms of inner peace and to think of death as a transition, or birth, into a different existence. From her *Course in Miracles* viewpoint, she argued persuasively that the life of the spirit didn't stop with the death of the body, but continued on, even if their physical senses couldn't perceive it. "The goal of the weekend is to increase our conscious contact with God as we understand him," explains Williamson. "What I'm trying to facilitate is a deeper experience of God and from that experience of God comes a deeper peace. There's a way to experience sadness with peace."

As she sat listening to Williamson, Rose couldn't help wishing Eddie would return to the Catholic Church in his time of need. Still, she could see that Williamson "understood her congregation," as she put it. "She seemed to take their fear of dying away by giving them a picture of life after," recalls Rose. "She spoke of this place of peace and light that was awaiting them."

Bill sat quietly, "his arms crossed," remembers Williamson, surveying the spiritual terrain of Eddie's illness. Rose, too, wanted to understand what Eddie was going through, but she was having trouble absorbing all the information coming at her. Her head was spinning and she'd occasionally doze off. "Eddie was furious at her for falling asleep," recalls Lissette, who was sharing Eddie's bed that weekend while his parents slept in her pullout bed downstairs. "He felt she didn't want to deal with his illness."

The next day, Rose and Bill listened to the men and women in the room share their stories. The particulars of the stories varied, but one theme kept coming up again and again: the fear that their parents would reject them if they knew they had AIDS. Hearing these accounts of abandonment made Bill feel closer to Eddie. "I'd never do that to Ed," he thought. Rose, however, was troubled by what she heard and raised her hand. Williamson nodded to Rose at once. "Go ahead, Mom!" Eddie urged her. "This is Eddie's mother, Rose," Williamson announced as Rose stood up and addressed a roomful of strangers.

"Being a parent of eight children," she began, "I'd like to speak on behalf of the parents of all of you in this room. Give your parents a chance to be supportive. Parents are strong people. They're like the palm trees we have in Florida. They've weathered severe storms and they're bent, but they're still standing. Ask your parents to be there for you now when you really need them." She took her seat to the sound of applause.

Handing out index cards around the room, Williamson asked everyone to write two letters: one to the AIDS virus, and one a response from the AIDS virus. She hoped that by addressing their disease directly, they would feel less like victims. She advised them to envision the AIDS virus as a gentle, loving being dressed in fearsome armor. "Imagine the AIDS virus as Darth Vader," she suggests in *A Return to Love*, referring to the *Star Wars* villain, "and then unzip his suit to allow an angel to emerge." Williamson preferred her own version of the AIDS acronym: Angels In Darth Vader Suits. When they had finished composing their letters, Williamson called on Eddie to read aloud what he had written.

Dearest AIDS Virus,

These are my honest feelings. For a time you had really brought so much uncertainty, so many questions about my life, the greatest being, Why? Well, I must say even with all of these uncertainties and questions, you have brought my life strength and answers, the great answer being Love. What a Life I have. You are teaching me to forgive, you are teaching me to contribute at the great level, and you are teaching me to love unconditionally. With every passing day I feel closer and closer to God so I thank you for bringing me this transformation. The only question I have left now to you, my teacher, is, Can I graduate?

Next, he read the response he had scripted for his virus.

> Dearest my friend Eddie,
>
> I know this has been tough for you and all of your loved ones especially your parents, but I really must tell you that you really didn't like yourself very much and I just found a place to be. What I really wanted to teach you was all of those things you mentioned but most importantly, I wanted to teach you hope. You know, I really can't handle the power of God, so I now give you your diploma. Eddie, you have passed with flying colors. I'll be gone real soon.

As Rose took in the scene and watched yet another audience focus on her son, she was overcome with pride. "Look at how he shines," she thought. Even here, he was setting the standard.

That night, Rose called Rosemarie and gushed about Eddie's stellar performance in the workshop. "My mother didn't really understand why Eddie was being singled out," recalls Rosemarie. "Marianne's spiritual message was confusing to her." As a result, Eddie emerged from the weekend with his thinking "turned around," says Rosemarie. "He was disappointed that my mom, who had been 100 percent behind him as a child, wasn't on top of things at all. Whereas my dad, who had never been very supportive of his dancing as a child, came through in the crisis of his life. Eddie thought, 'He's here understanding every aspect of it and thinking as I do about it.'" On Tina Awad's massage table later that week, Eddie gave an account of the weekend. He told Awad it had given him a new insight into his father. Eddie, she recalls, "felt his father was saying, 'It doesn't matter if I approve or not, I see who you are and I understand who you are.'"

The day after the AIDS workshop, Rose and Bill flew home to Florida and Eddie awoke with throbbing pains in his lower back. He thought perhaps he had overtaxed a muscle in class, a natural occurrence for any dancer, but when he noticed a swollen, tender bump in his groin, he called John Oppenheimer for an appointment. The doctor gave him Valium for his back pain, prescribed a massage, and advised Eddie to monitor his symptoms closely. On

November 1, two days later, Eddie was back in his office. He was short of breath, he had a fever, and his cough was dry and frequent. His weight, which had been dropping steadily since September, was down to 128 from his usual 139 pounds.

After evaluating Eddie's symptoms and reviewing his chest X-ray, the doctor concluded that Eddie had PCP, a major killer of AIDS patients. Even though he'd been taking aerosolized pentamidine before switching to the sulfa drug dapsone, Eddie seemed to belong to the small percentage of people with AIDS who developed PCP regardless of prophylactic measures. Typically, those who broke out with PCP died more quickly than those who came down with other AIDS-related opportunistic infections. Eddie was admitted to the AIDS ward of St. Vincent's that afternoon and started on antibiotics to clear his lungs. He called Rosemarie from the hospital. He simply refused to see the diagnosis as a death sentence and convinced himself he would recover. "I've come up with a different meaning for PCP," he announced to Rosemarie. "I'm going to think of it as Positive Christ Power."

The day Eddie was hospitalized with pneumonia, his mother mailed him a package from Florida. Wrapped in brown paper was the secret elixir Rose hoped would restore Eddie to health. She, too, believed in miracles.

In the accompanying letter, she wrote:

> I would like to share with you the healing water from Lourdes. Our friend, Helen, brought me the Holy Water from her visit to Lourdes in June. I learned about Our Lady of Lourdes as a very little child. I pray to Her always for each of my children. Please accept the water from me and with Her blessing.
>
> Love,
> Mom

At St. Vincent's, Eddie was not responding to treatment. To determine whether or not he had PCP, Doctor Sukumaran was called in to perform a bronchoscopy, an uncomfortable procedure during which a tube is inserted into the lung to extract tissue sample. No evidence of *Pneumocystis* was discovered in Eddie's lung, leading his doctors to conclude that Eddie must then have some kind of bacterial pneumonia, which was equally serious. They switched his antibiotic and, gradually, he improved. From then on, Eddie and his doctors had a tacit understanding: "We never discussed the long term," says Dr. Sukumaran. "We focused on the immediate. I would say, 'You have a problem, but it's treatable.'" Eddie regarded his bout with pneumonia as an inconvenience, a hurdle to jump over en route to his next destination. Rather than focus on the hurdle, he insisted on looking ahead to the spot where he hoped to land. For Eddie, the next immediate goal was getting back on his feet and into class in time for the Joffrey's *Nutcracker* performances at City Center in late November.

To that end, he tried to keep himself in shape in his hospital room. As soon as he began to feel better, he got out of bed every few hours, laid a towel on the floor, and ran through his stretching exercises, even though an IV was attached to his arm. The nurses on the floor marveled at the sight of Eddie going through his paces, but to Rosemarie and Lissette, such displays of will were fast becoming commonplace. They knew it was pointless to try to dissuade him from preparing for the New York season, just as it was pointless to ask him to take a break from *Empyrean Dances*. The ballet was Eddie's painkiller: It took him far away from his sickbed and allowed him to see himself springing off ruins and hurtling through the sky. Propped up in his hospital bed, Eddie studied set and costume designs and reviewed choreographic details with Lissette, frequently asking her to demonstrate the steps they discussed. Pushing back the chairs, medical trays, and IV drip, she danced for him in his room at St. Vincent's, since he could no longer dance himself.

Despite their own heavy performing schedules, Rosemarie and Lissette supervised Eddie's day-to-day care and passed the long hours watching "Wheel of Fortune," playing Scrabble, and discussing Eddie's medical options. Rosemarie was then starring in *Red, Hot, and Rowdy*, singing and dancing six nights a week in the 1,500-seat Superstar Theater at Resorts in Atlantic City. Each morning, she boarded a bus for the two-and-a-half-hour ride from Atlantic City to Manhattan, spent the day on the AIDS ward at St. Vincent's, and traveled back to the casino in time for her eight o'clock show that night. While Lissette didn't have as far to travel, she was trying to juggle daily class and rehearsals along with her visits to the hospital. As they watched television, Lissette would sew pink ribbons on her new toe shoes, the ballerina's nightly ritual. "Rosie and I were trying to be optimistic," she recalls. "I wanted to be strong for Eddie, but I'm very emotional and it was hard for me to see him evaporate. He was still beautiful to me, but his eyes got dull." When the other Joffrey dancers would inquire after Eddie, Lissette would cover for him and say that he was at home with a terrible cold. "He wore himself out with *Empyrean*," she'd tell them, and few thought to wonder further.

While Eddie saw no need to divulge his medical condition to most of the Joffrey dancers, he knew he was going to need extra consideration from the artistic staff, and put in a call to Scott Barnard. "I was given a message at home that Edward had called and was in the hospital," recalls Barnard. "Well, to be perfectly honest, I never dreamed that Edward was really sick. He was so vital and healthy that I assumed he must be calling me for a conference, to tell me what he expected from the company for the next six months. When he said, 'I'm in the hospital, I need to talk to you right away,' I went over to the hospital immediately. He told me he was positive, but at that point, he thought he could beat it. He had that youthful feeling of being invincible. He had the whole scenario worked out. He told me that he wouldn't be able to make that week's rehearsal, but that he certainly intended to be back in a matter of days. He said, 'Of course, when we start *Nutcracker*, I'll be there doing all the performances.' I was stunned. I couldn't get over the fact that he'd known he was positive for three years, and that he'd already been in the hospital once before, and here he was telling me not to worry about him missing rehearsals." Recognizing that Eddie might not complete *Empyrean Dances*, Barnard went to Arpino and suggested that if Eddie didn't get the ballet done, they should show it anyway as a "work-in-progress." Arpino agreed.

Performances of *Nutcracker* were due to begin on November 15 and Eddie didn't leave the hospital until November 13. The day he went home, his parents came to town to look after him. Arriving at

Eddie's apartment, Rose was pleased to find the bottle of holy water from Lourdes lined up in Eddie's medicine chest alongside his myriad vials of pills. By then, she and Bill had conveyed bits and pieces about Eddie's condition to the rest of their children. They knew Eddie had wanted to visit each of his siblings to tell them himself, but they saw he was running out of opportunities. Rose called Patty at the hospital where she worked in Columbia, South Carolina, to say that Eddie had pneumonia and was very sick, but she never once mentioned that Eddie had AIDS. As a critical care nurse, Patty didn't need long to put the puzzle together. Eddie soon called Patty himself to confirm what she had suspected.

Except for Patty, none of the other Stierle kids had ever seen AIDS up close, and the news that their youngest brother had the disease hit them in different ways. As the religious figurehead of the family, Michael Galligan-Stierle assumed the role of father-confessor, trying valiantly to help his parents cope with their guilt about Eddie's illness and their panic about losing him. "I was at dinner when my dad called me, crying," remembers Michael, who had just moved to Wheeling, West Virginia, to head the Campus Ministry program at Wheeling Jesuit College. "He was alone in my parents' apartment and he said, 'Eddie has AIDS and he's gonna die.' I remember just listening and asking questions about what his status was and how much time he had. A while later, my mom called, because Edward was going to call me and she wanted to prep me. I didn't tell her that Dad had already told me. She was sad, but she wasn't broken up like Dad was because she didn't understand the larger implications."

Bill, Jr., who was then teaching biology and coaching football at a high school outside Los Angeles, immediately went out and bought books on self-healing, having decided that he would "devise a strategy" to help Eddie "think" himself well. He listened to Louise Hay lead him through positive guided imagery on her assorted tapes and he read books by the surgeon Bernie Siegel, another evangelist of hope, about his experiences with exceptional patients. He wanted to try to understand what his brother was going through. Fired up by his research, he called Eddie with recommendations and became frustrated when Eddie failed to respond enthusiastically. "I would say, 'Eddie, this is what I found out,'" Bill recalls, "and he'd say, 'Oh, yeah, I know about that already.'" While Bill and Eddie had gone out to dinner after Joffrey performances whenever they were in the same city, Eddie regarded his brother as something of a dreamer. Eddie couldn't understand why Bill hadn't dedicated himself to a singular ambition and would roll his eyes as his brother vaguely sketched his plans to become a writer, playwright, or screenwriter. "I felt Eddie wasn't taking care of himself," he says. "He was just turning on the jets and burning the fuel trying to finish his ballet. When I called to ask if I should come and see him, he said, 'No, I have too many people here. Don't come now. Come in January.'"

Meanwhile, Eddie's sister Kathy had a different dilemma to confront. "I wasn't surprised I was going to be one of the last people Eddie told because we weren't close, we didn't have that rapport going." Still, she was shocked to learn that Eddie had AIDS. In the beauty salon where she worked in Gainesville, Florida, she'd heard stories about hairdressers who'd developed AIDS and then stopped working. She was worried that her clientele would fall off if word got out that her brother had AIDS. She talked to her husband about Eddie and when he asked her whom she was going to tell, she said she wasn't going to tell anyone, not even their best friends or her husband's family. "He felt that was a good idea," she recalls. "I knew that it had to be kept quiet because of the small community we live in. Things can get turned around. People here aren't really open-minded about AIDS. They still think you can get it by sitting on a toilet. We didn't want things to be said about us in the community."

No sooner was he back in his apartment than Eddie began preparing for his return to the Joffrey. Though he was still taking his antibiotics intravenously and had come home with an IV needle taped down to the top of his hand, Eddie thought only of regaining the muscle tone he had lost after two weeks of bed rest. "I've got Snow Prince coming up," he'd told Lissette his first morning home. The first performances were two days away. "I've got to get back in shape." He made an appointment for the next day at White Cloud Studios and scheduled massages with Tina Awad and Jan Epstein. Since he was too weak to negotiate the stairs to the bathroom, Eddie gave up his room to his parents and slept downstairs with Lissette and their dog, Missy Joe, on the pullout sofa. When Eddie awoke during the night, coughing, Lissette massaged his chest and legs and jumped out of bed to get him one of the five medications he was then taking every few hours: ddI, Zovirax, Fluconazole, Megace, and dapsone. "I couldn't sleep because my headaches were so bad," he told Adam Sklute that week at the White Cloud Studios. "Lissette stayed up with me and stroked my head." In an ironic twist of events, Lissette was finally sharing Eddie's bed, but as his nursemaid, an arrangement that worried Bill and Rose, who feared Lissette would get sick. "I wasn't versed on AIDS," recalls Bill, "and when Eddie would start coughing, I'd tell Lissette, 'You really shouldn't sleep with Ed. You're going to wind up dying too,' and she'd say, 'No, Pop, don't worry, I'm all right.' "

On his sixth day home from the hospital, Eddie took a nosedive. He had a fever, he was short of breath, his cough was worse, and he had swollen lymph nodes in his armpits and the back of his neck. Brushing his hair in the bathroom mirror, he got a terrible scare: He noticed a raised purplish lesion on his scalp, which he knew was a sign of Kaposi's sarcoma. His parents rushed him to John Oppenheimer's office on that cold, rainy afternoon and sat anxiously in the waiting room as Eddie underwent yet another checkup. The doctor told Eddie he'd have to order a biopsy of his scalp lesion and lymph nodes. He thought it might be either TB or KS, but he wouldn't know until they ran some tests.

Ushering his parents out of the waiting room and into the drizzling rain on Twelfth Street, Eddie began to cry. "They think I might have TB or KS. Dad, I don't think I can handle KS." Eddie had never felt so frightened and off-balance. "Let's not dwell on what it might be," Bill answered, trying in vain to bolster Eddie. "Let's just take it one step at a time and think about what we need to do next." As soon as they got home, Eddie stuffed his pajamas, pills, contact lenses, and dance notebooks into a bag, and headed back downtown to St. Vincent's. There, he, his mother, and Lissette sat in the emergency room for four hours before Eddie was given a bed in the AIDS ward. "I hope it's not KS. That would be terrible," Eddie said over and over to Lissette as they waited. "What's KS?" she asked. "I can't explain it to you right now," he replied.

The biopsies and chest X-ray showed KS on his scalp and in his lymph nodes and lung. "Eddie fell apart as soon as he heard he had cancer," says Bill Stierle. "He was really afraid." His doctors tried to reassure him, even though they privately thought that Eddie's prognosis "looked bleak," says Muthiah Sukumaran. KS most commonly showed up on the skin first and patients could go for years with KS skin lesions without having any medical complications. But in Eddie's case, the KS showed up on his scalp and lungs simultaneously, suggesting that the course of his illness was severe and aggressive.

Rosemarie pulled Dr. Sukumaran aside and asked how long Eddie had to live. "A few months?" she ventured. "I don't know if we can talk about months," he told her. Reading Eddie's despair about his KS diagnosis, Sukumaran tried to cheer him by telling him that several of his KS patients had responded very well to treatment and he saw no reason why Eddie wouldn't as well. "That was all Eddie needed to hear," says Rosemarie. "He decided he was going to be one of those cases." But first he had to endure five days of continuous chemotherapy. When his father heard that Eddie needed immediate chemotherapy, he called Patty, who offered to fly up at once. He wanted Patty on hand as the family nurse, although he worried that her unexpected presence would frighten Eddie into thinking that his situation was dire.

Patty insisted on coming. Despite the circumstances, she was happy finally to have the opportunity to showcase her own special talents to her family. "Most nurses I know have split personalities," says Patty. "Work is work and personal life is personal life. With Eddie, my first concern was with how they were treating him. I thought of myself as a sister first and a nurse second."

The chemo treatments exhausted Eddie and left him nauseated. Patty conferred daily with Eddie's doctors in his room and bathed

Eddie at night. "Make sure you wear your gloves," Eddie would warn her as she helped him into the shower. "I don't want anyone else going through this." Rosemarie fielded calls from family members and protected Eddie from unwanted intrusions, while Rose took care of meals, sometimes popping into the hospital's ground-floor chapel to pray on her way back from an errand. "Eddie, I'd really like to take you to Lourdes," Rose told him one day after seeing how drained he looked after a round of chemo. "I know you would, Mom," Eddie answered her, gently. "But I don't think Lourdes is the place for me to heal right now. I feel better when I go to Marianne's support group." While Patty, Rosemarie, and Rose could sit for hours by Eddie's bedside, Bill preferred to have an activity to keep him occupied and frequently passed the time tending to home improvements in Eddie's apartment. Each day, he'd give Eddie an update on the shelf he'd built for him or the crack in the wall he'd plastered. "Don't worry, Ed, you'll be out by Thanksgiving," he'd spur him on. "We're all going to Rosemarie's." When it became clear that Eddie wasn't going anywhere for Thanksgiving, his family brought Thanksgiving to him. That afternoon, Rose, Bill, Patty, Rosemarie, and Lissette sat in a circle around Eddie's bed, dining on turkey, stuffing, and pumpkin pie, their plates propped on their laps.

A week into his hospital stay, Eddie began to emerge from his chemo haze, although his doctors remained uncertain about his chances for recovery. "The doctors told me it was the fastest-growing KS they'd seen," recalls Patty Stierle, who one day had to take Eddie for an echocardiogram to determine whether the KS was affecting his heart. As Patty wheeled him down the corridor for his test, Eddie listened to the Howard Hanson score on his Walkman, determined to work out the remaining steps for *Empyrean Dances* in time for the final week of rehearsals in January.

Another day, Jerry Arpino came to visit and Eddie's spirits perked up within seconds of his arrival. "Hey, kid! You're going to be all right. I know you'll be out of here soon," he chimed before handing Eddie a gift box containing a rabbit-fur hat with earflaps that had belonged to Robert Joffrey. For the next few minutes, Arpino proceeded to fill him in on the latest news from the Joffrey. "I hear your piece is good," he said encouragingly. "The season is going to be great!"

Dr. Sukumaran also stopped by to see him. Eddie described the new ballet he was making and told the doctor how excited he was that *Lacrymosa* was going to have its New York premiere in March. You should get tickets for it, Eddie urged him. Neither Sukumaran nor Oppenheimer was convinced that Eddie was going to live until March. "We knew he wanted to be at the premieres of his two ballets and it somehow became his focus," recalls Dr. Oppenheimer. "We were all working to get him there, but at times, I really didn't think he was going to make it. Not everyone responds well to chemo. He could have died a few days after starting treatment."

By the end of November, eleven days after beginning chemotherapy for KS, Eddie was back in his apartment. The cancer in his lung and lymph nodes had responded well to the treatments. On his first day home, Rose and Bill flew back to Florida and a few hours later, Eddie made out his will. The rights to *Lacrymosa* he intended to leave to Rosemarie and Lissette; the rights to *Empyrean Dances* were to go to Rosemarie and Barbara Forbes; and his apartment and most of his personal belongings he bequeathed to his parents.

That same night, he took Patty and Rosemarie to hear Marianne Williamson lecture at Town Hall and afterward waited in the long line to introduce his sisters to Williamson. "How *are* you, Eddie?" asked Williamson, who had missed him that month in her support group. He told her he had just been in the hospital with KS. "There was such a radiance that came from him that you thought, 'Oh, no, he's not sick,'" recalls Williamson. "Even though I know how the whole thing goes, I was tempted to think, 'He's got such a positive feeling, he's not going to die.' But," she adds, after a moment's reflection, "that's my own lower level of understanding."

Encouraged by his improvement and growing strength, Eddie began inching his way back into shape. In between chemo treatments, blood tests, and massages, he stretched his body at White Cloud and honed his technique in classes at the Joffrey. The dancers noticed that Eddie had lost weight, but most of them assumed, as Tina LeBlanc did, that he had "run himself ragged working on *Empyrean Dances*" and was suffering from a bad bout of the flu. It wasn't uncommon for dancers to look thin and tired in the midst of preparations for a major season and Eddie's colleagues, when they had time to think about him at all, didn't make much of his changed appearance. If they *had* looked more closely, they would have noticed that Eddie was having trouble completing class and could barely manage the jumps he had once tossed off, one after the other. Nausea and dizziness, the aftereffects of chemotherapy, made class a struggle and, with his energy still in short supply, Eddie decided to talk to Scott Barnard about cutting back his *Nutcracker* performances during the Joffrey's Iowa and Los Angeles engagements. The company was to fly to Iowa on December 6 and to Los Angeles on December 19.

The day he met with Barnard in early December, Eddie had already missed the two-week *Nutcracker* season at City Center and consoled himself with the thought that perhaps he'd be back onstage sometime during the Hancher Auditorium engagement in Iowa. He had never before missed a performance in his career and the timing couldn't have been worse: The Snow Prince was his signature role and the fact that he couldn't dance the one role in the Joffrey repertoire that had been tailor-made for him served as a painful reminder of his waning physical powers. That moment of reckoning is one all dancers must confront, yet Eddie was facing it a dozen years ahead of schedule. "It's like growing old far too early," former ballerina Toni Bentley has written of the anguish that inevitably accompanies physical decline. "Instead of one's mind dwindling, one's body dwindles, with one's mind totally intact, filled with the same desire and energy as ever—probably more."

With a view toward rekindling Eddie's dampened spirits, Scott Barnard worked out a schedule with Eddie that allowed him several days of rest between performances. Barnard seriously doubted that Eddie would be joining the company onstage anytime soon, but he continued to keep Eddie's name on the casting list all the same because he saw how important it was to make Eddie feel that he was still a vital member of the Joffrey. The list was posted on the company bulletin board where Eddie could see his name. "I saw in his eyes that he was asking me to do that for him," recalls Barnard. "I knew he was not able to dance, but I couldn't cut the spirit out of him by saying, 'I don't think you can make that.' So I cast him. And then he would call me a few days in advance and say, 'I'd better not try and do that.' So I'd say, 'Okay, just get over that and you still have the next week.'"

Unbeknownst to Eddie, Barnard kept a second casting list ready, so that when Eddie called to cancel his performance, Barnard wouldn't throw the company into turmoil with last-minute changes. The alternate scenario created a lot of extra work for Barnard because Eddie danced three roles in *Nutcracker* and in replacing him, Barnard had to rearrange the assigned roles of several other dancers as well. Barnard had never gone to such lengths for any other Joffrey dancer. "Edward was such a presence in the company. There was no question but for me to cast him just as I would have normally," he says. "It helped his strength, somehow, to see his name still on the casting."

Barnard's unqualified support surprised Eddie and forced him to regard Barnard in a new light. "There's more to him than I thought," he told Rosemarie after his meeting with Scott. "He's really on my side."

The Joffrey's Iowa appearances came to a close on December 12 without any sign of Eddie Stierle in his signature role. Some of the dancers suspected that Eddie had AIDS and was recuperating from a more serious illness than he let on; others had no idea that there was anything amiss. Concluding that he had misjudged his rate of recovery, Eddie simply adjusted his target date: He would join the company in Los Angeles in mid-December. When he missed that deadline, he told himself he'd make sure to finish out the Dorothy Chandler season.

And so it went, week by week.

Rehearsal of *Empyrean Dances*. Eddie is reclining on the floor in the foreground.

24

SCOTT'S CAP

By late December, his weight had dropped to 120, down twenty pounds from his usual dancing weight, and he couldn't take a shower without seeing clumps of his auburn hair swirling around the drain. With his L.A. performances looking ever more unlikely, Eddie skipped ahead to the next significant date on his agenda: the first week of January, when he was to finish making *Empyrean Dances*. If he couldn't dance himself, he still had other bodies to make dances for and he was determined to show what he could do when he devoted all his energy to his choreography. Unable to sit still in his apartment while Lissette and the rest of the Joffrey dancers were performing in L.A., Eddie flew home to Florida for a few days of sun before heading to Atlantic City with his parents for Christmas. Tom and Patty Stierle also came in for the holiday and the family spent the week together at the home of Rosemarie and Kit.

Eddie had taken to wearing bandannas and hats and his siblings did their best not to dwell on how much hair or weight he'd lost since they'd last seen him. Instead they offered encouragement while he worked out steps for *Empyrean* in the living room and made a show of their enthusiasm whenever he mentioned the next ballet he wanted to make. Much as he loved *The Nutcracker*, Eddie hoped to provide an alternative to the annual Christmas classic with a dance version of Dickens' *A Christmas Carol*, the story's themes of regret and redemption having piqued his interest.

On Christmas Day, Eddie couldn't wait for Rosemarie to open his gift. "I got you something really special," Eddie whispered. Rosemarie had trouble stifling her disbelief when she opened Eddie's card and found two tickets to the Broadway hit *The Phantom of the Opera* for a performance in June. He told her that he had bought tickets for himself and Lissette too, so that they could all go together. "June?" wondered Rosemarie. "I was floored," she says. "Here I am hoping he'll make the week and Eddie is buying theater tickets for six months ahead." He surprised her again the next morning when he bounded down the stairs to her living room and announced: "Rosie, I've decided to have a big birthday party this year. Help me come up with ideas." Since his twenty-third birthday, the world premiere of *Empyrean Dances*, and the second performance of *Lacrymosa* fell within the same week in March, Eddie decided to invite everyone he knew to New York to celebrate all three occasions. He came up with a list of 120 people he planned to invite, including the friends, relatives, dance-world figures, and former teachers who had contributed to his career. Acting as his own press agent, he outlined a schedule of events revolving around himself. By summoning them all to Lincoln Center, he appeared to be orchestrating his own grand finale, the fitting coda to a life lived in performance.

That week, Eddie called Eric Castellano in L.A. to give him ample notice of his plans. "It's probably going to be my last birthday. I hope you can make it," Eddie said matter-of-factly. "Eddie wasn't saying it to be dramatic," says Castellano. "He just accepted it. He said, 'I just want to have this blowout party and have fun.'"

Eddie's last Christmas, with Rosemarie and his dog, 1990

January 25, 1991

Dear Family and Friends,

I invite each of you to share in the joy of celebrating my 23rd
birthday, the New York Premiere of Lacrymosa, and the World
Premiere of Empyrean Dances. My birthday party will take place
Saturday night March 2nd at the Gingerman Resturant following
the performance of Lacrymosa at New York State Theater. I would
also like to invite you to the World Premiere of Empyrean Dances,
Tuesday night March 5th. This new work is part of the Joffrey Ballets
Gala Celebration which includes a formal dinner following the performance. It would give me great pleasure for you to attend any or
all of these occasions.

Lacrymosa Premiere	March 2nd Saturday	8:00	New York State Theater W 62nd between Columbus&Amsterdam
Birthday Celebration	March 2nd Saturday	10:30	Gingerman Resturant 51 W 64th Street
Empyrean Dances Premiere	March 5th Tuesday	7:30	New York State Theatre
Joffrey Gala Dinner	March 5th Tuesday	10:00	New York State Theater On The Promenade

Please RSVP for birthday party by February 16 (212-269-8731).
Tickets for performances can be purchased through the Joffrey
box office (212-870-5570). For Joffrey Gala and dinner contact
Jane Emerson (212-265-7300). Thanks so much for your endless love
and support and I look forward to sharing this special time with
you.

All My Love,

Edward Stierle

On January 3, Eddie was back in the studio with the Joffrey dancers for the final week of rehearsal. The dancers hadn't seen him in over a month and, to them, he looked markedly skinnier. His once thick, powerful thighs lacked any muscular definition and his high-voltage speech had now dwindled to a barely audible whisper. Then there was the business of the blue bandanna on his head. "When did he start wearing those?" the dancers wondered. They didn't have to wait long for an answer.

The dancers were rehearsing Charles Moulton's *Panoramagram* when Eddie walked into the studio and quietly informed Scott Barnard that he thought it was time he talked to the dancers. Eddie remembered how they had felt when Robert Joffrey had gone missing from rehearsal for weeks on end without explanation, and he had no intention of veiling his own predicament. Barnard was relieved, because AIDS rumors had begun circulating and he hoped that Eddie might address them himself. "I know some of you have heard that I've been in the hospital," Eddie told his colleagues, nearly all of whom were under the age of thirty. "I want to be really up-front and let you know that I've been fighting AIDS. I'm feeling better now but I really want all of you in *Empyrean* to give me everything you've got. I need you to work with me to finish my ballet." Several dancers had to get back to the *Panoramagram* rehearsal, but many others crowded around Eddie offering their support. No other Joffrey dancer had ever brought them face-to-face with AIDS: Gregory Huffman, a former leading dancer, had died in 1988 at the age of thirty-five, several years after he had left the Joffrey; former soloist Ernie Horvath had died at age forty-six in January 1990; while forty-seven-year-old Burton Taylor, another ex-Joffrey principal, was then dying of AIDS, but few among the current crop of dancers knew him.* With Eddie's announcement, illness and mortality intruded for the first time into the dancers' daily lives.

---

*Burton Taylor died on February 13, 1991. Former Joffrey stars John Wilson, sixty-four, and Glenn White, forty-two, died of AIDS in 1992.

When they saw how calmly Eddie delivered his news and how optimistic he seemed, the dancers tried to respond in kind by going about their business as usual. "Everybody was supportive," remembers Kyle Ahmed. "Nobody freaked out." From then on, they took their emotional cues from Eddie and kept whatever despair they felt to themselves. "I was shocked," says Brent Phillips, then twenty-one, "because everyone I knew who had AIDS was older. They were part of the gay scene in the seventies. The fact that little Eddie from Hollywood, Florida, had it brought the whole thing crashing home to me. You expect to see your friends die when you're eighty. I thought, 'We should not have to deal with this.'" For several of the dancers, Eddie's illness brought on remorse. It didn't take long for them to do the math in their heads and realize that Eddie had known he was HIV-positive for virtually his entire career at the Joffrey. "At first I was really hurt," says Carl Corry, who regularly competed with Eddie for the same parts. "I felt I had treated him badly. In reality, though, I didn't know he was dying, I was dealing with the cards as I knew them. In hindsight, I must say, I have a completely different perspective of why Eddie was the way he was. It makes perfect sense to me that he would have been barreling through, grasping for any second of attention or artistic life that he could have. He went from a real whiny kid to a mature young man very quickly."

Tina LeBlanc, Eddie's favorite partner, remembers the profound sense of loss she felt the moment Eddie revealed the nature of his illness. In their performances together, she and Eddie had always shared a mutual rapport and symmetry and he was the first person close to her to be struck by AIDS. "It came as a total shock that my dear friend was going to die. Like everybody else, I associated AIDS with death. But Eddie didn't feel that way, or at least he didn't show it. He knew that word was going to get out that he was sick and he wanted everybody to hear it from him that it was indeed AIDS, but I never got the feeling that he felt it was terminal."

What struck them most profoundly was Eddie's refusal to hide anything from them. From his frank displays of his emaciated body to his determination to complete *Empyrean Dances*, he literally bared himself body and soul, and in the process, took the dancers step-by-step through his own experience with dying. The daily view of his deterioration unsettled them and made an indelible impression. Before morning class on his first day back at the Joffrey, Eddie peeled off the three different-colored turtlenecks he was wearing, in order to show off his body, then sheathed in a long-sleeved black unitard. To the dancers' amazed horror, he stood in front of the mirror admiring his skinny body. "Look, my butt is almost gone," he said, genuinely pleased with his reflection. "Eddie looked so emaciated," recalls Cynthia Giannini. "His legs were brittle because his ligaments had tightened up. Some people thought he should cover himself up, but he seemed to be proud of the way he looked. It was really weird." Brent Phillips remembers watching Eddie study himself in the mirror. "He kept saying he was so happy because he finally had the body he'd been wanting his whole life. We thought it was a little sick, but we were relieved that he was making light of the situation." In his attempt to cut through their discomfort, Eddie may have inadvertently added to it by dealing with AIDS in the same way he had approached every other taboo subject at the Joffrey: directly and defiantly. Not even his bandanna was meant as camouflage: "He'd take it off," recalls Barbara Forbes, "and say, 'Look at this, I have three hairs left. Can you believe it?' Eddie put the other person where he was, and allowed them to experience what he was going through. He didn't try to conceal the extent of the battle he was waging, though we probably had no idea of what his suffering really was." The dancers, in turn, made every effort not to treat Eddie as an invalid. "We tried to be really normal," says Adam Sklute, "which is what Eddie wanted most of all. He never let his being sick get the most of him."

Despite their knowledge of his illness, none of the dancers thought Eddie had only a short time left. "There was such a discrepancy between the way he looked and the way he acted," says Cynthia Giannini. "He never faltered throughout the day." In fact, Eddie did such a good job of masking his effort that his colleagues never realized how close to death he was. A portable oxygen tank would have quickly eased his discomfort when he

grew short of breath, yet Eddie refused to appear handicapped
before his colleagues. As a ballet dancer, he was practiced in the
fine art of masking pain, having forced his body beyond its natural
threshold, night after night, on the stage. Unlike the Olympic
athletes and thoroughbred racehorses with whom they are often
compared, dancers learn early not to grunt, grimace, or even hint
at the strain involved in creating the illusion of effortless grace.
Eddie's daily presence throughout all of the six-hour rehearsal
sessions for *Empyrean Dances* only reinforced the dancers' sense of
his fortitude. "It was monumental that he made it to those rehearsals," says Barbara Forbes, "but the dancers soon came to expect
that he'd be there because he always showed up. At the same time,
he made us feel that he needed our support to continue. That's
what brought the company together in experiencing his illness."
Now when Eddie jumped up to demonstrate a chain of steps, the
dancers would urge him to rest. "At that point," says Scott Barnard, "the dancers were ready to pull their socks up and give
Edward any extra help he needed." But their pleas were often
ignored: Cynthia Giannini gently reprimanded him for eating
powdered doughnuts and for drinking only water instead of vita-
min-rich fruit juice. And Barbara Forbes remembers urging him to
protect himself against the chilling January temperatures. "It was
cold in the studio," she says, "and Eddie would be wearing a
unitard. I'd have to say, 'Don't you feel cold? Shouldn't you put
on a sweater?' And he'd say, 'Oh, yeah.' We needed to remind him
to take care."

Cast in the role of Eddie's caretaker was Bill Stierle, who sat
quietly off in a corner of the studio each day, paying close attention
to his son's progress on the ballet. Throughout Eddie's life, his
mother had been the one to ferry him between home and studio.
This time, it was his father who packed him into a taxi and escorted
him to rehearsal, his father who counted out his pills and gave
them to him hourly, his father who brought him water and chewing
gum and ran out to get him the lunch he barely touched, and his
father who patiently sat out the six hours of rehearsal, waiting to
take Eddie home.

Bill had taken a leave of absence from his maintenance job at

Bill Stierle during rehearsals of *Empyrean Dances*

Chaminade. "My son is terminal," he told the school's principal. "He has lung cancer from AIDS. I'm going to go up to New York and spend time with him. I don't know how long it's going to take." Bill understood how important *Empyrean Dances* was to Eddie and wanted to help him get his work done. Father, like son, couldn't bear the thought of not completing a job he'd set out to do. "I knew the ballet would probably cost him his life," he acknowledges, "but I had to help him accomplish what he needed to do."

Bill's offer to accompany Eddie to the Joffrey each day took the rest of the family by surprise. "It's not something we'd ever expect my father to do," says Rosemarie. "He'd never been able to sit through a whole day of rehearsal. He always had to be doing something." Behind his silent, solid demeanor, Bill was hard at work studying the ballet and trying to come up with ideas about how best to photograph it. Just as he had done at Liana's ballet studio, he put a frame around the images that interested him and learned to anticipate the high point of the action so that he would know at precisely which moment to snap the shutter. "Eddie's father seemed to express a lot of emotion just sitting there quietly," remembers Barbara Forbes. The dancers were equally moved by the figure in the black baseball cap. "We were thinking, 'Oh, God, there's Eddie's father out there and his son is dying,' " says Brent Phillips. "It was too much to comprehend what both of them must have been thinking."

The sadness and despair they imagined were far from Eddie's thoughts. "I've never had this relationship with my father before," he happily informed Lissette one night as they were lying in bed, talking. "It's great to see him sitting there."

Each night around 7 P.M., before he, Eddie, and Lissette set off for home, Bill would call Rose to alert her that they were on their way. By the time they reached Eddie's apartment, Rose had dinner on the table, having spent the day cooking, mending Eddie's dance clothes, and "wiping everything down so it was hospital clean," as she proudly put it. Though she desperately wanted to be with Eddie at the Joffrey, Rose saw that her husband and son needed their time together and willingly removed herself to the sidelines. "My mother had been trying to draw my father into Eddie's world her whole life," says Rosemarie. "She was always dragging him to see Eddie perform. It was the first time she didn't have to convince him to be part of Eddie's world."

At home, Eddie would review the day's work on video with Lissette and his parents and make endless revisions. "Then he'd start coughing," says Bill, "and I'd get him his medicine. He became incoherent after taking the pills because there were so many different drugs. I'd say, 'Eddie, what the hell are you doing taking so many pills?' We worked out a system where he could space them out more. They'd just knock him out for a while and then he'd get up and say, 'Where's the video? I've got to go over the video.' "

Eddie was under terrific pressure to finish *Empyrean Dances* in a six-day rehearsal period and amid an intense flurry of activity at the Joffrey. While the majority of new ballets were staged in roughly three weeks, Eddie's ballet involved a large cast, complicated group patterns, and unusual set pieces. In addition to *Empy-*

rean Dances, the dancers had three other new works to learn as well as twelve ballets to prepare for the New York season. Not surprisingly, energy was in short supply. While the overall shape of *Empyrean* had emerged by the end of the first rehearsal period in October, its edges remained unfinished and the last movement had still to be choreographed.

On Eddie's good days, he conveyed an air of calm and managed to indicate the kind of movements he wanted, though he was too weak to perform them himself. Among the images that most pleased him was the culminating moment of the ballet in which the dancers line up in an ascending diagonal, their arms stretched up and out toward a celestial glow emanating from the wings. It was Eddie's view of Elysium, the final resting place of the blessed after death.

On his bad days, he'd need to sit down to catch his breath after giving a few instructions and would become easily frustrated when he couldn't find the transition he needed in between patterns. "We watched him deteriorate as his ballet was growing. He was killing himself with *Empyrean,*" says Brent Phillips. Adam Sklute remembers that often "Eddie didn't have the strength to show us what he wanted and didn't have time to fix certain problems. He wanted us to form a big pinwheel, where the girls are hanging on the guys' arms. For us, it was most unpleasant. The girls were hanging off us and our arms were breaking. We needed to work out who went where and how we could get into the pattern. Eddie would say, 'No, that's not the way,' and when he got frustrated, he'd throw his hands up in the air and say to Scott, 'You just do it because I can't.'"

Eddie had come to rely increasingly on Scott Barnard to help him work out the ballet's trouble spots. In several passages, the dancers weren't getting into position on time, and Eddie recognized that he needed help rephrasing their counts and revising some of their transitional steps. For the first time in their edgy relationship, Eddie took Barnard's recommendations without resistance. But not without a few amendments. "It was a fight to finish the ballet," recalls Barnard. "Edward was feeling the time racing on him. I urged him to finish each section, so that he'd have something completed in case he didn't finish the whole ballet." While Eddie worked on one section of the ballet, Barnard polished another in a separate studio.

Eddie always thanked Barnard for his support and welcomed his input, but, according to Barnard, on several occasions Eddie reviewed his changes only to dismiss them. "That's lovely, Scott," he'd say. "It works very well, but it's not what I wanted." To which Barnard would reply: "Well then, you must fix it." Eddie feared that his ballet had too many of Scott's touches and not enough of his own imprint. "That was just Edward being young," Barnard says. "He began to feel all of a sudden that he was getting too much help on something that he so very much wanted to do *all* himself."

One morning en route to his seventh-floor office, Barnard poked his head into studio six to see how Eddie's rehearsal was progressing. It was a cold, blustery day and having just come indoors, Barnard was still wrapped in his wool coat and brown leather cap. The cap was the one dapper item in Barnard's otherwise unstudied wardrobe and he rarely ventured outside the Joffrey's offices without it. On planes to distant engagements, the dancers always knew where Barnard was sitting by the brown leather cap peeking over his seat.

Eddie spied Barnard at the door and came over to greet him. "I've always liked that hat," he said.

Without ceremony, Barnard whisked off the cap and placed it on Eddie's head.

"Oooh," Eddie said, stroking the leather. "That feels so good."

"Then you must wear it," replied Barnard.

"No, no, no," Eddie protested. "It's your favorite cap. I couldn't take it away from you."

"I've had that old hat long enough. *You* wear it for a while," Barnard insisted.

And with that, Eddie accepted the hat. "Look what Scott gave me," he remarked with boyish delight as he modeled the hat for the dancers. For the rest of the week, it stayed on his head throughout rehearsals. "Eddie sent me a card thanking me for the hat," says Barnard. "He said that he saw the hat as a token of my true friendship. It was then that he realized that I had always been his friend and was not simply a director trying to make him do something he didn't want to do."

The day Eddie finished *Empyrean Dances*, he and the dancers invited several friends to come to the Joffrey to watch a run-through of the work. It wasn't customary for dancers to invite outsiders in to see rehearsals of a new ballet, especially on occasions when the company's artistic director had yet to see the final draft. In his excitement about his work, Eddie overlooked company protocol and once again broke the rules, but this time unwittingly. He not only invited an agent at William Morris he hoped to cultivate, but he also asked his mother to bring wine and cookies. By the time Gerald Arpino marched into the studio at the end of the day to review the ballet, he found people crowded into the room and wine bottles and trays of cookies laid out on a table in the corner. The Joffrey's director was not amused.

"What is this?" he grumbled under his breath to Barbara Forbes. "How could Eddie think to invite all these people without my approval? What is he thinking? This is my company and *I* haven't even seen the ballet yet."

"Jerry felt that Eddie was trying to upstage him by taking matters into his own hands," says Jodie Gates, recalling the darkening dismay on Arpino's face as he crossed the room to his seat. "He felt that Eddie wasn't respectful."

There was little to be done though, for as soon as he took his seat next to Forbes the dancing began.

Having learned of Arpino's displeasure, Eddie ran over to apologize to him the moment the run-through finished to loud applause. By now accustomed to such moments with Eddie Stierle, Arpino listened patiently to Eddie's apology, his exasperation overwhelmed by admiration for the feat Eddie had just pulled off. "You always do what you're going to do, don't you, Edward?" he said finally as he hugged him.

Although impressed that Eddie had managed to complete *Empyrean Dances*, the Joffrey dancers were mortified when he showed up the following week to join rehearsals for the New York season. It was one thing to see the frail Eddie walking around in his unitard giving instruction and quite another to watch him attempting to propel himself through his bravura roles. Not seeing himself as his colleagues did, Eddie decided to begin his comeback with a rehearsal of *Trinity*, a ballet with great personal resonance. Gerald Arpino's rousing rock homage to the spirited sixties, *Trinity* concluded with a stage dotted with lit candles in memory of those who died in Vietnam. The day Eddie came to rehearsal, Carl Corry was supposed to be dancing the leading role, but Corry was late.

Eddie stepped forward. "I'll do it, Scott," he offered.

The dancers looked askance. "*Trinity* is a sexy ballet and Eddie didn't look at all sexy," says Cynthia Giannini. "His physicality wasn't there anymore and there was so little life left in his body, yet he was trying to defy what his body was capable of doing. I couldn't believe that he had the mental strength to want to go out there and do a variation in front of the whole company. We were thinking, 'Are they going to let him go out there and perform during the season?' "

Scott Barnard was leading the rehearsal and seriously doubted that Eddie could get through such a strenuous ballet. Eddie hadn't danced full-out in two and a half months. This was a delicate matter and he knew enough to tread cautiously.

"Are you sure you want to try this?" he asked gently.

"Yes, let me try," Eddie answered, gearing up for his entrance as if his body had lost none of its brio. Eddie took off on his running jump. He was to turn in the air and fly backward with one foot extended out in front of him. Just as he was turning himself around in midair, Eddie crumpled to the floor, doing a full backward somersault before landing on his shins with his head tucked into his chest.

A horrified hush fell over the room. No one dared move, when suddenly, Eddie's laughter shattered the uneasy silence. Their relief palpable, the dancers laughed along with him as he picked himself up off the floor. "Edward's initial instinct was to laugh about it," recalls Scott Barnard. "He helped everyone else through that moment."

If Eddie's fall surprised the dancers, "it surprised him even more," remembers Tom Mossbrucker. "He was always the most energetic dancer in the company." Though the dancers were never to know it, Eddie later told Rosemarie that his fall had deeply embarrassed him.

Carl Corry soon appeared in the doorway and Eddie gave up the floor to him. In a bittersweet turn of events, the thirty-two-year-old Corry had finally made it into the first cast of *Trinity*. Corry had been "absolutely sure" that he would be assigned the first cast of *Trinity* since he had seniority over Eddie and had already danced the role. Instead, Eddie won the coveted slot ahead of him, just as Eddie had won the role of Alain in *La Fille Mal Gardée*, and the first casts of *Clowns*, *The Dream*, and *The Nutcracker*. Now at twenty-two, Eddie was too weak to finish out the *Trinity* rehearsal and Corry stepped in for him. But Eddie refused to stop moving. For the rest of the rehearsal, he stood in the back of the studio, indicating with his hands the movements that Corry was dancing. When Lissette came by to check up on him, he shooed her away. "Are you sure you're okay?" she asked. "Yeah, I'm fine," he said, though she recalls he was short of breath and there was disappointment in his voice.

For the rest of the week, Eddie pushed through classes and rehearsals, still intent on learning new roles for the spring season. Just months earlier, during the first series of rehearsals, he had sailed through them. Two ballets being prepared for the Lincoln Center engagement had been earmarked especially for Eddie: Balanchine's *Tarantella*, a pas de deux in which technical flights of fancy are performed at breakneck speed; and Robert Joffrey's *Postcards*, a lyrical, poetic suite of dances set to the music of Erik Satie.

Even when other dancers were assigned the roles he was meant to dance, Eddie preferred to believe that they were simply filling in for him, not taking his place. He honestly assumed that he would return, fully, to form. "Eddie had come through so many hurdles that seemed to be final," observes Barbara Forbes, "that he thought it was possible that he was going to get better one more time, enough to dance again." He even went as far as to tell Scott Barnard that he planned to join the company on its tour to Taipei and Hong Kong later that month. When Barnard advised him against the long journey and requested a doctor's note, Eddie was heartbroken, imploring, "But I really want to go to China. I've never been there." Without further discussion, he soon dropped the idea.

Still, he continued to rehearse, his addiction to dancing overriding the pain he endured daily as he tried to come to grips with his enfeebled body. During rehearsals for *Tarantella,* and for a new ballet by Alonzo King called *Lila,* Eddie mirrored the movements of the dancers as they danced, but never left the floor. And yet his shadowy presence proved unsettling to the dancers, who had trouble dismissing the memory of Eddie's fall from their thoughts. "Eddie was such a fireball," says Tina LeBlanc, Eddie's intended partner in *Tarantella.* "To see him so weak and yet so optimistic was very disturbing. I felt saddened and uncomfortable because I didn't know how to deal with it." One day, Eddie decided to rehearse the central duet of *Lila* with the female lead, Beatriz Rodriguez. At certain moments, the woman partners the man. "Bea was holding Eddie up completely," recalls Adam Sklute. "Afterwards I remember talking to Bea and she started crying and said, 'I would love it if he could hold on just until the premiere, even if we have to change some of the steps.' "

But soon, his lungs started giving out. A close call in class that week finally convinced Eddie to rest awhile longer before pushing his body to perform. He had been doing only the barre portion of class and sitting out the "grande allegro" or jumping section. On this day, however, he tried to jump, one last time. Suddenly, he bent over in pain from a chest cramp and hobbled out into the hallway. Cynthia Giannini rushed out behind him and found him lying on the sofa, gasping for air. "I can't breathe, I can't breathe," he struggled to tell her. For the next several minutes, the ballerina massaged his chest and helped him to release the tightness in his lungs so that he could once again breathe more easily.

Well, if he couldn't dance entire ballets, Eddie thought, perhaps he could dance excerpts from them. He informed Tom Moss-brucker that since he wouldn't be strong enough by February to dance in the New York premiere of *Lacrymosa*, perhaps he would just dance the solo and let Mossbrucker perform the rest of the role. Clinging to his identity as a dancer, Eddie was scaling down, not giving up.

In an interview with Jennifer Dunning of *The New York Times* that ran on March 3, two days before the premiere of *Empyrean Dances*, Gerald Arpino pointed out that Eddie still hoped to dance. "He lives for it," said Arpino. "He makes facing boards of directors and the reality of life seem just stepping over a small fence. He is a big influence on the growth of the company. He adds to the whole ambiance with his style. He is Joffrey, in a sense."

25

ENTR'ACTE

As the Joffrey dancers were making their way from Taipei to Hong Kong at the end of January, Eddie was packing his overnight bag for a return trip to St. Vincent's. Despite chemotherapy, his chest was filling up with fluid, making it difficult for him to breathe. Back in the AIDS unit, he had the fluid drained from his chest and underwent another bronchoscopy, only to learn that he had developed MAI, a deadly form of tuberculosis found in up to 50 percent of people with AIDS. Worse still, the cancer in his lungs and lymph glands was spreading "like wildfire," according to Dr. Sukumaran, who started Eddie on radiation and put him back on chemotherapy. Endless rounds of medications were also administered to do the job Eddie's immune system could no longer do for itself. In the course of a day, he was taking five different antibiotics just for the TB alone, plus eleven other pills meant to retard the virus, build up his appetite, and fight off cryptococcus, PCP, and herpes.

Eddie was only momentarily deflated. "What are our options?" he'd ask Rosemarie, his spirits brightening as his sister rattled off the possible treatments available to him. As long as something, anything, could be done, Eddie was convinced he would make it past whatever obstacle stood in his way. Rather than clear his schedule as many terminally ill patients are wont to do, Eddie packed his calendar with important occasions and marked them, unequivocally, in red ink: He had the dress rehearsal of *Lacrymosa* and *Empyrean Dances* on February 27, the premiere of *Lacrymosa* that same night, his twenty-third birthday party on March 2, and the gala premiere of *Empyrean Dances* on March 5. Flipping ahead to June, he made note of the tickets to *Phantom of the Opera* tacked to the bulletin board in his kitchen.

Though bedridden, he was rarely still. He addressed and stamped envelopes for the 120 invitations to his birthday party, he reviewed *Empyrean Dances* with Lissette, and he played Scrabble with his father. "You can just sit there for so long and then you run out of things to say," recalls Bill Stierle, whose description of Eddie's approach to Scrabble aptly sums up his son's approach to life. "I wasn't very good at it because I never had the time to play. I said to Ed, 'You're going to beat my butt.' I would get a long word, but I wasn't good at putting them in the right places, whereas Ed would do a short word and get forty-two points."

Lissette was supposed to be in China with the Joffrey, but fearful of leaving Eddie and never seeing him again, she feigned a bad ankle sprain so that she could stay behind and take care of him. "I'm dancing for both of us," she told him in December before leaving to dance *The Nutcracker* in L.A., but once onstage, she found his absence impossible to bear. Lissette had called him every night during the L.A. engagement, always in tears. As the downward spiral of Eddie's illness had accelerated, Lissette's life had changed, irrevocably, along with it. Her day still consisted of class and rehearsal, but after putting in seven hours at the Joffrey, she would throw on her street clothes and head down to St. Vincent's, where she'd wait out the rest of the night by Eddie's bed. "I wish he could have loved me the way I love him," she confided to Rosemarie one night while Eddie slept. Cynthia Giannini recalls asking Lissette to suggest a good day for her to come visit Eddie, and says Lissette never gave her an answer. As far as

Lissette was concerned, there was no time with Eddie she wished to give up to others. "Lissette loved Eddie so much that she didn't want anyone else around," says Giannini. "I didn't want to impose on her time with him. It was so precious."

That week, Joe Brown stopped by to see Eddie, his first meeting with him since their breakup in the summer of 1989. Joe was still healthy and dancing with Feld Ballets/NY. Although frequently away on tour, he was still friendly with Kyle Ahmed and, through Kyle, had kept up with news of Eddie. Hoping to tie up loose ends with Eddie, to whom he owed $900 in back rent, Joe brought a check with him to the hospital, an act that both pleased and annoyed Eddie. For most of Joe's visit, Eddie treated him coolly.

"Why did it take this long for him to come to see me?" he complained to Rosemarie after Joe left.

Joe was soon followed by Senta Driver, with whom Eddie passed an afternoon discussing *Petrouchka*. He continued to rehearse his roles in his mind, determined to keep himself in shape mentally for the day he could dance them again. "Eddie was sitting in bed nearly bald," she remembers of her visit. "He was on oxygen and not allowed to drink anything, and he was talking to me about his Petrouchka. I had a question for him. 'What is Petrouchka doing in that image at the end?' I asked him. 'Above the house he's making all these flailing gestures. What's your take on it? Is he sneering at the magician?' And Eddie said, 'No, he's not sassing the magician at the end. He's triumphing because he knows so much about all kinds of human feeling. So he can't die. You can't kill him.' And he looked at me and he said again, 'You can't kill him. He can't die.' And suddenly I realized what he was saying to me and it was sort of awkward. He was saying, You can't kill *me*. And he knew he was going to die. It flashed by. We had a lot else to talk about."

The one subject Eddie did his best to avoid was AIDS. He loved receiving calls from his friends, but dreaded that opening moment when the caller invariably asked him how he was. It was depressing, this business of bedside reports, especially when each day brought little to cheer about. Still, Eddie managed to keep up his bright patter for visitors, and reserved his more sullen and withdrawn self for his sister and Lissette. "He'd perform for everybody else," says Lissette. "We reminded him of his sickness."

"Why don't we talk," Rosemarie finally said to him during one of his blacker moods. "What's going on?"

He was trying to stay positive, Eddie explained between shallow breaths, but he couldn't help feeling angry at the same time. He expected to be dancing, not spending his days in some hospital ward. He was only twenty-two, why wasn't he dancing? The frustration spilled out of him. "I've stayed 'up,' I'm doing all these treatments, and nothing seems to be working. You don't know how hard it is not to cry and feel angry all the time."

"But, Eddie," she protested gently, "it's okay to cry. You don't always have to be up. I'm trying to stay positive because that's what you said you wanted. It's fine to be sad. You've been through a lot."

"But I feel like I'm letting everyone down," he continued. "I'm afraid I'm hurting the family." He was used to his independence and hated having to rely on Rosemarie to take care of him, particularly when it meant that she had to give up everything else she was doing. He tried to go on, but his voice broke without warning. For the first time in months, Eddie sobbed inconsolably.

"You're not letting anyone down," Rosemarie answered, struggling to hold back tears. "You need to feel whatever you're feeling. But you need to stay positive because it's your best medicine."

Eddie's despair gave way to anger, which reached a fever pitch the day Gary Chryst came to see him. Chryst had been in Europe for seven months touring in a production of *West Side Story*, and had just gotten back into town when he heard that Eddie was in St. Vincent's. He lived across the street and rushed over. Desert Storm was then in high gear and the war on most people's minds was the one being fought in the Persian Gulf. "Most people go right into this sickness, but Eddie was just sitting up and fighting like a war hero," says Chryst. "He said, 'I am just so fucking angry. Look at all the money the government is spending on this war. Billions and billions. Why aren't we spending money on programs for kids in schools about AIDS? Why didn't I know about it when

I was younger? I was just experimenting. If someone had told me it could kill me, I would have been more careful.'"

The next day, a phone call from Melissa Hayden pulled Eddie out of his funk. "Hi, Eddie, I hear the new ballet is terrific," she spurred him on from Winston-Salem. The sound of her voice carried him far from St. Vincent's and back to the stage. For the next several minutes, Eddie enthusiastically described *Empyrean Dances* to his former teacher. "I hope you can make it to the premiere," he said before hanging up.

Nine days after being hospitalized, Eddie checked out of St. Vincent's on February 8, 1991, and was soon back at the Joffrey teaching his beloved Snow Prince to other dancers. One night after a costume fitting for *Empyrean Dances*, Eddie shared a cab home with Jodie Gates and, though weak and short of breath, never once mentioned his health. "All he talked about were the costumes and how beautiful they were," she says. "He was so excited about the ballet."

But that week, Eddie got a jolt when Joffrey II director Richard Englund died of cancer at the age of fifty-nine, amid rumors of AIDS. A few days later, Eddie gave an interview to *Newsday*'s dance critic, Janice Berman, to acknowledge publicly his battle with AIDS. Though shadowed by death, Eddie was far from somber and nowhere in his answers are there traces of the despondency he had expressed to his sister and Gary Chryst only days earlier. In reply to a question about the impact of AIDS on his life, Eddie told Berman:

> This is a tiny part of me. It bothers me that so many people make it so big. They give it so much power. The mind-set, if you want to stay well, is you are bigger than it, you have the power. And if you give it all that power, then forget it, you are doomed.

Eddie added that he hoped to be able to dance his Profiteer role in *The Green Table* during the last week of the New York season, then a month away.

However, after a brief, twelve-day respite from St. Vincent's, Eddie found himself back in the emergency room on February 20. The radiation and chemotherapy had failed and the KS was fast destroying his lungs. "Out of nowhere you go from light to dark," Paul Monette writes in *Borrowed Time*, his memoir of his lover's battle with AIDS,

> from winning to losing, go to sleep murmuring thanks and wake to an endless siren. The honeymoon was over, that much was clear. Now we would learn to borrow time in earnest, day by day, making what brief stays we could against the downward spiral from which all our wasted brothers did not return.

Despite the dire prognosis, Eddie refused to give in to depression. He still had his sights set on making it to the premiere of *Lacrymosa* and reminded his doctors daily of the coming event. They were swept along by his enthusiasm. "His positive thinking was contagious," says John Oppenheimer. "At that point the goal was the premiere on the twenty-seventh. Eddie was determined to do this and we all would have felt bad if he couldn't make it. The timing was incredible, that he was so sick and there were these two major things he wanted to do. He was racing to experience them."

That week, Rose Stierle flew back to New York to give her daughter and husband a break from Eddie's bedside. Each day, when Eddie was wheeled away for tests, Rose slipped into the main-floor chapel to pray. The world of medicine left her baffled and she preferred to let Rosemarie handle the specifics of Eddie's care. Though she was still going weekly to an AIDS support group for families in Fort Lauderdale, Rose couldn't get past the shame of AIDS, nor bring herself to tell relatives or friends that Eddie had a "gay disease." Instead, she said Eddie had either pneumonia or cancer and didn't elaborate.

Now that Eddie was alone with his mother, a sense of urgency overcame him. He thought it was time to settle childhood accounts. For years he had kept the resentment he felt toward her largely to himself, fearing the pain he would inflict in unleashing his litany of grievances. "Why did you keep me so isolated from my brothers and sisters?" he now demanded. "I missed that time with them. It's taken me so long to rebuild those relationships. I wish you hadn't kept me away from them."

Rose didn't argue. "I did the best I could," she said. Later that night she called Rosemarie from a hospital pay phone. "I wish Eddie was old enough to forgive me and understand why I thought I was doing the best for him," she told her daughter. "I was trying to protect him so he wouldn't be too tired to dance." Once again she was watching over him, only now he *was* too tired to dance. Rose felt utterly helpless. It had never occurred to her that there were limits on her ability to take care of him.

One afternoon after Eddie had drifted off to sleep, she stepped out into the hallway and approached a nun she had glimpsed many times on the ward. "I was crying very hard," recalls Rose, "and I said, 'Sister, I really need to speak with you.' We went into this little room and I said, 'You know, Sister, I found out that my son was gay back in 1985 and I was really hoping that he would change his sex preference. Now he has the virus, but I really don't know if he contracted it from a male or female.'" Once again, the Church's representative didn't give Rose Stierle the answer she expected. Instead, she imparted a cautionary tale about the men and women she had seen die, alone, abandoned by their families. Many of them, she told Rose, had wanted to kill themselves after their families had rejected them when they had first told them they were gay. "That's not right," she said. "That's not fair."

On the morning of February 24, the phone rang in Richard Register's Manhattan apartment. "There's an article about Eddie in today's *Newsday*," a friend told Register, Eddie's first boyfriend. "It says Eddie has AIDS." Register didn't know anything about it. He hadn't seen Eddie in nearly two years. "Even though I'd been tested many times and was negative, I felt the shock for both of our mortalities at that moment," he remembers. Register ran out and got the paper and there in the "Arts" section was a large rehearsal photo of Eddie in his blue bandanna, helping Lissette to balance on a pedestal on one knee. He was positioning her on a pedestal, and yet preparing her for the moment when he would not be there to support her. "Reaching Into Deep Soul Places," the headline announced. A second, starker phrase ran just beneath it: "Edward Stierle's works are his answer to a 'wake-up call': AIDS." In the article, Janice Berman reported that *Lacrymosa* was dedicated to the memory of Robert Joffrey, who died in 1988, she noted pointedly, "after a long illness whose nature was never made public."

The day after Eddie Stierle went public in *Newsday*, Rosemarie boarded the bus for Manhattan to make arrangements for his release from the hospital. The New York premiere of *Lacrymosa* was now only two days away and she had many details to attend to. For starters, there was Eddie's outfit. At Macy's she had bought two suits for him to choose from, one blue, the other maroon, and she had them packed in her bag along with the sewing machine she planned to use to alter them. Of course, there were no guarantees that Eddie would be granted permission to leave St. Vincent's. Earlier that week, Drs. John Oppenheimer and Muthiah Sukumaran had determined that the only way they could keep draining the fluid from his lungs was through a tube they had inserted in his chest. No patient in recent memory had ever left St. Vincent's with a tube implanted in his or her chest, but knowing Eddie's goals and the time he had left, his doctors wanted to do everything possible to accommodate him. When Rosemarie got to Eddie's room, she heard the first bit of good news she'd had in a while: Eddie could leave the hospital the following day. The doctors had arranged for him to use a portable fluid sac. Except for trips to the bathroom, he hadn't walked in over a week and he could breathe easily only when tethered to his bedside oxygen.

"We knew Eddie was not going to get better," says Dr. Sukamaran. "A lot of doctors would probably not have wanted him to go home as sick as he was, but we felt happy for him that he was accomplishing what he wanted to. We took a chance by letting him go."

Early the next morning, Rosemarie came to take Eddie home. It was her thirty-third birthday and she spent it waiting and waiting for the resident on the floor to sign Eddie out. At four P.M. a doctor neither of them knew marched into the room, demanding to know why Eddie thought he could check out. He sounded annoyed and edgy and Rosemarie was about to let him have it. "This is really against hospital policy," he rebuked Eddie. "If you were my patient, I'd never allow you to leave here in your condition. I'd put you on more chemo."

Eddie sat upright in bed. "Look, Doctor," he said with a calm that surprised his sister, "I don't know how much you know about me, but I'm twenty-two years old and I have two ballets that are premiering this week at Lincoln Center. It's one of the biggest moments in my life and Dr. Oppenheimer got permission for me to leave."

The doctor blanched, backtracked, and signed the release.

It took Rosemarie one hour to get Eddie from his room on the seventh floor to the street below. His body frail and weakened by drugs and bed rest, Eddie had difficulty standing on his own, and could barely manage more than a few teeny steps before he had to pause. The plastic sac taped to his chest jostled as he walked, adding to his discomfort. Rosemarie wrapped her arm around his waist and literally carried him down the hall on her hip. "I never realized how sick he was until that moment," she says.

Sixteen hours later, Eddie was sitting in the orchestra of the New York State Theater running back-to-back technical rehearsals of *Lacrymosa* and *Empyrean Dances*. Going it alone, without his portable oxygen, he wore a headset and microphone, which helped amplify his corrections to the dancers onstage. "Hi, guys! I'm here. I made it," the Joffrey dancers heard Eddie say, as they peered into the orchestra looking for him. From 10 A.M. to 4 P.M., Eddie carried on as if it were just another preopening run-through. "Afterwards, he was totally wiped out," remembers Barbara Forbes, who, along with Scott Barnard and lighting designer Tom Skelton, conferred with Eddie throughout the day. "It was as though there was no more energy left in his body. He was aware of how sick he was, but he was desperate to make it for the opening."

With only four hours to go before showtime, Eddie, Rosemarie, and Lissette hurried back to the apartment to get ready for the evening. The night before, Lissette had informed Eddie that she wasn't going to the premiere. *Lacrymosa* had special meaning for her, she told him, and since she wasn't able to dance because of a sprained foot, she didn't want to sit in the audience and watch it. She and Eddie had argued. "I was crying because I was injured and couldn't dance and Rosemarie said, 'Stop being a baby. He's doing all of this and you don't want to support him.' And I said, 'Hey, wait a second. How can you say that? I've been here the whole time for him. What about me?' But I went anyway. Everything was like that. All for Eddie."

It took them two hours to get Eddie ready, for any sign of sickness was to be hidden from view. Rosemarie slipped Eddie's plastic sac into a cloth bag she'd made and tied it firmly around his waist. She then helped him into his gold shirt, and the maroon suit he had picked out for the night. Next came the wig Eddie and his father had custom-ordered. Applying glue to the mesh cap on Eddie's scalp, Rosemarie then brushed the wig this way and that to make it look as natural as possible before securing it in place.

Although he felt shooting pains in his chest, Eddie refused to take painkillers. They made him groggy, he protested, and he didn't want to "miss anything." His parents had ordered two tanks of oxygen for the night but Eddie insisted on going to the State Theater on his own steam. Rosemarie decided to bring the oxygen along anyway, *just in case*. She never allowed herself to finish sentences like that.

Once inside the theater, Eddie walked without assistance to his seat in the orchestra. Only when he was sure no one could see him would he deign to let Rosemarie or Lissette steady him. "All these friends were rushing to say hello to Eddie, not realizing how sick he was," says Rosemarie. "Very few people knew he had just come out of the hospital." Drs. Oppenheimer and Sukumaran were both in the audience that night, accompanied by their wives.

Moments before the curtain went up on *Lacrymosa*, Eddie made his way backstage to talk to the dancers. Huddling around him, they held on to one another, their arms circling one another's shoulders. "You all know what the ballet's about," he said simply. "I'm really happy with what you guys have done with it." Seeing him now in a wig, his once-muscular body tiny inside his suit, the dancers acknowledged to themselves for the first time that Eddie was dying. Just then, the overture to Mozart's *Requiem* began, leaving them no time to collect themselves. "We were running around onstage, tossing our heads and crying," says Adam Sklute. "*Lacrymosa* lends itself to those kinds of emotions."

Indeed, in her review of that performance, Anna Kisselgoff would write: "Deep down, dance is an art of exaltation and *Lacrymosa*, an astonishingly impressive premiere for the Joffrey Ballet by a twenty-two-year-old novice choreographer, Edward Stierle, makes the case in the most compelling terms. . . . We have seen a great many recent ballets about accepting death. But few have Mr. Stierle's gift for creating images that simultaneously surprise but never ring false. . . ." In *The Village Voice*, dance critic Deborah Jowitt would observe that *Lacrymosa* was "a death song, strong and unsentimental in its group passages, more tentative in its choreography for three soloists: a stern death figure (Daniel Baudendistel); one who is suddenly pulled from the ensemble to confront death (Tom Mossbrucker); and a mysterious woman (Jodie Gates)—perhaps death's handmaiden, perhaps a loved one or an impotent mourner. . . ."

As the figure of death parted Jodie Gates from Tom Mossbrucker, Eddie returned backstage for the curtain calls. This time, he took Rosemarie's arm, but once in the wings, let go of her and walked to center stage alone for his bow. He looked out into the audience and smiled shyly. He had made it, after all.

Dr. Oppenheimer and Dr. Sukumaran came toward him as he came off the stage. Bowled over by Eddie's performance, they searched for words to describe it. Such moments were rare in *their* profession. "I felt very emotional watching his ballet," says Dr. Oppenheimer. "That he could use his lungs as well as he did and get up there for his bow was pretty remarkable. It was amazing that anybody could do that. He had so much dignity and presence." Dr. Sukumaran had always thought that dramatic comebacks like Eddie's happened only in the movies. "I'd heard stories, of course, but I'd never actually seen a dying person summon the energy and courage to go through with something like that the way Eddie did. You could see the surge of adrenaline in his face. His eyes lit up and he looked peaceful."

When Kyle Ahmed came out into the orchestra to congratulate Eddie, he was struck by how "meditative" he seemed. Hospitals unnerved him, so he hadn't been to see Eddie in several weeks. "He wasn't the Eddie I knew before," he remembers.

Carried along by the momentum of the night, Eddie insisted on staying on for the next ballet on the program. It was *Trinity* and he wanted to see the votive candles. "You always said the only thing a man can leave behind on this earth is the light of himself," he had remarked to Arpino in the theater's Green Room during intermission. "Tonight, I want to see the candlelight."

The following morning, Eddie awoke from a fitful sleep in his apartment. He couldn't lie flat without feeling pressure in his chest and his breathing was so labored that rest came only intermittently. He still had one last matter to resolve with his parents and, reluctant to put it off any longer, he addressed it the moment Lissette went off to see the doctor about her sprained foot. The subject was life support and Eddie made it clear that he didn't wish to be kept alive by machines. "I don't want to live in a body that can't dance," he said. When his parents showed little resistance, Eddie proceeded to the next issue at hand. He wanted his life celebrated, he told them, not mourned. For two hours, he outlined the memorial tribute he envisioned for himself, leaving no detail unattended. "I want to be cremated," he said. "Mom, you can keep my ashes if you want them. I want a big celebration with everyone in white. I want pictures, flowers, balloons."

Later that day, Eddie awoke from a nap gasping for air and was rushed to the emergency room, where John Oppenheimer and Muthiah Sukumaran were there to meet him. Twelve hours earlier, they had all been chatting about ballet at the New York State Theater. "Can you believe how well it went last night?" Eddie asked happily. Dr. Sukumaran tried to drain the fluid from Eddie's chest to help him breathe, but there was little that could be done for him. The KS completely covered his lungs. The doctor called Rosemarie into the hallway. "Eddie is really dying now," he told her.

But the dying often hold on for significant events and Eddie had a world premiere to attend. As he and Rosemarie sat waiting for a bed, Eddie called her attention to a potential glitch in his plans. "Maybe we should postpone my birthday party," he suggested. His birthday was two days away, his next premiere three days after that. "I just want to get to *Empyrean Dances.*"

The final moment of *Empyrean Dances,* March 1991

26

FLIGHTS OF ANGELS

The disease was gaining on him with terrifying speed, despite medicines, despite prayers. His body had withered to one hundred pounds and his cheeks, stripped of their padding, looked bony and white. A few strands of hair hung loosely from his downy scalp, the remnants of his youthful self. Hooked up to his bedside oxygen, Eddie could muster only shallow breaths and, with drugs coursing through him intravenously, he found it difficult to stay awake. Nonetheless, Eddie's strength of spirit carried him forward. Day after day, he talked of little else but returning to Lincoln Center. Anyone who spent a moment at his bedside in early March came away convinced that Eddie was willing himself alive for the premiere of *Empyrean Dances* on March 5.

Among them was Gerald Arpino, who took time out from his company's hectic New York season to visit his protégé. Having only recently recovered from his own series of setbacks—from the loss of Robert Joffrey to the thwarted board coup—Arpino was struck by Eddie's halo of calm. He arrived to find Eddie sitting up in bed in the lotus position, dressed in baggy pajamas and wire-rimmed glasses. Eddie preferred wearing his glasses in the hospital; his contact lenses were too much trouble. He looked "like Mahatma Gandhi," Arpino remembers thinking. Within minutes, they were in deep conversation about Arpino's artistic leadership—or rather, Eddie was. "He lectured me about what I should do with the company. He said, 'You don't realize what you bring to us when your presence is there.' The whole essence of his being was love. He talked about the classes, his costumes for the new ballet. Oh, he was my mentor."

That week, there were plenty of people who were hoping to catch a moment with Eddie. At his request, Rosemarie had postponed his party, but many of those invited decided to come to town anyway to see Eddie and his ballet. He had touched their lives and they needed to tell him so. From Florida came his teachers, Liana and Mitzi, and from North Carolina came Duncan Noble. On March 1, his brothers and sisters streamed into Manhattan from disparate parts of the country and took rooms at the Comfort Inn next to Eddie's apartment building on Thirty-fifth Street. They, too, needed time alone with their brother, each dimly aware that he might not last the week.

To bolster him, they covered the stark walls of his room with green, blue, and red posters on which they'd drawn his favorite images with colored markers. There had been no beds available on the AIDS floor, so Eddie had been given a private room on Cullman 11, the Ear, Nose, and Throat floor. As he lay propped in bed, he saw the Manhattan skyline out the picture window to his left and directly ahead his eyes feasted on the images his brothers and sisters had culled from his life: a map of Florida, a figure at the beach, his dog, Missy, an architectural plan of his apartment. On one poster, his brother Bill had written simply, "Just Breathe."

"I think we really confused the medical staff," recalls Patty Stierle. "I deal with dying people all the time and most families don't deal with death the way we did. As a nurse looking at my family, I would say, 'They are in complete denial. They're not coping with this.' But we *did* know what was going on, it was just that we had decided we were going to make it as happy and as stressless for Eddie as possible."

The same day his children gathered in New York, Bill Stierle went to the final dress rehearsal of *Empyrean Dances*. With Eddie too weak to go along, Bill offered to take pictures of the rehearsal for his son to review from his bed. On his way back to St. Vincent's, Bill stopped by Westside Cottage, Eddie's favorite Chinese restaurant, to retrieve the deposit Eddie had laid out for his birthday party. But the moment he arrived, he changed his mind. He decided that the family should go ahead and celebrate Eddie's birthday, even if Eddie couldn't be there. He would include the handful of Philadelphia relatives who were driving in to see *Lacrymosa* the next night. The party was back on, he told the owner, only now there would be thirty coming, not one hundred.

It was well past dusk when Bill began walking back to St. Vincent's in the rain. As he headed east along Forty-second Street, his hands warming in his pockets, his mind on Eddie, a young man suddenly whisked by him, just barely brushing his hip. Something told Bill to check his back pocket. Gone was the twenty-dollar bill he had stashed there. Out of his mind with fury and fatigue, Bill sprinted after the robber, chasing him down into the Forty-second Street subway station, where he disappeared. He decided not to tell his family that he'd been robbed, afraid of contributing to the chaos. More drama awaited him on his return to Eddie's room. Lissette was in tears, having just learned that she was not to dance the opening-night performance of *Empyrean Dances*. In class that morning, she had sprained her ankle again and been forced to sit out the final dress rehearsal of Eddie's ballet. She was beginning to be accident-prone, the result of undue strain. The Joffrey, however, had a long-standing rule that dancers who hadn't rehearsed with lights, costumes, and sets were not to dance the first night of a new ballet. On this particular occasion the edict had come down from Scott Barnard and no sooner did Lissette relay the news to Eddie than he was on the phone to Gerald Arpino's assistant, Roberta Stewart. He was furious. "I'm the choreographer," he reminded her, indignantly. "It says in my contract that changes have to be approved by the choreographer. I want Lissette in the piece. It's very important to me. How can they make changes without my approval?"

The message was promptly delivered and an exception soon granted. Arpino called Scott Barnard and told him to let Lissette dance opening night. According to Barnard, he agreed at once, though he was uneasy about bending such a long-standing rule. "I said to Jerry, 'If her dancing is that important to Edward, it doesn't bother me.' So, for the first time, in however long it has been, someone went on the stage opening night without having done the final rehearsals."

The next day, March 2, Eddie turned twenty-three. As it happened, *Lacrymosa* was on the Joffrey's mixed bill that evening and while Rosemarie stayed behind with Eddie, the Stierle family trooped off to Lincoln Center, before going on to Westside Cottage for Eddie's birthday party. Despite missing the night he'd spent weeks planning, Eddie didn't appear depressed. As he saw it, he was not incapacitated, but conserving strength for the premiere of *Empyrean Dances*. He thanked Rosemarie for her help with the party, full of gratitude now for even the smallest gestures. That morning, a few of the nurses had surprised him with a birthday muffin, a Q-Tip standing in for a candle.

Eddie was the only AIDS patient on the Ear, Nose, and Throat floor and he quickly became a favorite with the nurses, who, unaccustomed to dealing with the terminally ill, regarded his optimism with awe and affection. They also welcomed the services of his family, who had quickly supplanted them as Eddie's support staff. They were thrilled to have a star on the floor.* Each morning, it seemed, another article about Eddie or his ballets appeared in some newspaper, which Eddie or his mother would proudly show

---

*The award-winning lyricist Howard Ashman was also dying of AIDS in St. Vincent's Hospital at the time. Like Eddie, Ashman was on the verge of a breakthrough in his career: He had already won an Academy Award for Best Song for *The Little Mermaid* and he had just completed work on Disney's *Aladdin* and *Beauty and the Beast*. He also died in March 1991, and his sister later wrote Rosemarie a condolence letter after reading about Eddie in *The New York Times*. A year after his death, Ashman was awarded his second Oscar for his lyrics to the title song "Beauty and the Beast."

off to each nurse on duty. By the week's end, the nurses had tacked all the clippings about Eddie to the bulletin board in their station. There were the reviews of *Lacrymosa*, a reprint of Janice Berman's interview in *The Los Angeles Times* accompanied by a large photograph of Eddie, and a *New York Times* piece about the Joffrey's four new ballets, which also made mention of Eddie's AIDS diagnosis.

At Eddie's twenty-third birthday party, Bill Stierle had struggled to say a few words about the absent guest of honor, but he couldn't get out more than a sentence without breaking down. Still, he got through his toast, pausing now and then to let the difficult moments pass. "Pop, the man of few words, stood up to speak," Tom Stierle would later write in his journal. "He managed to summarize all of our feelings in the simplest way possible." To Tom, the occasion suggested "a going-away party," though one filled with awkward moments. His brothers and sisters were in an unfamiliar setting and city "without the one person who was responsible for bringing us all together." In Eddie's stead, Lissette blew out the lone candle on his vanilla and chocolate ice-cream cake, making sure to cut him a big slice. Afterward, she and Tom brought it to him at the hospital. It cheered them that Eddie ate the whole piece.

Worried that Eddie would be overwhelmed by visitors, Rosemarie did her best to limit them and, with the help of Tom and Patty, had divided the family into round-the-clock shifts of complementary teams: Bill Stierle was paired with his son Mike; Rose Stierle with Tom and Kathy; Bill, Jr., with Terri; and Patty with Rosemarie. Since Patty was a night nurse in South Carolina, she was already accustomed to the hours and soon offered to go it alone to give the others a chance to rest. One night, when Patty, Lissette, and Rose Stierle were discovered in Eddie's room after visiting hours, the nurse on duty told them they would have to leave. Enraged by the nurse's haughtiness, Patty demanded to see her supervisor. She would set *her* straight, she thought. "I'm a critical care nurse," she told the supervisor in the hallway. "I know all about policy. My brother is very sick. He might be dying. What's best for him is that someone stays with him." The supervisor readily agreed, provided that Eddie's visitors left the room whenever the nurses needed to tend to him.

Snatching moments of sleep wherever she could, Rosemarie oversaw the changing of the guard, a delicate job given that there was competition among friends and family for Eddie's attention. While she was careful to give everyone time alone with him, she also tried to surround Eddie with the people he considered the most positive-minded. Among these, Eddie now counted his brother Bill, who used taped recordings of ocean sounds to transport Eddie to Hollywood Beach, his childhood playground. It was there he wanted his ashes scattered.* Bill also led Eddie daily through visualization exercises designed to help him heal himself. Of course, it was unlikely that Eddie could heal himself, but Bill thought otherwise. "I felt he had the power to lick the KS," he says. "People lying on their deathbeds with cancer do get better. I believed I just needed time with him." Naturally, some family members were bound to feel excluded from Eddie's care. "I was not assigned a specific watch," recalls his sister Terri, who held his hand one afternoon while he slept, as she had done when he was a baby. "I felt pushed out and robbed of that time with Eddie."

When she wasn't marshaling the family forces, Rosemarie was frantically investigating any experimental treatment that might keep Eddie alive a little longer. A few weeks before her family's arrival in New York, she had come across an item about a potential new treatment for KS in an AIDS newsletter and had called the reporter to find out more information. A doctor in Los Angeles claimed to have had success in prolonging the lives of skin cancer patients by administering therapeutic heat in combination with low

---

*Several days after telling his mother she could keep his ashes, Eddie changed his mind and decided it would be better for her if they were scattered at Hollywood Beach. He worried that she would make a shrine to him at home.

doses of radiation. He had just initiated an experimental study to apply the same treatment to KS patients when Rosemarie called him at the Valley Cancer Institute. Convinced the treatment sounded promising, she had called her brother Bill, still in Los Angeles, and asked him to drive over to the institute to check it out before flying east. He thought it seemed legitimate, he informed her, and the news was soon conveyed to Eddie. "We're going to fly you to California to get you well," they told him. "It sounds great," he answered, "but not till after my premiere." Anxious for a second opinion, Rosemarie sounded out John Oppenheimer, who was unfamiliar with both the doctor and his treatment. Dr. Michael Gottlieb, Eddie's Los Angeles physician, was next on her list. For several days, they traded calls, she from a hospital pay phone, the doctor on his car phone. Hearing the desperation in her voice, he agreed to look into it. "It was a bizarre cancer-type cure," recalls Michael Gottlieb. "I called the man and discussed his ideas with him and did not have a favorable opinion. I called Rosemarie and said, 'I don't think this is going to save him.' "

Having been on the front lines from the start, Michael Gottlieb knew a great deal about Eddie's odds for survival. Even so, he began hatching a radical strategy of his own to help him. To his mind, what Eddie needed was a new set of lungs. "What about a lung transplant?" he suggested to a surgeon he knew at Johns Hopkins Hospital. A lung transplant had never been performed on an AIDS patient. It was the first time Gottlieb had entertained such a plan and he knew he was going to draw fire for attempting it. "Most people would say, 'He should have his head examined,' Gottlieb would later acknowledge. "For most patients with AIDS and KS of the lung, society would say, 'You don't spend $150,000 and subject them to this kind of surgery, because they don't have much of a prognosis.' But when it came to Edward, I felt that unusual measures were entirely appropriate. If he had a few more years to choreograph, it seems to me that the transplant would have been worth something." Gottlieb was encouraged when the staff at Johns Hopkins expressed interest. "They thought it was feasible, but they weren't quite ready to go. If Edward had lived a few more weeks, I'd have tried to pull it off."

He was still alive on March 5, the day of the premiere, but just barely. The night before, he had been in terrible pain and had asked Patty to hold him. "I'm just having such a hard time breathing," she heard him say through his oxygen mask. Patty took him in her arms and rocked him. "In the morning, we'll get you a shot of morphine," she offered. "You'll be able to rest, so you'll have your strength—for later on." By the time Rosemarie heard about the morphine shot, it had already been administered and she was furious. To her, morphine spelled sure death and, with the gala still hours away, she feared that Eddie's body would begin shutting down.

Eddie, however, was not about to miss his eight o'clock curtain, not on the opening night of his own ballet. Besides, so much planning had gone into this day. His brothers had even driven to and from Lincoln Center on a trial run and rehearsed the steps they would take to get Eddie from the car to his seat in the State Theater. Every maneuver had been timed with a stopwatch. Nothing within their control was to be left to chance. As Paul Monette has written of attending his dying lover:

> We were all so close and so alert, like a troop of sentries. I've never before experienced the feeling of having to physically keep Death away, as if he would actually come in the door if I let down my guard for an instant.

Eddie's reprieve arrived that afternoon. When his brother Bill came by his room to give him a pep talk, he found Eddie listless from the morphine. Thinking he might be able to revive him, Bill led Eddie through some of the visualization exercises he had read about, and slowly, Eddie's strength returned. Bill couldn't help marveling at the startling disparity between the ruin of Eddie's body and the vitality of his spirit. "It was as if Eddie was back from the dead, right there," he says.

And yet Eddie prepared for the evening with an air of solemn purpose, his vanity very much intact. So many old friends were coming to the gala, he wanted to look good. Patty, Kathy, and Rosemarie helped him get ready. While Patty was bathing him, she offered to give him a shave. "But I'm not very good at it," she said, teasingly, "so I may leave a few marks on you." Eddie turned her down. "Don't get close to me with that razor," he replied, clearly "not his joking self," remembers Patty. "I felt he was saying, 'You can't mess up my face tonight.'" Not tonight.

It fell to Kathy the beautician to shave Eddie and apply his hairpiece, which, she was quick to assure him, didn't look like a wig. Kathy had come from Gainesville without her husband, who was having trouble accepting the fact that his brother-in-law had AIDS. They had tried to keep the nature of Eddie's illness hidden from everyone they knew, and only when her mother-in-law asked to join her in New York for the gala did Kathy finally tell her that Eddie had AIDS. She agreed not to repeat the news to others back home. All the same, she was surprised that anyone in her family had AIDS.

By the time Eddie was dressed in his tuxedo and black cowboy boots, nearly every nurse on the floor had popped into his room to have a look. It wasn't every day that a dying patient left the hospital in a tuxedo. John Oppenheimer knew it would likely be Eddie's last night out. "He was so sick. I thought he might die that night. You could see him using the muscles between his ribs to breathe."

At the State Theater, Eddie and his entourage were met by Scott Barnard. "I just want you to know that I've taken care of the bows," Barnard told him. "The dancers know you're here. Jodie will come to get you, so you can bow with the company."

"But I want to take a bow by myself," Eddie informed Barnard, catching him by surprise.

Could Eddie walk? Barnard wondered. He was in a wheelchair, after all, and strapped to an oxygen tank.

"If that's what you want," he assured Eddie. "I'll tell the dancers then."

As *Empyrean Dances* was coming to a close, Kyle Ahmed caught sight of Eddie in the wings. He was due to go on in the next ballet and two thoughts struck him simultaneously: He'd never seen

Eddie in a tux before and Eddie looked like an old man. Eddie seemed to have aged years in the week since *Lacrymosa*. Stunned by the sight of his friend's cadaverous frame, he assigned the two thoughts equal weight. He couldn't lose his composure now; he had to go onstage in a few minutes.

Jodie Gates had just exited to stage left when she saw Eddie in the darkness. "I was practically in the same position I was in when Mr. Joffrey came to take *his* bow for *Nutcracker*," she recalls. "It was an incredibly emotional moment. Eddie wanted to be out of that wheelchair like nobody's business. He took off the tubes from his nose and started walking on his own. He reminded me so much of Mr. Joffrey. Neither of them wanted to seem paralyzed."

When the curtain came up on the cast, Eddie was standing center stage. Letting go of the hands stretched out to him for support, he broke from the line and stepped forward, into his own circle of light. With upturned palms, he acknowledged the applause. It was vintage Eddie Stierle, a tour de force of will.

As soon as the curtain fell, Eddie barely made it to the wing before Rosemarie had to help him into his wheelchair. Reconnected to his oxygen, he struggled to thank the dancers for the joy they had given him. He smiled at Lissette, who had managed to get through the performance on an injured ankle. "We stood around Eddie crying, the same way we had stood around Mr. Joffrey," remembers Cynthia Giannini. "And Eddie tried to thank us, the way Mr. Joffrey had. It was a lot for everyone to have to go through again."

"I made it, I made it," Eddie repeated, drawing strength from the incantation. The dancers knew they were seeing him for the last time. "He was talking as if he was already someplace else," says Jodie Gates.

Two days later, on the morning of March 7, Eddie sat up in bed and read his reviews. In *Newsday*, Janice Berman noted that "the overall theme of rebirth and hope came across with touching

Bowing at the
premiere of
Empyrean Dances

With Gerald Arpino and Lissette at the gala dinner following
the premiere

clarity," while in *The New York Times*, Anna Kisselgoff announced the arrival of a promising new choreographer. "Yet Mr. Stierle is no ordinary novice and proves in *Empyrean Dances* . . . that dance can still grab an audience by its collective throat. His is a stunning talent, delving unabashedly into images of emotional turbulence—a ceaseless outpouring of passions that both disturb and thrill. [The ballet] is a rarity, a visionary ballet, and the vision of the Empyrean or highest heaven that Milton extolled is translated by Mr. Stierle into a burning onrush of hope."

Satisfied, Eddie turned to his father. "Well," he said, "at least I've left something to be remembered by."

That night Bill and Rose returned to the State Theater to see *Lacrymosa*, the ballet their son had made about accepting mortality. It was the final performance of the ballet during the Joffrey's spring season and Lissette was dancing. Bill had urged Rose to go with him. "I want to see it one more time before we go home," he told his wife. Eddie had been holding steady all day, and Bill thought they needed a break from his bedside. In fact, just about everyone in the family was taking a break that night: Terri, Kathy, and Michael had just flown home, and Patty, Tom, Bill, Jr., and Kit had gone out to eat. Only Rosemarie stayed behind, standing guard.

Ten minutes into *Lacrymosa*, Rose sensed something was wrong. Earlier that afternoon, Eddie had fallen asleep with his head on her shoulder and she had refused to budge until he awoke two hours later. "We've got to get out of here," she told Bill at intermission. He wanted to stay, but hearing the urgency in her voice, he left with her at once.

In their absence, Eddie had cried out for morphine. The stabbing pains in his back had become unbearable. "Don't be mad at me, I'm not giving up, but it hurts so badly," he begged Rosemarie once he had started the morphine drip. "I don't think you're giving up," she said. She could see that he was beginning to feel what was happening to his body. "You've carried more physical pain than is humanly possible." John Oppenheimer had approved the drip to make Eddie more comfortable. Eddie's lungs were clogged with fluid and the doctor knew that suffocating was among the worst ways to die. As soon as Eddie had fallen asleep, Rosemarie stepped out into the hallway to await her parents' return. "Eddie asked for morphine," she told them. Throughout the night, as Bill, Tom, Patty, Kit, and Lissette trickled back to the hospital, the news was repeated. "Eddie asked for morphine," they whispered to one another. The phrase became a death knell.

For the next five hours, Eddie drifted in and out of consciousness, all the while fighting to stay awake. Braced for loss, his family crowded around his bed, trying to anticipate his needs. Lissette rubbed his back, Tom held his hand, and Rose applied cool cloths to his forehead. Suddenly, at around 3 A.M., Eddie awoke with a start and asked for a bowl of Cap'n Crunch, his favorite cereal as a child. "Mom," he said, "will you feed it to me?" The night before, Patty had gone out to get a box after Eddie mentioned that he might like some; now they all watched their mother spoon-feed Eddie from a cup, while their father massaged his feet.

Bit by bit, as the morphine kicked in, Eddie turned increasingly euphoric and struggled to express all that he was experiencing. His brother Bill turned on the small cassette recorder he had brought with him, placing it on a tray where Eddie couldn't see it. Through the oxygen mask covering his nose and mouth, Eddie's voice sounded curiously hollow, despite the fervor of his tone. At one point, he began reciting Marianne Williamson's prayer about golden light, but grew frustrated when he couldn't recall the words. "I see in my mind a little ball of golden light, I see a little ball of golden light," he kept repeating, unable to get any further.

As the night wore on, Eddie slept intermittently, each time awakening, fully alert, to address unfinished business. Even in dying, he was choreographing his final moments, summoning energy from—who knew where.

"I need all of you in here," Eddie commanded through his oxygen mask. "I want to talk to you."

He turned first to Lissette. "You're a beautiful dancer, Lissette," he told her. "I want you to shine up there onstage. You know how much you mean to me. It's too bad I'm gay."

Slowly, he began working his way around the room. He thanked Rosemarie for caring for him and called her his best friend. He thanked his father for teaching him the value of service. "Go tell them about AIDS," he goaded his father, who was resting his chin on Eddie's foot. "You were a great dad, but you're a lousy masseur," he added, prompting laughter. "Your fingers are too stubby."

Then he fixed his eyes on his mother and absolved her. "I don't care what anybody says, you were a great mom," he said. "You cared for me and drove me to ballet class and were always there to support me. You're beautiful and I love you." Rose couldn't answer. Numb with despair, she smiled at him.

"Eddie said exactly what each person needed to hear," remembers Rosemarie. "He could hardly breathe, but he kept talking." But when he got to his brother Bill, he drew a blank. "Bill, you'll always be . . . Bill," he said, exasperated, and they all laughed once more.

"Dad," Eddie continued, meting out tasks yet to be done, "I want lots of pictures at my celebration. I want them up all over the place. And, Mom, I want lots of articles and lots of flowers. I want lots of white balloons and lots of jokes and lots of partying. I want a celebration, so no crying. Mom, make sure you wear a white dress. Promise me. You guys help her look nice."

Then he began to sing in a loud voice, "I love life, life loves me. . . ."

His father tried to give him something to hang on for. "I've got beautiful pictures of the gala coming for you in the morning, Ed. Big eleven-by-fourteens. You gotta stick around for them."

"Oh, that's too long, Dad," Eddie answered. "I think it's time for me to go."

"Do you think we can get another ballet out of you?" Patty asked him.

"Noooo," he said slowly.

By the time Dr. Oppenheimer arrived at the hospital at daybreak, Eddie was nearly delirious. "John! John!" Eddie screamed. "This is so great. It's beautiful. I'm flying. It's incredible. Incredible!" The scene before him touched the doctor profoundly. It wasn't one often played out at St. Vincent's. "Eddie was holding on with this last burst of life," he recalls. "He was saying good-bye to everyone, which is amazing. Usually that doesn't get done."

An hour later, a priest arrived. No one in the room had sent for him, not even Rose, but the moment he appeared, Rose muttered quietly, "I'm so glad you're here." Eddie, however, backed away with his eyes, too weak to move. The priest made the sign of the cross over Eddie's forehead, mouth, and heart. "This is what you do? You bless people?" Eddie asked, faintly. "Yes, Eddie, I'm here to bless you," the older man whispered and quickly left the room.

"Will everybody let me go?" Eddie asked a few moments later. "Everybody has to let me go."

"You can go," they answered in unison.

Two hours later, Eddie awoke again with a sudden start. "Where are those pictures, Dad?" he demanded. His family scrambled to find the pictures for him, never believing that he'd remember. The enlargements wouldn't be ready for another day. Finding a small photo in his pocket, Bill handed it to his son. But as the morning light began filtering through the blinds, Eddie faded away. His breathing became irregular, short breaths followed by long pauses. The spaces between each breath grew longer and longer, until finally at 8:14 A.M. on March 8, 1991, Eddie exhaled for the last time, in his mother's arms.

On March 10, between a matinee and an evening performance of *Romeo and Juliet*, Eddie was remembered by his family, friends, and colleagues on the promenade of the New York State Theater. Five days earlier, he had taken his final bow just steps away; now everywhere the three hundred mourners looked were mementos from his life. Giant photo collages and Joffrey posters sat on easels near the grand staircase and tables displayed his medals, his trademark T-shirt ("Life is not a dress rehearsal. . . . Go for it," it said), and his favorite stuffed animal, Mousie. Bouquets of white balloons floated throughout the room. Lissette and Eddie's sisters all wore white. So did Rose Stierle, who had gone shopping at Macy's the day before to buy a white dress.

The Stierle family at Eddie's memorial service at Lincoln Center

Eddie's obituary had run in all the local papers, trailing reviews of his two ballets by days. Deborah Jowitt of *The Village Voice* had just turned in her weekly dance column when Eddie died. "Those who wail over the dearth of up-and-coming ballet choreographers—meet Edward Stierle," she had written, noting in her review-turned-obituary that she'd had to amend "is" to "was" and "may become" to "could have been." Unfulfilled promise was an oft-repeated theme in the tributes that followed. Soon, the Joffrey would take *Empyrean Dances* on tour, and critics would lament the loss of a choreographer who, to borrow the words of poet Thom

Gunn, had died "as only an apprentice to his trade, the ultimate engagements not yet made."

And yet, that month, Eddie's was just one of the 2,570 AIDS deaths reported to the Centers for Disease Control and just one of the thousands of artists who had died while still becoming, their sensibilities irreplaceable. Audiences could only wonder about works that might have been, while future generations of dancers, playwrights, designers, and composers lost valuable mentors, who were themselves the trustees of legacies handed down. In 1991 alone, the disease would claim the lives of 31,715 Americans, 497 of them young males between the ages of fifteen and twenty-four. From the beginning of the AIDS epidemic in 1981 through December 1991, 148,216 Americans had died from AIDS-related illnesses.

From a podium in the center of the promenade, Eddie's oldest brother, Michael, led the service he had written following a family meeting the previous day. Terri, Bill, Jr., and Tom spoke for the family; Gerald Arpino spoke for the Joffrey; and Kim Sagami read aloud reminiscences from the Joffrey dancers, including a brief tribute to Eddie that Lissette had written but couldn't bring herself to deliver. Edward Morgan, another Joffrey dancer, improvised a solo with a tambourine to Eddie's favorite song, "That's What Friends Are For."

The ceremony closed out-of-doors, on the balcony of the promenade. One by one, Rose Stierle, Lissette, and Gerald Arpino stepped forward and released a white balloon into the air: the first for family, the second for friends, and the last for dance.

Eddie's piece of the AIDS quilt, made by Rosemarie

EPILOGUE

A MAN OF FEW WORDS

The week his youngest son would have turned twenty-four, Bill Stierle was addressing a class of seniors at Chaminade-Madonna College Preparatory, the Catholic high school where he had served as head maintenance man for twenty-six years. On Eddie's birthday two days earlier, Bill and his wife, Rose, had spent the early morning hours at nearby Hollywood Beach, where their son's ashes had been scattered in a family ceremony.

All of Bill's children, save for Eddie and Kathy, had attended Chaminade-Madonna. In his work pants and black cap, Bill was a familiar presence on the grounds, and no one greeting him would think to call him anything but "Pops."

"Hi, I'm Pops Stierle," he told the thirty teenagers shifting in their seats. "I'm the father of eight children and I'd like you to look at my photos of my kids."

Positioned around the room were large laminated poster boards that Bill had spent weeks assembling. Most of the photographs featured Eddie, modeling, dancing, choreographing. One poster was devoted to family photos taken the night of Eddie's final bow at Lincoln Center.

"This is a work of art by someone who knew he was going to die," Bill told the students over the music of Mozart's *Requiem*, as *Lacrymosa* ran on the television monitor. "It's by my son. In a short amount of time, he did a lot of things. He contracted HIV when he was eighteen. AIDS is not a gay thing. You get it from sex. In this day and age, you have to pay attention or it'll cost you your life."

Biting his lip, he turned away for a moment to collect himself.

"I just want you to live past the age of twenty-three."

AFTERWORD

As of this writing, nearly three years have passed since Eddie's death.

Among Eddie's lovers, Eric Castellano died in Seattle on July 29, 1993, at the age of thirty-two. Joseph Brown, who had joined Oregon Ballet Theatre in the fall of 1991, retired from dancing in April 1993 owing to health reasons. He died at home in Portland on April 14, 1994, at the age of twenty-eight. Richard Register is an actor in New York City.

Lissette Salgado, now in her fifth season with the Joffrey Ballet, made her debut as the Sugar Plum Fairy in Robert Joffrey's production of *The Nutcracker* in December 1993.

The Joffrey Ballet itself continues under the direction of Gerald Arpino. In 1992, the company was forced to cancel its New York season due to financial problems and its Los Angeles season as a result of the riots that erupted the week the company was to begin its engagement. In 1993, however, the company scored a success with *Billboards*, four contemporary ballets set to the music of Prince. Though many critics and cognoscenti dismissed it as choreographically slight, *Billboards* proved enormously popular with new audiences and helped get the company back on firmer financial footing.

In the fall of 1993, Kyle Ahmed left the Joffrey Ballet for the Zurich Ballet in Switzerland, while Brent Phillips left the Joffrey to begin studying for a career as a physical therapist at New York University. He also joined the artists' committee of Dancers

Responding to AIDS, a new organization providing financial assistance to people in the dance world with AIDS.

Dr. Michael Gottlieb was awarded a Lifetime Science Award by the Center for the Study of Immunology and Aging in 1993. He has yet to perform a lung transplant on an AIDS patient. As of 1994, it has never been attempted. He now says that if he had known the full measure of Eddie's opportunistic illnesses, he would not have considered it.

Marianne Williamson's celebrity has grown considerably since the publication of her bestselling book, *A Return to Love.* In 1993, Williamson followed up with *A Woman's Worth* and is currently at work on a book of prayers and a book about America. She continues to lecture in Los Angeles and in New York City, where she also leads HIV support groups at the Manhattan and L.A. Centers for Living.

Senta Driver reluctantly disbanded her company in March 1991 owing to financial strain and the loss of a valued dancer to AIDS. She is now a registered nurse in Manhattan working with critically ill newborn babies at Beth Israel Medical Center.

Among Eddie's Joffrey colleagues and friends, Pennie Curry now heads her own arts management and production company in New York City, while Ashley Wheater and Tina LeBlanc are both principal dancers with the San Francisco Ballet. Patrick Corbin is now in his fourth year with the Paul Taylor Dance Company, and Parrish Maynard, who left the Joffrey in 1988, is currently a soloist with American Ballet Theatre.

Millicent Hodson and Kenneth Archer reconstructed and staged Nijinsky's last—and lost—1916 ballet, *Till Eulenspiegel,* for the Paris Opera Ballet. The work was unveiled at the Palais Garnier in Paris in February 1994.

Eddie's brother Bill conducts AIDS prevention workshops at high schools and businesses under the auspices of AIDS Project L.A.

Eddie's sister Rosemarie and her husband adopted a baby girl in January 1994.

Bill Stierle has spoken about AIDS to numerous classes of high school students since Eddie's death.

SOURCE NOTES

Given that Edward Stierle lived such a brief life, nearly everyone linked to his story was alive when I began my research, their recollections still vivid. As a result, much of this book is drawn from numerous interviews, not only with the Stierle family and Eddie's closest friends, but also with the myriad people who knew Eddie and wanted to share their memories and impressions. Eddie provoked strong reactions, even from those who knew him only casually.

In a few instances a name has been changed or omitted to grant anonymity where requested.

For written materials, I was particularly fortunate in finding an archivist in Rose Stierle. Throughout Eddie's life, she collected and catalogued his report cards, recital programs, modeling composites, dance school applications, competition materials, plane tickets, Joffrey Ballet itineraries, and gala invitations, which she generously loaned to me. She also lent me Eddie's two journals as well as three full scrapbooks of news clippings and reviews. Rose and Bill Stierle also made Eddie's medical records available to me. After Eddie's death, his spiritual healing tapes and books as well as his private papers, all of them unpublished, were bequeathed to his sister Rosemarie Worton, who provided me with complete access. These comprised his letters, date books, personal photographs, contracts, mortgage papers, choreographic drawings, and good-luck notes from Robert Joffrey. Flavia Carnevale, Chrissie Guastella, and Richard Register helped to fill in important details and dates by supplying me with letters Eddie had written to them; Joseph Brown, Lissette Salgado, and Kyle Ahmed supplied many personal reminiscences over the course of my interviews with them. Despite its brevity, his was a remarkably well-documented life.

That documentation extended to his final hours in St. Vincent's Hospital, which were tape-recorded and later replayed for me by Rosemarie Worton.

The Stierle family's extensive collection of photographs also helped enormously in re-creating key events in Eddie's life. Most of them were taken by Bill Stierle.

The details of Eddie's medical history were conveyed to me in interviews with Dr. John Oppenheimer and Dr. Muthiah Sukumaran in New York and with Dr. Michael Gottlieb in Los Angeles following approval from the Stierle family.

1

EMPYREAN DANCES

Details on Eddie's farewell at Lincoln Center were provided in interviews with his parents, his sister Rosemarie Worton, his brothers Tom and Bill, and the Joffrey Ballet dancers Lissette Salgado, Kyle Ahmed, Jodie Gates, Adam Sklute, and Brent Phillips.

p. 3   *"so that when I . . .":* Janice Berman, "Reaching into Deep Soul Places," *New York Newsday,* February 24, 1991.

p. 5   *"His is a stunning . . .":* Anna Kisselgoff, "A High-Energy Feast of New Choreography at the Joffrey's Gala," *The New York Times,* March 7, 1991.

2

GIRLS' TAP

The material relating to Rose and Bill Stierle's early life and courtship was based on interviews with the subjects themselves and corroborated by several of their children.

4
BALLET CONCERTO

p. 43   *"I spent more time with him . . .":* Ken Williams, "Edward Stierle, 23,
Joffrey Ballet's Little Big Man," *The Hollywood Sun,* March 22, 1991.

5
EPIDEMIC

The information about the history of the AIDS epidemic is culled from numerous
sources, among them Randy Shilts' *And the Band Played On: Politics, People, and the
AIDS Epidemic* (New York: Penguin Books, 1988), assorted newspaper and maga-
zine stories listed in the Bibliography, statistics provided by the Centers for Disease
Control, and "Medical Answers About AIDS" (New York: Gay Men's Health
Crisis, Inc., 1989).

p. 50   *"the fact that these . . .":* Shilts, p. 67
p. 50   *"no previous association . . .":* Shilts, p. 77.
p. 51   *"when it was not . . .":* Shilts, p. 213

6
BALLET BODIES

pp. 55–56 *"the West Point . . .":* Christine Temin, "Ballet's Commander In Chief,"
Harvard Magazine, November–December 1981.
p. 64   *"surrounded by people who . . .":* Debbie Blaylock, "Determination Pays Off
for Teen Ballet Dancer," *The Sun-Sentinel,* April 2, 1985.
p. 65   *"Not quite kosher.":* Duncan Noble, notes on Eddie's Audition Sheet,
School of Dance, North Carolina School of the Arts, June 15, 1983.
p. 66   *Watching Eddie dance . . . :* Robert Lindgren, notes on Eddie's Audition
Sheet, June 15, 1983, and to author.

7
STAR SEARCH

p. 68   *"Miss Hayden" quickly earned . . .* and *"Melissa would tell us . . .":* background
and quotations regarding Hayden's reputation among her students are
taken from off-the-record interviews with a number of Eddie's classmates.

p. 70   *Baryshnikov was not immediately* . . . : John Fraser, *Private View: Inside Baryshnikov's American Ballet Theatre* (New York: Bantam Books, 1988), p. 48.

p. 71   *The idea for a* . . . : Information on the founding of the school is based on interview with Robert Lindgren and on Leslie Banner, *A Passionate Preference: The Story of the North Carolina School of the Arts* (Asheboro, North Carolina: Down Home Press, 1991).

p. 72   *"It's new here . . .":* Banner, p. 152.

p. 74   *"Hollywood's teenage ballet sensation . . ."* Ken Williams, "The Comeback Kid: Foot Surgery Doesn't Keep Dancer Eddie Stierle Down," *Sun-Tattler,* May 12, 1986.

p. 76   *"I heard a lot of . . .":* videotape made in Washington, D.C., 1989.

p. 78   *an encounter with* . . . : [Eddie's lovers] Richard Register and Joseph Brown both related this story in interviews with author.

p. 78   *4,177 U.S. AIDS cases:* Centers for Disease Control.

p. 79   *It wouldn't be until 1992* . . . : "Teenagers and AIDS," *Newsweek,* August 3, 1992.

p. 83   *"The male dancing . . .":* Jennifer Dunning, "Dance: Prix de Lausanne Contest," *The New York Times,* January 28, 1985.

p. 84   *"Wait . . ."* and following scene: Stierle family videotape of Eddie's final performance at the 1985 Prix de Lausanne competition and his exit into the wings.

8

PAS DE TROIS

p. 89   *Hudson's doctor,* . . . : Shilts, p. 582.

p. 90   *the means by which one acquired AIDS* . . . : the story of Kimberly Bergalis, the first patient known to have contracted AIDS from a dentist, was given front-page focus in "Doctors with AIDS," *Newsweek,* July 1, 1991.

p. 90   *when Magic Johnson went public* . . . : "Magic's Message," *Newsweek,* November 18, 1991.

p. 90   *12,067 Americans* . . . : Centers for Disease Control.

p. 90   *"[AIDS] brings to many . . .":* Susan Sontag, *Illness as Metaphor and AIDS and Its Metaphors* (New York: Anchor Books, 1990), p. 122.

p. 91   *European health authorities* . . . : Shilts, p. 564.

9

DISTANT STAGES

p. 100   *overlapping relationships* . . . : Linda Roth to author as well as a postcard from Stefan to Eddie (February 16, 1986) and a letter from Catherine to Eddie (August 17, 1989).

10
AMBITION

p. 109   *"It's about being judged . . .":* Ken Williams, "The Comeback Kid: Foot Surgery Doesn't Keep Dancer Eddie Stierle Down," *Sun-Tattler*, May 12, 1986.

p. 109   *"God's forgiveness":* Betsy Kennedy, *The Voice* (newsletter of the Catholic Archdiocese of Miami), August 8, 1986.

p. 111   *"I'm going to shoot . . .":* Kitty Oliver, "Winning Dancer Home to Perform," *Miami Herald*, May 15, 1986.

11
THE JOFFREY

p. 125   *"The wonderful surprise . . .":* Anna Kisselgoff, "Dance: Proclamation Opens Joffrey's 30th Season," *The New York Times*, October 17, 1986.

p. 125   *"the right sort of grotesqueness . . .":* Tobi Tobias, *New York*, November 3, 1986.

p. 125   *"Another of the performance's . . .":* Clive Barnes, *The New York Post*, October 18, 1986.

12
THE MAN MAGNET

p. 135   *took up with a blond actor . . . :* this information based on interviews with Joseph Brown and Rosemarie Worton.

p. 135   *20,000 Americans had died . . . :* Centers for Disease Control.

p. 141   *"I'm Catholic . . .":* Sasha Anawalt, "It's Time Again to Send in 'Clowns,' " *The Los Angeles Herald Examiner*, April 26, 1987.

p. 144   *"put a body like that . . .":* Interview with Joffrey dancer.

p. 147   *"made the most brilliant . . .":* Allan Ulrich, "Slow Windup, Fast Break for Joffrey's Opening Night," *The San Francisco Examiner*, July 9, 1987.

13
FREE FALL

p. 151   *"I'm not happy about . . .":* Patrick Corbin, Kyle Ahmed, and Rosemarie Worton related this story to author.

p. 154   *"I just found out . . .":* Joseph Brown, Kyle Ahmed, and Linda Roth related this story to author.

p. 155   *President Ronald Reagan delivered . . . :* Shilts, pp. 589–596.

p. 158n.   *As Susan Sontag writes . . . :* Sontag, *AIDS and Its Metaphors,* p. 148.

p. 159   *"Every possible ingredient . . .":* Francis Steegmuller, *Cocteau* (Boston: Little Brown, 1970), p. 86.

p. 159n.   *"As Diaghilev's lover . . .":* Lynn Garafola, *Diaghilev's Ballets Russes* (New York: Oxford University Press, 1989), p. 51.

p. 160   *"the soul of nature . . .":* Millicent Hodson, "Searching for Nijinsky's Sacre," *Dance Magazine,* June 1980.

p. 163   *"exposed the barbarism . . .":* Lynn Garafola, *Diaghilev's Ballets Russes* (New York: Oxford University Press, 1989), p. 68.

p. 164   *"into New Age healing . . ."* and details of Eddie's relationship with John: Kyle Ahmed and Lissette Salgado to author.

14

CURTAIN CALL

p. 172   *"seemed to split . . .":* Sasha Anawalt, "Joffrey's Moments of Dreamy Truth," *The Los Angeles Herald Examiner,* October 5, 1987.

p. 175   *"almost stole the show . . .":* Clive Barnes, "To Dance, Perchance to 'Dream,' " *The New York Post,* October 29, 1987; Janice Berman, "The Joffrey, Doing What It Does Best," *Newsday,* October 29, 1987.

p. 175   *"Never have the clarity . . .":* Anna Kisselgoff, "Joffrey Ballet Opens at City Center," *The New York Times,* October 28, 1987.

p. 175   *"the superlative dancing . . .":* Anna Kisselgoff, "Diversity Was Partnered by New Talent," *The New York Times,* December 27, 1987.

p. 177   *"The rumors about . . .":* several Joffrey dancers to author.

p. 178   *"Bob wouldn't acknowledge . . .":* Joffrey board member to author.

p. 181   *"That Bob would die . . .":* Gerald Arpino quoted in Allan Ulrich, "Joffrey's Living Legacy," *The San Francisco Examiner,* July 3, 1988.

p. 183   *"as if all . . .":* Alan Kriegsman, "A Gem of a 'Nutcracker,' " *The Washington Post,* December 17, 1987.

p. 183   *"one of the most pleasant . . .":* Richard Philp, "In Touch with Tradition," *Dance Magazine,* December 1987.

p. 183   *"Well, I believe . . .":* Philp, *Dance Magazine,* December 1987.

p. 185   *"breathtaking jumps . . .":* Alan Kriegsman, "A Gem of a 'Nutcracker,' " *The Washington Post,* December 17, 1987.

p. 187   *"Mr. Joffrey had been . . .":* Jennifer Dunning, "Robert Joffrey, 57, Founder of the Ballet Troupe, Is Dead," *The New York Times,* March 26, 1988.

15

LACRYMOSA D'AMORE

p. 195   *"Losing Mr. Joffrey . . .":* Ken Williams, "Joffrey II Company to Perform Stierle Ballet," *The Sun-Tattler,* April 14, 1988.

p. 195   *"[Lacrymosa] came about . . .":* Libby Slate, "Stierle Dedicates His 1988 Work 'Lacrymosa' to Joffrey's Memory," *The Los Angeles Times,* May 12, 1990.

p. 195   *"[Lacrymosa] paralleled . . .":* Jennifer Dunning, "New for the Joffrey: Five Works, Four Styles," *The New York Times,* March 3, 1991.

p. 206   *"the most fertile mind . . .":* Anna Kisselgoff, "Structure Informs Kudelka Work," *The New York Times,* October 29, 1988.

16

SELF-HELP

p. 213   *"by-the-numbers . . .":* Interview with Joffrey dancer.

17

ENDLESS SIREN

p. 219   *"bouncing, rebounding . . .":* Laurie Horn, "Twin Pleasures: Cotillon and Stierle," *Miami Herald,* November 10, 1988.

p. 220   *"Suddenly the Joffrey . . .":* Anna Kisselgoff, "The Joffrey Lives Up to Its Past," *The New York Times,* November 27, 1988.

p. 220   *"made a breakthrough . . .":* Anna Kisselgoff, "Year's Best: 1988 in Review," *The New York Times,* December 25, 1988.

p. 220   *"a distillation of . . .":* Anna Kisselgoff, "The Joffrey Ballet's Personalized 'Nutcracker,'" *The New York Times,* November 21, 1988.

19

BEING POSITIVE

p. 237   *"Good . . .":* Interview with Joffrey dancer.

20

PETROUCHKA'S CRY

p. 240   *"I use Clowns . . .":* Ann Crittenden, "The Joffrey Returns, Spotlighting a Virtuoso," *The New York Times,* October 22, 1989.

p. 242   *"Petrouchka must live . . .":* Olga Maynard, "Petrouchka," *Dance Magazine,* February 1970.

p. 242   *"the personification . . .":* Richard Buckle, *Nijinsky* (New York: Simon & Schuster, 1971), p. 159.

p. 242   *"began to discern . . .":* Olga Maynard, "Petrouchka," *Dance Magazine,* February 1970.

p. 242   *"a Hamlet among puppets":* Buckle, p. 161.

p. 242   *"The metamorphosis took place . . .":* Buckle, p. 199.

p. 243   *"Many people will say . . .":* Romola Nijinsky, ed., *The Diary of Vaslav Nijinsky.* (Los Angeles: University of California Press, 1968), p. 112.

p. 243   *"I did a lot . . .":* Valerie Takahama, "Young Dancer Takes Big Steps," *Orange County Register,* December 10, 1989.

p. 245   *"rewound the fabric . . .":* Anna Kisselgoff, "Fan Dances, Charlestons and Other Flapper Fare," *The New York Times,* October 26, 1989.

p. 245   *"poignant, yet indomitable . . .":* Janice Berman, *Newsday,* November 1989.

p. 245   *"an always angry . . .":* Anna Kisselgoff, "At the Joffrey, a Pearl in a Classical Setting," *The New York Times,* November 7, 1989.

p. 251   *"spiritual psychotherapy":* Leslie Bennetts, "Marianne's Faithful," *Vanity Fair,* June 1991, p. 131.

p. 252   *"You are not your virus . . ."* and other quotations relating to Williamson's HIV support groups and lectures are taken from meetings attended by the author and from Williamson's book, *A Return to Love: Reflections on the Principles of A Course in Miracles* (New York: HarperCollins, 1992).

p. 255   *"There was such a radiance . . .":* Marianne Williamson to author.

21

COUP DE THÉÂTRE

p. 259   *"I refuse to participate . . .":* Jennifer Dunning, "Artistic Chief Quits, Taking His Dances," *The New York Times,* May 3, 1990.

p. 260   *The trouble had started . . . :* Background and quotations regarding the Joffrey board are based on off-the-record interviews with a number of former members of the Joffrey's board of directors.

p. 261   *"The odds are . . .":* Memo to the managing directors of the Joffrey Ballet, May 1, 1990.

p. 262   *"measure up to . . .":* Cathy Curtis, "Unexpected Premiere by Joffrey," *The Los Angeles Times,* May 8, 1990.

p. 263   *"I don't consider . . .":* Libby Slate, "Stierle Dedicates His 1988 Work 'Lacrymosa' to Joffrey's Memory," *The Los Angeles Times,* May 12, 1990.

p. 263   *"This is like losing . . .":* Judith Michaelson, "Gerald Arpino—Waiting in the Wings," *The Los Angeles Times,* May 17, 1990.

22

GHOSTS AND RUINS

p. 272   *"Eddie seemed to personify . . .":* Marianne Williamson to author.

23

HITTING HOME

p. 285   *"em.py.re.an . . .":* The American Heritage Dictionary (Boston: Houghton Mifflin, 1982), p. 450.

p. 286   *"The dancers complete . . .":* Janice Berman, *Newsday,* February 24, 1991.

p. 291   *"It doesn't happen very . . .":* Marianne Williamson to author.

p. 292   *"We see in the middle . . .":* details of Williamson's AIDS workshop are based on Rose and Bill Stierle's recollections and on information supplied by Marion Edmonds of the Manhattan Center for Living in an interview on May 12, 1993.

p. 292   *"The goal of the weekend . . .":* Marianne Williamson to author.

p. 292   *"his arms crossed":* Marianne Williamson to author.

p. 293   *"Imagine the AIDS virus . . .":* Marianne Williamson, *A Return to Love: Reflections on the Principles of a Course in Miracles* (New York: HarperCollins, 1992), p. 209.

p. 304   *"It's like growing old . . .":* Toni Bentley, *Winter Season* (New York: Random House, 1982), p. 51.

24

SCOTT'S CAP

p. 322   *"He lives for it . . .":* Jennifer Dunning, "New for the Joffrey: Five Works, Four Styles," *The New York Times,* March 3, 1991.

25

ENTR'ACTE

p. 327   *"This is a tiny part . . .":* Janice Berman, "Reaching Into Deep Soul Places," *Newsday,* February 24, 1991.

p. 328   *"Out of nowhere . . .":* Paul Monette, *Borrowed Time: An AIDS Memoir* (New York: Avon Books, 1990), p. 183.

p. 330   *"after a long illness . . .":* Janice Berman, *Newsday,* February 24, 1991.

p. 333   *"Deep down, dance . . .":* Anna Kisselgoff, "A 22-Year-Old's Joust with Death," *The New York Times,* March 1, 1991.

p. 333   *"a death song . . .":* Deborah Jowitt, "Forests, Trees," *The Village Voice,* March 11, 1991.

p. 334   *"You always said . . .":* Sid Smith, "Joffrey Accomplishes a Most Difficult Feat," *The Chicago Tribune,* May 5, 1991.

<u>26</u>

FLIGHTS OF ANGELS

p. 344   *"We were all so close . . .":* Monette, p. 210.

p. 346   *"the overall theme . . .":* Janice Berman, "Sculptural Stillness and Locomotion," *Newsday*, March 7, 1991.

p. 348   *"Yet Mr. Stierle is no . . .":* Anna Kisselgoff, "A High-Energy Feat of New Choreography at the Joffrey's Gala," *The New York Times*, March 7, 1991.

p. 349   *Eddie's voice sounded . . . :* details of Eddie's death scene are based on the tape recording made by the Stierle family as well as on recollections supplied by each family member present.

p. 352   *"Those who wail . . .":* Deborah Jowitt, "Forests, Trees," *The Village Voice*, March 11, 1991.

p. 353   *"as only an apprentice . . .":* Thom Gunn, "The J Car," *The Man with Night Sweats* (New York: Noonday Press, 1993), p. 77.

p. 353   *one of the 2,570 . . . :* Centers for Disease Control.

EPILOGUE

A MAN OF FEW WORDS

p. 355   The author was present at the AIDS talk given by Bill Stierle to a class of high school seniors at Chaminade-Madonna College Preparatory in Hollywood, Florida, on March 4, 1992.

SELECTED
BIBLIOGRAPHY

Altman, Lawrence K. "Federal Health Officials Propose an Expanded Definition of AIDS." *The New York Times*, October 28, 1992.

————. "Researchers Report Much Grimmer AIDS Outlook." *The New York Times*, June 4, 1992.

Ansen, David, et al. "A Lost Generation." *Newsweek*, January 18, 1993.

Banner, Leslie. *A Passionate Preference: The Story of the North Carolina School of the Arts*. Asheboro, North Carolina: Down Home Press, 1991. (Originally published 1987.)

Bennetts, Leslie. "Marianne's Faithful." *Vanity Fair*, June 1991.

Bentley, Toni. *Winter Season: A Dancer's Journal*. New York: Random House, 1982.

Berkow, Ira. "The Changing Faces of Arthur Ashe." *The New York Times*, October 25, 1992.

Berman, Janice. "Even as the Show Goes On, It's Wait-and-See." *Newsday*, May 8, 1990.

Bernheimer, Martin. "The Board, Arpino, and the Turmoil at the Joffrey." *The Los Angeles Times*, May 26, 1990.

Bonham Carter, Mark, ed. *The Autobiography of Margot Asquith*. London: Eyre & Spottiswoode, 1962.

Buckle, Richard. *Nijinsky*. New York: Simon & Schuster, 1971.

Callen, Michael. *Surviving AIDS*. New York: HarperCollins, 1990.

Camus, Albert. *The Plague*. Great Britain: Penguin Books, 1960. (Originally published in English by Hamish Hamilton, 1948.)

Cunningham, Michael. "After AIDS, Gay Art Aims for a New Reality." *The New York Times*, April 26, 1992.

Driver, Senta. "Edward Stierle (1968–1991)." *Ballet Review*, Fall 1991.

Dunning, Jennifer. "Why a Dance-World Veteran Decided to Pack It All In." *The New York Times*, April 28, 1991.

————. "Its Repertory in Turmoil, the Joffrey Dances On." *The New York Times*, May 7, 1990.

———. "Bliss Quits Joffrey Board and Says Others Will Go." *The New York Times,* May 11, 1990.

———. "Arpino Re-establishes His Links with the Joffrey." *The New York Times,* May 21, 1990.

———. "Arpino Argues for Role in the Artistic Future of the Embattled Joffrey." *The New York Times,* May 10, 1990.

Egan, Timothy. "Creating a Pleasant Stop on the Journey to Death." *The New York Times,* January 8, 1992.

FitzGerald, Frances. *Cities on a Hill.* New York: Simon & Schuster, 1981.

Fraser, John. *Private View: Inside Baryshnikov's American Ballet Theatre.* New York: Bantam Books, 1988.

Garafola, Lynn. *Diaghilev's Ballets Russes.* New York: Oxford University Press, 1989.

Goleman, Daniel. "If Hidden Depression Is Halted, Patients May Get Better Faster." *The New York Times,* August 5, 1992.

Goodman, Mark. "One Final Mystery." *People,* September 28, 1992.

Goreman, Christine. "Invincible AIDS." *Time,* August 3, 1992.

Graubard, Stephen R., ed. "Living with AIDS." *Daedalus,* Vol. 118, No. 2, Spring 1989.

———, ed. "Living with AIDS: Part II." *Daedalus,* Vol. 118, No. 3, Summer 1989.

Green, Jesse. "This School Is Out." *The New York Times Magazine,* October 13, 1991.

———. "Day of the Locust." *Premiere,* February 1992.

Greenberg, Michael Miles. "Blood Ties: Life in an HIV Support Group." *QW,* July 5, 1992.

Grigoriev, S. L. (translated by Vera Bowen). *The Diaghilev Ballet: 1909–1929.* London: Constable, 1953.

Gross, Jane. "In Age of Cancer and AIDS, Therapists for the Dying." *The New York Times,* August 9, 1991.

Gross, Michael. "Sex in the '90s." *New York,* June 8, 1992.

———. "Lost Angel." *New York,* March 2, 1992.

Gunn, Thom. *The Man with Night Sweats.* New York: Noonday Press, 1993.

Hawthorne, Nathaniel. *The Scarlet Letter.* New York: Penguin Books, 1986. (Originally published by Ticknor, Reed, and Fields, 1850.)

Hay, Louise L. *You Can Heal Your Life.* California: Hay House, 1984.

Hendrickson, Peter A. *Alive & Well: A Path for Living in a Time of HIV.* New York: Irvington Publishers, 1990.

Henry, William A., III. "An Identity Forged in Flames." *Time,* August 3, 1992.

Hilts, Philip J. "Dying Member of Panel on AIDS Wants Her Illness to Lift Stigma." *The New York Times,* August 4, 1991.

Hoare, Philip. *Serious Pleasures: The Life of Stephen Tennant.* London: Penguin Books, 1992.

Hodson, Millicent. "Nijinsky's Choreographic Method: Visual Sources from Roerich for *Le Sacre du Printemps.*" *Dance Research Journal,* Winter 1986–87.

Holden, Stephen. "For Alan Menken, A Partnership Ends but the Song Plays On." *The New York Times,* March 15, 1992.

Horn, Laurie. "The Spirits Come to Dance." *Miami Herald,* March 23, 1991.

Hull, Anne V. "The Last Dance." *St. Petersburg Times,* May 5, 1991.

Jampolsky, Gerald G. *Love Is Letting Go of Fear.* Berkeley: Celestial Arts, 1979.

Kaminer, Wendy. *I'm Dysfunctional, You're Dysfunctional: The Recovery Movement and Other Self-Help Fashions.* New York: Addison-Wesley, 1992.

Kasindorf, Jeanie Russell. "The Plague." *New York,* April 19, 1993.

Kirkland, Gelsey. *Dancing on My Grave.* New York: Doubleday, 1986.

Kirstein, Lincoln. *Nijinsky Dancing.* New York: Knopf, 1975.

———. *Ballet: Bias & Belief: Three Pamphlets Collected and Other Dance Writings of Lincoln Kirstein.* New York: Dance Horizons, 1983.

Kisselgoff, Anna. "Despite Sorrow, the Joffrey Season Soars." *The New York Times,* March 17, 1991.

Kübler-Ross, Elisabeth. *AIDS: The Ultimate Challenge.* New York: Collier Books, 1987.

Lahr, John. *Prick Up Your Ears: The Biography of Joe Orton.* New York: Knopf, 1978.

Monette, Paul. *Borrowed Time: An AIDS Memoir.* New York: Avon Books, 1990. (Originally published by Harcourt Brace Jovanovich, 1988.)

Navarro, Mireya. "The Search for Romance in the Shadow of AIDS." *The New York Times,* October 10, 1991.

Nijinsky, Romola, ed. *The Diary of Vaslav Nijinsky.* Los Angeles: University of California Press, 1968. (Originally published by Simon & Schuster, 1936.)

Ostwald, Peter. *Vaslav Nijinsky: A Leap into Madness.* New York: Carol Publishing Group, 1991.

Pierce, Charles P. "Magic Acts Up." *GQ,* February 1993.

Pogash, Carol. *As Real as It Gets: The Life of a Hospital at the Center of the AIDS Epidemic.* New York: Birch Lane Press, 1992.

Pristin, Terry. "The Power, the Glory, the Glitz." *The Los Angeles Times,* February 16, 1992.

Rosenthal, Elisabeth. "To a Drumbeat of Losses to AIDS, a Rethinking of Traditional Grief." *The New York Times,* December 6, 1992.

Schemo, Diane Jean. "Where AIDS Advances, Understanding Lags." *The New York Times,* August 12, 1993.

Schindehette, Susan. "The Divine Miss W." *People,* March 9, 1992.

Schmalz, Jeffrey. "Call Him Earvin: 'I Can't Be Magic.'" *The New York Times,* November 19, 1992.

Segal, Lewis. "Joffrey Marks 35th Year: Focus Is on the Future, Not Past." *The Los Angeles Times,* May 9, 1991.

Seligmann, Jean, et al. "The HIV Dating Game." *Newsweek,* October 5, 1992.

Servin, James. "Prophet of Love Has the Timing of a Comedian." *The New York Times,* February 19, 1992.

Seymour, Lesley Jane. "Mom, I Have AIDS." *McCall's,* January 1993.

Sherrill, Martha. "A Course in Marianne." *Mirabella,* April 1993.

Shilts, Randy. *And the Band Played On: Politics, People, and the AIDS Epidemic.* New York: Penguin Books, 1988. (Originally published by St. Martin's Press, 1987.)

Siegel, Bernie S. *Love, Medicine & Miracles.* New York: Harper & Row, 1986.

Smith, Dean. "AIDS and the Arts." *The Charlotte Observer,* March 31, 1991.

Smith, Sid. "Joffrey Offering Has Undercurrent of Real-Life Tragedy." *The Chicago Tribune,* April 19, 1991.

Solway, Diane. "Mustering Creative Power in the Face of Death." *The New York Times*, March 24, 1991.

———. "How 'Cotillon' Was Reborn." *The New York Times*, October 23, 1988.

Sontag, Deborah. "Haven in the Grim World of AIDS." *The New York Times*, March 12, 1992.

Sontag, Susan. *Illness as Metaphor and AIDS and Its Metaphors*. New York: Anchor Books, 1990. (Originally published by Farrar, Straus & Giroux, 1989.)

Steegmuller, Francis. *Cocteau*. Boston: Little, Brown, 1970.

Stevenson, Richard W. "Magic Johnson Ends His Career, Saying He Has AIDS Infection." *The New York Times*, November 8, 1991.

Stewart. Thomas A. "Gay in Corporate America." *Fortune*, December 16, 1991.

Thom, Rose Anne. "Tragedy and Triumph." *Dance Magazine*, June 1991.

Tobias, Tobi. "Gains and Losses." *New York*, March 25, 1991.

Webb, Marilyn. "The Art of Dying." *New York*, November 23, 1992.

Williamson, Marianne. *A Return to Love: Reflections on the Principles of A Course in Miracles*. New York: HarperCollins, 1992.

———. "My Life Is Driving Me Crazy." Transcript of appearance on "The Oprah Winfrey Show," Harpo Productions, Inc., February 4, 1992.

———. "A Message of Love." Transcript of appearance on "Larry King Live," Cable News Network, Inc., February 14, 1992.

ACKNOWLEDGMENTS

While I had seen Edward Stierle dance on numerous occasions with the Joffrey Ballet, I knew little of his life until March 1991, when Gene Lambinus, dance editor of the "Arts & Leisure" section of *The New York Times*, asked me to write a piece about the Joffrey's promising choreographer and leading dancer, who had died a few days earlier at the age of twenty-three. His second ballet had just had its premiere that week and I was asked to write about the challenges he faced in making dances while dying.

That article would not have evolved into a book had it not been for the enthusiasm and interest of Bill Grose, Pocket Books' editorial director, who saw many stories in that first story and encouraged me to look further. His support and faith are especially appreciated.

My gratitude also extends to Lisa Queen, who prodded, coddled, and calmed me throughout the process of writing this book, and to Ann Shortell, from whose experience and astute judgment I benefited enormously. I would also like to thank my agent Barney Karpfinger for providing care and wise counsel at every turn, and Tom Miller, an engaging and thorough editor.

From the moment I set out in search of Edward Stierle and the many people who populated his life, I was fortunate in securing the cooperation of all nine members of the Stierle family, who not only gave unstintingly of their time and impressions, but provided introductions, insight, and hospitality to me during the many months of research. I am particularly grateful to them for granting me not only complete access to Edward Stierle's papers, but authority over the telling of his story, even when it meant that intimate details about their own lives might be revealed. This concession was not given lightly and I thank the Stierles for their trust.

I owe a special debt of gratitude to Bill and Rose Stierle, whose detailed recollections and generosity of spirit proved inspiring. Eddie's sister Rosemarie Worton was another invaluable resource and guide. She thoughtfully answered hundreds of questions, many of them involving painful recent memories, fielded phone calls from every member of her family, decoded family dynamics, tracked down materials and phone numbers, and challenged easy assumptions about her youngest brother.

Lissette Salgado, Kyle Ahmed, and Joseph Brown were also crucial to my research. Their candor, trust, and patience are greatly appreciated.

For information about Eddie's teenage years, I would like to acknowledge the assistance of Liana Navarro, Chrissie Guastella, Anita Intrieri, Richard Register, and Duncan Noble, and the hospitality of Melissa Hayden and Donald Coleman during my visit to the North Carolina School of the Arts in Winston-Salem.

Despite their hectic schedules, Eddie's Joffrey Ballet colleagues, both past and present, couldn't have made themselves more available. While many of them had found Eddie trying in his first years at the company, his talent, his drive, and his approach to his illness had made a profound impression on them and they were eager to talk about him. I am particularly grateful to Scott Barnard, Gerald Arpino, Pennie Curry, Barbara Forbes, Val Golovitser, Parrish Maynard, Ashley Wheater, Brent Phillips, Adam Sklute, Jodie Gates, Carl Corry, Mark Goldweber, Tina LeBlanc, Rima Corben, and Elaine Brand. Herb Migdoll, the Joffrey's resident photographer, generously provided several performance photos.

For their seasoned perspective on significant strands of Edward Stierle's life, I would like to thank the following for their contributions: Marianne Williamson, Millicent Hodson, Senta Driver, Eric Castellano, Dr. John Oppenheimer, Dr. Michael Gottlieb, and Dr. Muthiah Sukumaran.

A number of other people nurtured this book into being: Gabrielle Glaser gave the manuscript a close reading and made numerous helpful suggestions at key moments; Gerard Raymond transcribed tapes; and Aaron Betsky and John Carrafa discussed ideas and approaches. Pam Allen and David Zitzerman also provided assistance.

While the writing process is isolating, a writer invariably relies on a few well-chosen friends and relatives to listen patiently to recited passages over the telephone and to offer words of encouragement, enthusiasm, or consolation at various crossroads. For these and other services rendered, I am grateful for the support of my parents, Herb Solway and Elaine Solway; my brothers, Gary and Michael; my grandmother, Sophie Bassin; and my extended family, the Moores.

Several friends also deserve special mention and thanks—in particular, Laura Coverson, Isabel Bassett, Eva Haller, Wendy Weinstein, Fred Schroeder, Jennifer Fischer, Sharon Messitte, and Dennis Freedman.

Perhaps no one understands the arc of this project better than my husband, David Resnicow, whose humor, advocacy, and cooking helped me to see it to completion. He read this manuscript carefully during each stage of its preparation, helped me sort through thorny issues, and offered his valued support along the way. His contribution goes far beyond editorial scrutiny, and to him I owe the greatest measure of thanks.

INDEX

°ES = Edward Stierle.